WALKING THE BYPASS

WALKING THE BYPASS

NOTES ON PLACE FROM THE SIDE OF THE ROAD

KEN WILSON

University of Regina Press

Printed and bound in Canada. The text of this book is printed on 100% post-consumer recycled paper with earth-friendly vegetable-based inks.

Cover art: Ken Wilson
Cover design: Duncan Campbell, University of Regina Press
Interior layout design: John van der Woude, JVDW Designs
Copyeditor: Kelly Laycock
Proofreader: Rachel Taylor
Indexer: Patricia Furdek

Library and Archives Canada Cataloguing in Publication

Title: Walking the bypass : notes on place from the side of the road / Ken Wilson.
Names: Wilson, Ken (Kenneth Clayton), author.
Description: Includes bibliographical references and index.
Identifiers: Canadiana (print) 20250137445 | Canadiana (ebook) 20250137526 | ISBN 9781779400772 (hardcover) | ISBN 9781779400765 (softcover) | ISBN 9781779400796 (PDF) | ISBN 9781779400789 (EPUB)
Subjects: LCGFT: Creative nonfiction.
Classification: LCC PS8645.I47428 W35 2025 | DDC C818/.6—dc23

10 9 8 7 6 5 4 3 2 1

U OF R PRESS

University of Regina Press, University of Regina
Regina, Saskatchewan, Canada, S4S 0A2
TEL: (306) 585-4758 FAX: (306) 585-4699
WEB: www.uofrpress.ca

We acknowledge the support of the Canada Council for the Arts for our publishing program. We acknowledge the financial support of the Government of Canada. / Nous reconnaissons l'appui financier du gouvernement du Canada. This publication was made possible with support from Creative Saskatchewan's Book Publishing Production Grant Program.

Canada Council for the Arts | Conseil des Arts du Canada | Canada | creative SASKATCHEWAN

For Christine

CONTENTS

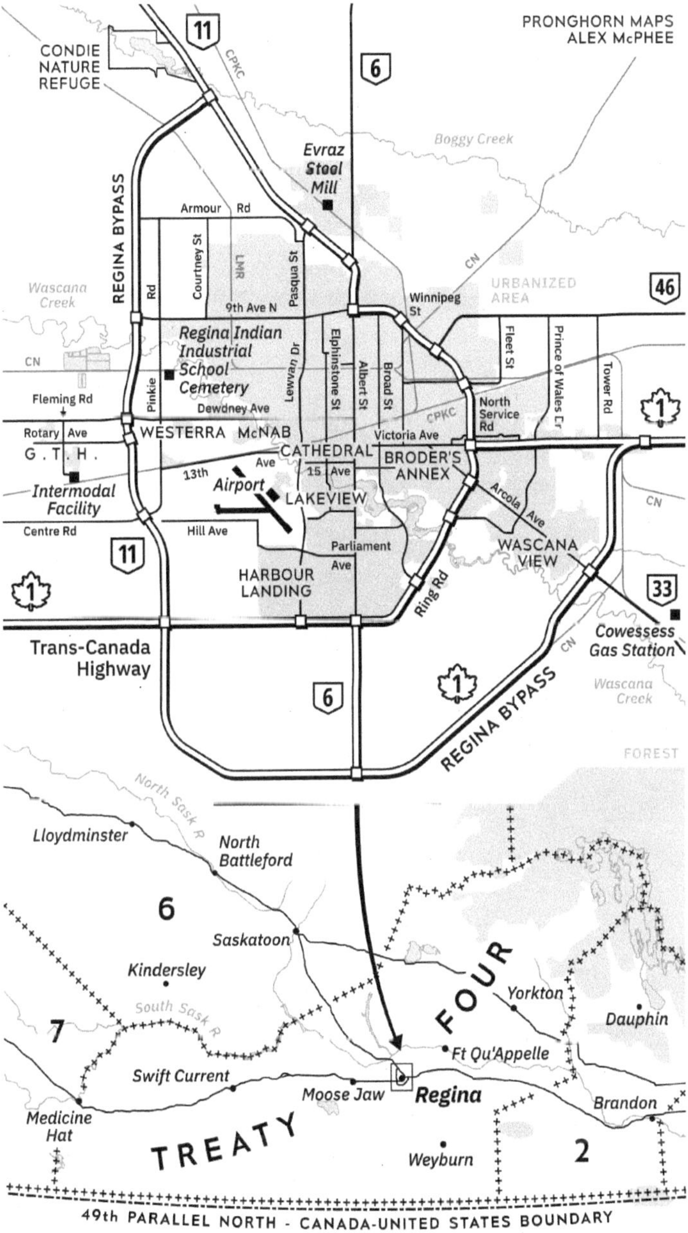

PRONGHORN MAPS
ALEX McPHEE
CONDIE
NATURE
REFUGE
11
6
CPKC
Boggy Creek
Evraz
Steel
Mill
REGINA BYPASS
Armour Rd
Courtney St
LMR
Pasqua St
Rd
Wascana
Creek
9th Ave N
Winnipeg
St
CN
URBANIZED
AREA
46
Regina Indian
Industrial
School
Cemetery
Lewvan Dr
Elphinstone St
Albert St
Broad St
Fleet St
Prince of Wales Dr
Tower Rd
CN
Fleming Rd
Pinkie
Dewdney Ave
CPKC
North
Service
Rd
1
Rotary Ave
WESTERRA
McNAB
Victoria Ave
G.T.H.
CATHEDRAL
BRODER'S
ANNEX
13th Ave
15 Ave
Airport
LAKEVIEW
Intermodal
Facility
Arcola Ave
CN
Centre Rd
Hill Ave
Parliament
Ave
WASCANA
VIEW
11
HARBOUR
LANDING
Ring Rd
33
1
Trans-Canada
Highway
Cowessess
Gas Station
CN
6
1
REGINA BYPASS
Wascana
Creek
FOREST
North Sask R
Lloydminster
North
Battleford
6
Saskatoon
Kindersley
FOUR
Yorkton
South Sask R
Dauphin
7
Ft Qu'Appelle
Swift Current
Moose Jaw
Regina
Brandon
Medicine
Hat
TREATY
Weyburn
2
49th PARALLEL NORTH - CANADA-UNITED STATES BOUNDARY

You road I enter upon and look around, I believe you are not all that is here,
I believe that much unseen is also here.

—Walt Whitman, "Song of the Open Road"

Place and a mind may interpenetrate till the nature of both is altered.

—Nan Shepherd, *The Living Mountain*

PROLOGUE

THE REGINA INDIAN INDUSTRIAL SCHOOL CEMETERY

APRIL 25, 2020

It's a cool, sunny morning in Regina, Saskatchewan, about six weeks into the COVID-19 pandemic. You might know this place, the provincial capital, home to about a quarter of a million people, built on the flat, heavy gumbo clay of the Wascana Plains. Maybe you've visited this city, briefly, on a car trip across the country; it's a reasonable day's drive from Winnipeg to the east, or Calgary to the west, a sensible spot to stop for the night. My family stayed here once, the summer I was four years old. My parents thought I might enjoy the museum at the Royal Canadian Mounted Police's Depot Division, where new recruits are trained. I'm told we went there. I don't know what else we might've seen. I imagine it was also an opportunity for us to sleep in a motel instead of in the tent trailer we pulled behind our black Volkswagen Beetle. Before I moved here twenty-five years ago, that was my only experience of this place, and I remember nothing about it.

Regina is situated on the northern Great Plains. That term, "the Great Plains," like its synonym, "the prairies," denotes the grasslands (or former grasslands) of the interior of western North America, which stretch from the deserts south of the Rio Grande in Mexico north to the transition between the aspen parkland and boreal forest in northern Canada, and from the Rocky Mountains in the west to the 98th or 100th meridian in the east, depending on who you ask. That eastern boundary line roughly parallels the place where the tall-grass prairie gave way to the shorter mixed-grass prairie, although both of those grassland ecosystems are mostly gone now, and establishing such a clearly defined line ignores the subtle transitions that happen between the more humid areas of the eastern parts of the continent and the drier region to the west, lying in the rain shadow of the mountains. The Great Plains are vast and complex; Ian Frazier describes them as "so big you can never know all there is to know about them—your fantasies could never wear them out."[1] The more I learn about this city and the prairies where it's located, the more I realize how much they go beyond my understanding.

As Trevor Herriot points out in the introduction to *Grass, Sky, Song: Promise and Peril in the World of Grassland Birds*, Regina is unusual because it's "one of the only prairie cities built upon utterly treeless grassland."[2] Other cities on the northern Great Plains were built on large rivers, "where ravines sheltered a few poplars and willows," he explains, "but the stretch of Wascana Creek where Regina sprang up did not incise deeply enough into the tableland of its glacial lake bed to allow woody growth of any kind."[3] Archival photographs of the creek taken in the 1880s, when settlers first arrived here, show it looking more like a ditch, so shallow that its water occasionally disappeared during the hot, dry summers. Other photographs of the first town site depict, in Herriot's words, "a landscape in which the highest vegetation is an exuberant patch of spear grass."[4] Now Regina is a city of some 400,000 trees, each one deliberately planted, and Wascana Creek has been widened and deepened into Wascana Lake, its hydrology controlled by dams and weirs so it doesn't dry up in the summer anymore, even if it moves so slowly that it appears to be stagnant.

I'm not from Saskatchewan. I grew up in southwestern Ontario, in the Haldimand Tract, a territory encompassing most of the Grand River valley.[5] The Haldimand Tract was deeded to the people of the Six Nations—in English, the names of the Six Nations are known as the Seneca, Cayuga, Onondaga, Oneida, Tuscarora, and Mohawk—by Sir Frederick Haldimand, the governor of Québec, in 1784. They had supported the British during the American Revolution, and as a result had been driven from their home territories in upstate New York by American troops, their crops and villages burning behind them. The people of the Six Nations named George Washington, who had ordered General John Sullivan to carry out that scorched-earth campaign, *Hanadagá•yas* ("Town Destroyer")—a name they've applied to American presidents ever since.[6] After the revolution, most of the Haudenosaunee—that's what they call themselves, a word meaning "the People of the Longhouse"—were living as refugees along the Niagara River. Haldimand knew that the Haudenosaunee were important allies against the Americans, and so he negotiated with Joseph Brant, a Mohawk Pine Tree Chief, selected for leadership because of his abilities rather than, as was more usual, inheriting it through his mother's family line. The result was the treaty that guaranteed the Haudenosaunee could live in the Haldimand Tract forever. Within a few decades, though, settlers had taken back 95 percent of the land in the Haldimand Tract through a series of thefts and forced surrenders.[7] So like most settlers in this country—all settlers, really—I grew up on stolen land.

You won't find the Haldimand Tract on most maps. You will find Brantford, the small, industrial city between Hamilton and London, named after Brant, where I grew up. Later I lived in Ottawa, on unceded Algonquin land, and then in Toronto, on land shared (or not, depending on who you ask) by the Michi Saagiig and the Haudenosaunee and transferred to settlers through the unjust Toronto Purchase.[8] Now I live in Regina, on Treaty 4 land: the territory of the nêhiyawak, Anihšināpēk,[9] Dakota, Lakota, and Nakoda, as well as the homeland of the Métis or Michif Nation.[10]

I'm telling you these things because over the past few years I've learned how important it is to understand whose land you live on, to recognize the people who were pushed aside—and that's the politest way to describe what happened; one could use other language—by the settlers who came to what's now called Canada looking for a better life. Nobody can blame those people, my ancestors included, for running from poverty and landlessness and hunger, from pogroms and tyranny and war, and seeking a new beginning here, but at the same time, the people who were living in this place originally were deeply wronged by that invasion. Our invasion. And, because settlers are still here—and still reaping the benefits of the lands we occupy—that invasion continues, and so the wrongs done by our predecessors continue, too.[11] We might prefer to pretend otherwise, but isn't it better to face the facts? To be honest about the situation in which we find ourselves?

Since I wasn't born in Regina, I'm still something of an outsider. I've tried to root myself, gardening with native wildflowers and learning about the history and geography and botany of this place. Perhaps, because I came here from elsewhere, I see this place with fresh eyes. I've learned a little *nêhiyawêwin*, one of the Indigenous languages of Saskatchewan. I've even started cheering for the Roughriders, the province's professional football team—a big change for someone who's never cared much about sports. "Live anywhere long enough and the landscape will claim your loyalty, your heart," John Terpstra writes. That's harder in a city, he admits, where "[i]t can take a lifetime to discover and uncover the physical reality and beauty of the place."[12] Do my years in Regina count as a lifetime? Of course not. No matter how many football games I watch, how many bitter winters I survive, I'm not from here. I know that. I'm always learning more about this place, trying to figure it out as I go, particularly as I walk in and around this city. At the same time, I have to acknowledge the truth of Les Back's words about places: "There is never a single coherent definition of place and no definitive version of its history. Other stories can always be told and different paths taken."[13] The stories I tell about this place are inevitably going to be idiosyncratic, partial, and incomplete. Others walking on the same roads and sidewalks would find different stories to tell.

This morning, I leave our house, a Craftsman-style bungalow in the city's Cathedral neighbourhood constructed in 1929—just before the stock market crash and the subsequent decade of drought and economic depression that shaped Saskatchewan for generations—and start walking west. My destination: the Regina Indian Industrial School cemetery on Pinkie Road. At least once every year I make this journey. It's a way of paying respect to the children buried there. What's a person like me, a *môniyâw*, a white person,[14] doing walking to those graves? That's a good question. I don't have an answer. I just know that what happened at the Regina Indian Industrial School was wrong, and that those wrongs cannot be forgotten or consigned to unread history books.

Besides, I'm not the only môniyâw who remembers. In 2016, Regina's city council—settlers all—announced that the city was going to grant the RIIS cemetery municipal heritage status.[15] The following year, the provincial government named the site a provincial heritage property.[16] These designations protect the ground where the children lie from being developed into another subdivision. Both levels of government were pressured into action by a group of activists inspired by two filmmakers, Janine Windolph and the late Trudy Stewart, who made a documentary about the school, *RIIS from Amnesia*.[17] That group, the RIIS Commemorative Association, organized annual pilgrimages up Pinkie Road as part of their campaign. I participated in one and went to the feast afterwards. I remember the nêhiyaw Elder in charge reminding us all that we were at a serious ceremony, not a picnic. And I remember that we hadn't brought any food to share. Typical môniyâw behaviour, I suppose, coming to a feast empty-handed, but had I known, I would've brought something good. I hope someday I get a chance to make up for my ignorance.

I turn north on Elphinstone Street, where I pass a different kind of educational institution: Connaught School, the new elementary school built through a public-private partnership (P3) arrangement. That's the way governments prefer to build infrastructure these days. I cross the Canadian Pacific Railway tracks and trudge past the new football stadium, another P3 project. Then I turn west on Dewdney Avenue, walking alongside one of the city's hospitals and the RCMP's Depot Division, where the museum I was taken to as a boy is located. Soon I find myself close to the city's edge, at Courtney Street. There isn't much traffic. That's always a relief, particularly when the sidewalk disappears and I have to continue on the gravel shoulder. There's always the chance that someone, distracted by a text message or kids arguing in the backseat, will look away from the road at just the wrong moment and I'll end up broken and bleeding in the ditch. When I walked from Regina to Wood Mountain, a village 250 kilometres southwest of here, in August 2018—a journey I made in honour of the poet Andrew Suknaski, who was born there—I travelled on busy highways with narrow, sometimes nonexistent shoulders. On the ride back to the city, I was surprised at how close I had been to the traffic, at how the slightest error on the part of a driver could have killed me. I've had a couple of close calls over the years—not so close that I'm too frightened to walk, but just close enough to help me imagine more vividly what could happen.

The western edge of the city has moved. Regina used to stop at Courtney Street, but now a new development, Westerra, has pushed the boundary to Pinkie Road, named after a nearby village that was itself named after Pinkie Cleugh, the site of a sixteenth-century battle in Scotland.[18] Pinkie, Saskatchewan, was swallowed by the city a long time ago. Things change so quickly. The last time I walked this way, Westerra was only a sign and a sales office. Now it's two neighbourhoods: one of houses, the other of apartments. A retail development is supposed to be built between them someday. Large signs announce cheap rent for potential tenants and more new houses for people who can qualify for a mortgage. These suburban developments always make me think of the phrase "ticky-tacky" in Malvina Reynolds's satirical song "Little Boxes." I know that's unfair. People have to live somewhere. Why not in Westerra? Still, the neighbourhood has its drawbacks, including a strange concrete bunker that emits a ceaseless mechanical howling. I can't tell what its purpose is or why it makes such a loud noise, something like a giant vacuum cleaner. Is it a pump supplying Westerra with water or siphoning away its sewage? There's no sign, just a city truck parked inside the fence. I wonder what it would be like to live next to that thing, to open my apartment windows on a cool evening after a scorching summer day and be confronted by that terrible racket.

I stop for a minute on Dewdney Avenue and drink some water. Then I turn north again onto Pinkie Road. It's seen some recent work, and the gravel is thick and soft and hard to walk on. I slog along the road until I'm standing in front of the cemetery. In 2019, ownership of the one-acre plot of land was transferred from a private owner to the federal government. The RCMP, which owns an adjacent plot of land, agreed to make an exchange with the landowner—one piece of land for another—and then the federal government deeded the land to the RIIS Commemorative Association.[19] A permanent memorial is to be built on the site. The old rail fence, which was covered in plush toys, is gone; a new fence is being built, but so far only the posts have been erected. A hand-painted sign leans up against one of them, asking us to remember the forty or so children buried here.[20] Their graves are unmarked[21]—the wooden crosses over the graves burned during a grass fire some time before 1921[22]—and the ground over the graves is uneven. The hummocked lawn is the only visible evidence that children are buried here. There is one stone memorial, though, marking where the child of one of the school's principals is buried.

The Regina Indian Industrial School was operated by the Presbyterian Church for twenty years, from 1891 to 1910. It was a terrible place. Abysmal. A 1908 federal government report described the school as looking "more like a deserted place than a Government Institution."[23] The school's fire doors were kept locked with the students inside to keep them from running away,[24] its sewage system was inadequate,[25] the heating system didn't keep the building warm in winter,[26] and there was no running water, so the children couldn't wash.[27] Students were poorly fed and often hungry.[28] They were ill-treated in other ways, too. For instance, in 1903 a Methodist missionary, Reverend William W. Moore, complained that one of the teachers had given a revolver to a young student who had tried to commit suicide while being punished for attempting to run away, and invited her to pull the trigger. The gun was empty.[29] What kind of person would do that? Moore also told Presbyterian Church officials that two girls had been sexually assaulted in the school's basement by two other students, and that the principal had threatened to punish all the students involved if they told anyone, including their parents, about what had happened.[30] These are just two particularly awful examples; they hint at other traumatic experiences that didn't make it into the historical record but were carried by the school's survivors for the rest of their lives.

The school held more dangers. Tuberculosis and other diseases, including smallpox, ran rampant in the crowded dormitories, which lacked proper isolation facilities for students who were ill.[31] During a 1904 smallpox outbreak, the school waited five days to vaccinate the children living there.[32] No wonder 20 percent of the kids who entered the Regina Indian Industrial School died of disease or neglect.[33] Many others were sent home to die after contracting tuberculosis, a disease connected to the school's scanty rations. The connection between malnutrition and tuberculosis was well known in the nineteenth century, as James Daschuk points out in *Clearing the Plains: Disease, Politics of Starvation, and the Loss of Indigenous Life*,[34] and yet the people who ran residential schools ignored the link between the inadequate food they served their students and the tuberculosis that was killing them. Among the children who contracted tuberculosis at the Regina Indian Industrial School was Thomas Moore Keesick, an Anihšināpē boy who was the subject of a famous pair of staged photographs. In the "before" picture, as John Milloy writes, Keesick, whose surname means "Sky," is "posed against a fur robe, in his beaded dress, his hair in long braids, clutching a gun."[35] The gun appears to be a toy pistol: a symbol of his potential for violence, which the lessons he would learn there were supposed to contain—a horrific irony, since the school and the system it was part of were violent, not the children caught inside them. In the "after" picture, Milloy continues, "Thomas, with his hair carefully barbered, in his plain, humble suit"—probably his school uniform—"stands confidently, hand on hip, in a new context": he has been "reduced to civility in the time he has lived within the Regina Industrial School."[36] Keesick died of the tuberculosis he contracted there four years after going home with the disease.[37]

The school was in constant financial difficulty, mostly because it had trouble recruiting students. That's no surprise: it closed before 1920, when the law was changed to make attendance in such institutions mandatory for First Nations children,[38] so it depended on parents voluntarily sending their children there, since residential schools received a certain amount of money from the federal government for each student. People who lived on nearby reserves knew what the school was like, and they were reluctant to allow their children to attend. That only makes sense. The numbered treaties between First Nations and the Crown in Western Canada, including Treaty 4, which covers southern Saskatchewan, contained provisions that called for schools to be built on reserves so that First Nations children could be taught, in the words of Treaty Commissioner Alexander Morris, "the cunning of the white man."[39] The Regina Indian Industrial School was not the kind of institution the Chiefs who negotiated those treaties had in mind when they were talking about educating their children. These graves remind me of the haunting question Chief Kamooses asked during the Treaty 4 negotiations in September 1874: "Is it true that my child will not be troubled for what you are bringing him?"[40]

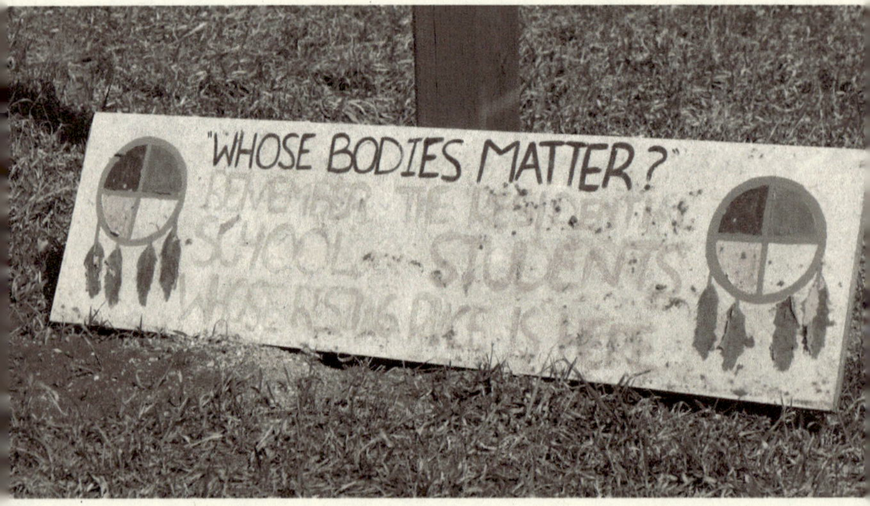

Calling these places "schools" isn't accurate. The Regina Indian Industrial School's main building became Regina's temporary jail in 1911,[41] and a youth detention facility in 1919.[42] The ease with which "school" became prison is telling. One of its principals admitted publicly that the children didn't get much of an education there, because they spent too much time outside of the classroom, working without pay on the institution's farm or in the laundry. The money earned by the farm and the laundry supported its operations.[43] Indeed, rather than using the term "school," Assembly of First Nations National Chief RoseAnne Archibald called them "institutions of assimilation and genocide."[44] The Regina Indian Industrial School finally closed because of declining enrolments, poor management, and parental opposition.[45] Other residential schools carried on operating, of course; the last one closed in 1998.[46] I've seen what's left of that place, the Qu'Appelle Indian Residential School in Lebret, a village east of Regina in the Qu'Appelle Valley. The Elder who reminded us that feasts aren't picnics was sent there when he was a boy. I heard him talk about the experience before he passed away. No one should have such memories.

I kneel and put down some tobacco as a sign of respect, as I was taught to do by the Elder who hosted the feast at the RIIS cemetery. To my surprise, it doesn't blow away in the strong west wind. I tell the children buried beyond the fence posts how sorry I am for what happened to them. Nothing they experienced here was right or fair. The colonialism that shaped their lives—that continues to shape the lives of Indigenous Peoples in this country, and that disfigures the minds and hearts of settlers—isn't right or fair. As a settler, I've benefited from the colonizing processes that sentenced these children to incarceration and death. After all, these institutions were intended to break the children's connection to the land, to eradicate their languages and cultures, a calculated strategy to eliminate their right to be recognized as having a claim to the land that competes with the one that settlers make. I'd rather not have to admit that shameful truth. In *My Conversations With Canadians*, the late Stó:lō Elder Lee Maracle notes that Canadians haven't asked questions about the colonialism that built this country, even as they claim they don't know what happened. "No one got curious about how the shift from Indigenous authority over the land to Canadian authority over the land occurred, nor did they become curious about how our access to the land and its wealth became restricted," she writes. "No one became curious about how Canadian law became the law that dominated the entire landscape. No one got curious about what was here before."[47] Maybe it's easier to remain ignorant than it is to know the truth, because that truth leads here, to this cemetery, to the others like it at residential schools across this country, to all of the evidence that the way we Canadians think about ourselves—that we're good people, that this is a good country—is at best a partial truth, and at worst a lie.

I stand up and look around. There's no evidence of the school buildings; they're long gone, demolished or burned down decades ago. They were actually a kilometre or more to the east, closer to Wascana Creek, on the spot where the Paul Dojack Youth Centre, a detention facility, now stands. The spatial continuity between the Paul Dojack Youth Centre and the Regina Indian Industrial School is a strange, disturbing historical fact. The school authorities made a deliberate decision to locate this cemetery far from the school's buildings: out of sight, out of mind.

A meadowlark on a nearby power pole is singing its liquid song.

I stretch, then pick up the small backpack that holds my water and a tube of sunscreen. It's time to start back towards home. In the distance, I see traffic moving along the Regina Bypass, the new highway that encircles the city, and over the bridge that crosses the Canadian National Railway line. What do I know about the Bypass? I know it was expensive and controversial. I know it took years to build. I know its purpose is somehow connected to the

Global Transportation Hub (GTH), a warehouse park built farther west, just south of Dewdney Avenue. That twelve-kilometre-long street, one of the city's major arteries, is named after Edgar Dewdney, a land developer, an author, the first lieutenant governor of the Northwest Territories, and the person responsible for making Regina—then known as Pile of Bones, a translation of the nêhiyawêwin word for this place, *oskana kâ-asastêki*, "where the bones are gathered together"—the territorial capital. He owned real estate here and stood to benefit from making Pile of Bones important. The naked self-interest in Dewdney's decision about where the capital would be located became a national scandal.[48] Dewdney's biographer, Brian Titley, calls that move the most egregious example of his "self-serving opportunism" and part of "the shady moral code of frontier capitalism"[49] that defined Canada's colonization of the plains. I remember reading about the reason Regina became the capital of the Northwest Territories in Bill Brennan's *Regina: An Illustrated History* shortly after we moved here. I was trying to learn about this new place, to find out why the houses in our neighbourhood in this small prairie city are as close together as they are where we lived in Toronto. The reason is simple: Dewdney wanted to maximize his profits by squeezing as many lots as possible into each acre of land. The land was a commodity for him, something to make money from. In that respect he's not much different from most settlers here. We see land as an asset, as property. The idea that there are other ways to think about land is hard for us to understand.

Dewdney was also one of the architects of the Indian residential school system, and he implemented the federal government's policy of starving First Nations as a way of coercing them into submitting to treaty and living on reserves.[50] Standing here, next to this cemetery, I decide those actions ought to disqualify him from having anything bear his name, including the street I walked on to get here. No wonder a group called the Buffalo People Arts

Institute, founded by Joely BigEagle-Kequahtooway, a Nakota/Cree/Saulteaux woman from the White Bear First Nations, has been pushing the city to take Dewdney's name off that street. He's not worth celebrating, BigEagle-Kequahtooway says.[51] The Federation of Sovereign Indigenous Nations' chiefs-in-council think so, too.[52] So far, though, the city has yet to agree.

Taking Dewdney's name off that street would be the right thing to do. Settlers need to understand the impact colonialism has had on those who were living here before we arrived. As nêhiyaw journalist Doug Cuthand says, taking down the statue of Sir John A. Macdonald in Victoria Park, or renaming Dewdney Avenue, would be the beginning of a new understanding of this country. "Canadians must understand that we are a product of an imperialistic Victorian past that is badly out of date," he writes. "It's time to decolonize ourselves."[53]

Scandalous land deals like Dewdney's are still part of the politics of this place: a few years back, two businessmen with connections to the governing Saskatchewan Party made millions of dollars in land deals in which the provincial government bought land for the GTH for far more than its appraised value. I don't know the details, except that the RCMP investigated without laying any charges.[54] The scandal hardly dented the provincial government's popularity. I don't understand why so few people cared about it.

I watch the trucks on the horizon, gliding across the overpass against the sky. At this distance, they're silent. I don't know much about the Bypass or the GTH, I realize, just as I didn't know about the Regina Indian Industrial School when I first arrived here. If I'm really going to belong here, to be part of this city, I tell myself, I need to learn more about it—including the kinds of places most of us don't think about, like the Bypass.

Then I turn and start walking back towards the city.

ONE

WEST/ PAHKISIMOTÂHK

APRIL 28, 2020

A *few days after my visit to the graves at the Regina Indian* Industrial School, I head towards the city's western edge again. I'm going to walk to one of the overpasses that crosses the Regina Bypass. I've decided to approach the Bypass from the four cardinal directions before taking a look at the Global Transportation Hub and then, finally, trudging around the forty-four-kilometre length of the Bypass itself—all on foot. That journey should take two days, but walking to and from the trailheads, if that's the right word to describe the points where the Bypass begins and ends, will add an extra day to the journey. I want to see what I can learn about the highway by walking. That's my plan—how I intend to spend a big part of this pandemic spring and summer.

I'm not the first person who has used walking to study a freeway. John Davies, an Anglican priest who made an epic, fifty-five-day walk in 2007 across northern England from Leeds to Liverpool, paralleling the route of the M62 motorway across northern England, later published *Walking the M62*, a book that gathers together the blog posts he wrote during that experience. Those posts range from poems and prayers to beautifully detailed accounts of things seen, places visited, and people encountered.[1] Iain Sinclair's book *London Orbital* also comes to mind. Sinclair and a group of friends shadowed the route of the M25 motorway around London on foot while he was researching that book.[2] I'm hoping to learn something about this place, about land deals, about what we settlers think is important, by doing something similar. My method will be like Sinclair's, too. He describes his process in his typically hyperenergetic prose: "Memory is a lace doily, more hole than substance. The nature of any walk is perpetual revision, voice over voice. Get it done, certainly, then go home and read the published authorities; come back later to find whatever has vanished, whatever is in remission, whatever has erupted."[3] Like Sinclair, I'll walk and then research the places where I've been and the thoughts I had while I was there. Unlike both Davies and Sinclair, though, I'll be able to walk on the generous shoulder of the Bypass, experiencing the texture of that highway directly; since highways in the United Kingdom lack shoulders, it would've been suicidal for them to attempt such a thing.

These walks will be "improvised pilgrimages," to use Robert Macfarlane's term.[4] I've made several pilgrimages, improvised and established, over the past several years. The first was my 2013 walk on the Camino de Santiago, from Saint-Jean-Pied-de-Port on the French side of the Pyrenees to the cathedral city of Santiago de Compostela in the Spanish province of Galicia and then on to the villages of Finisterre and Muxía on the Atlantic coast. To use the language of my Baptist childhood, I felt called to make that pilgrimage. Who or what was calling me I still can't say, but I was about to turn fifty that year, dissatisfied with my life and not sure how to change it, facing an uncertain employment situation and not convinced I knew how to do anything else. I figured a month away, walking in a foreign country, would give me time to think. It did that—and a lot more, too. I remember experiencing a joy I hadn't felt in years, talking to strangers as if childhood bullying hadn't made me wary of other people, and making new friends from all over the world—friendships I still enjoy, years later. Since then, I've taken long walks in Saskatchewan, in Ontario, in England, and in Scotland, with friends and by myself. That kind of travel has become something I love to do.

The Camino put me on a path—such metaphors are unavoidable when talking about walking—back to graduate school, to an MFA and then a second attempt at a PhD. I didn't finish my dissertation the first time, partly because my chronic depression got in the way, but also because I underestimated how much hard work it was going to be. Since I went back to school after finishing the Camino, I've published academic articles on pilgrimage and walking as a mode of performance and given papers at conferences in Canada and overseas. The Camino has also led me to the idea of walking, especially long and difficult journeys, as a way to connect with place, with land, with other people—especially here in Saskatchewan. I've participated in walks on historic paths in this province organized by my friend Hugh Henry: from Swift Current to Battleford, from Mortlach to Gravelbourg, from Humboldt to Fort Carlton.[5] Those group walks have also resulted in lasting friendships. Someday I'd like to go back to Spain; I think I have more to learn from the Camino. Perhaps I might follow a different route to Santiago de Compostela than the one I took the first time. Until then, I'm going to see what I can learn from walking closer to home.

As part of my research-creation PhD—that term, "research-creation," refers to scholarship that incorporates an artistic or creative component in some way[6]—I knew I wanted to go on a long walk in Saskatchewan. That's part of the reason why I walked from Regina to Wood Mountain in 2018; I wanted to see whether a long, solo walk here would even be possible. That nine-day journey was an improvised pilgrimage in honour of poet Andrew Suknaski. He grew up in Wood Mountain; his lovely first book, *Wood Mountain Poems*, published in 1976, is both important because it's one of the few books of poetry about that part of this province and politically suspect because of the way Suknaski, a settler, adopts (or appropriates) Indigenous voices.[7] That experience taught me that such a walk was just barely possible.[8] For me, at least. It was gruelling—nine days of blisters and heat exhaustion—but I survived. Since then, I've been thinking about walking across Treaty 4 territory and writing about the experience, as a way to consider what that treaty means. That long walk was going to be the centre of my research-creation doctoral project, but the pandemic has made it impossible. Everything I'd need to support that walk—restaurants, grocery stories, hotels—has been affected by the lockdown, so I've abandoned the idea. I'm not sure what to do next. To be honest, I'm afraid of not finishing another PhD; that would be a crushing failure. Perhaps these walks out to look at the Regina Bypass will help me come up with a new idea; perhaps they'll even become the project I'll end up writing about.

This walking won't be easy—not physically, not if any of the walks I've made in the past ten years are any guide. Not on any level. I'm not particularly fit. I'm about 100 pounds heavier than I'd like—weight I've gained slowly, a couple of pounds every year over the past three decades, and then quickly, after the lockdowns were announced. Now I have trouble bending over to tie my shoes; hell, when I look down, I can't see my feet. My blood pressure is too high, and every morning I take medication to control it. Maybe my weight isn't surprising for a man who's almost sixty, but I can feel how hard being this heavy is on my body. If I walk all day, for instance, my knees start to ache; I wore knee braces on the Camino, buying one for my right knee first, and then, a week later, another for my left. My feet blister, no matter what tricks I try: expensive silk liner socks, Vaseline or Vick's VapoRub as a lubricant. People seem to think I walk everywhere, but I don't; it's too easy to drive to work, especially in the winter, when the frigid wind makes the notion of strolling to the university across Wascana Centre, the huge park in the middle of south Regina, feel impossible. All of this means that an afternoon of walking quickly becomes an exhausting trudge. Circumnavigating the entire Regina Bypass on foot, a three-day, seventy-kilometre journey, might be more than I'll be able to accomplish.

I'm going to be alone today—and on the other walks I make to the Bypass—the way I was on that walk to Wood Mountain. I'd prefer to be with other people, but right now, just two months into the COVID-19 pandemic, that's difficult. We just don't know enough about the virus yet: how dangerous it is, how it's transmitted. And I'm afraid these walks are going to be too long and too dreary—not peaceful or restorative experiences, the way walking on native grassland or in a forest in a national park would be, nothing close to the Japanese idea of *shinrin-yoku* ("forest bathing"), a practice that brings natural environments together with physical and mental wellness.[9] Nor is the random juxtaposition of factories, warehouses, railway tracks, and highways against massive fields of wheat and lentils and canola likely to satisfy any desire for an aesthetically pleasing experience. So it's going to be difficult, this walking: noisy, ugly, exhausting, dangerous. To be honest, I'm half-convinced I'm out of my mind for attempting to do this. Thinking about the examples of Davies and Sinclair makes me a little less uneasy. If they could manage to finish their walks, maybe I will, too.

Along with a camera, I'm carrying a notebook and a pen. Taking careful notes, I've decided, will help me pay attention to where I am, to what I'm seeing and hearing, smelling and feeling. I'm not sure the camera will be as useful. This landscape is tough to photograph. Because people are rarely visible, my pictures end up being all ground and no figure. Occasional road signs or power poles or grain bins give the vast space some sense of scale, but otherwise it's just horizon and clouds and sky, an abstract in shades of grey brown on this spring day, before the crops are growing, with the huge blue and white sky above. As Jonathan Raban observes, these plains are "a region with no foreground, no background, no natural frame or lines of perspective," a landscape "more space than place."[10] To photograph these plains successfully would take more skill than I possess.

Compared to the journeys of pedestrians from previous centuries, my perambulations might be unsatisfactory: short, confined to roads, past fields dominated by industrial agriculture. I can't imagine Henry David Thoreau, for instance, who walked ten or twelve miles around his home in Massachusetts every afternoon, favouring the woods and avoiding roads as much as possible, thinking that my walk today would be worth making.[11] But I can't follow his example—not here. For one thing, there aren't many forests on the Wascana Plains, and although there are a few tame pastures, little wild grassland remains near this city. And, unlike Thoreau's Massachusetts, this province's trespassing laws and farming practices forbid public access to private land. Pastures are surrounded by barbed-wire fences, and few farmers leave space around the edges of their fields for passing pedestrians. The land and the crops that grow on it are too valuable for that, the profit margins of contemporary agriculture too narrow. In Saskatchewan, the law about trespassing recently changed. Landowners no longer need to post NO TRESPASSING signs to limit access to their land; instead, people must get permission to be there, which isn't easy, since it's often hard to know who to ask. Canada has no tradition of "the right to roam," and few people here advocate for the right of responsible access, something common in some European countries.[12] These new rules were part of the provincial government's plan to tackle crime in rural areas. Even though property crime in the country has been decreasing, violent crime has been going up, according to statistics, and rural people have to contend with lengthy response times when they call police.[13] The move to change those laws began after the death of a young nêhiyaw man, Colten Boushie, who was shot in August 2016 by a white farmer, Gerald Stanley, while trespassing with three friends in Stanley's farmyard. You might have heard about that incident; the behaviour of the police during their investigation and the acquittal of Stanley by an all-white jury were scandalous. The Saskatchewan Party government seems to have taken the wrong lesson from that event—or perhaps just the one that appeals to its political base. Instead of considering Boushie to be the victim of a crime, Premier Scott Moe and his cabinet see him as a perpetrator.[14] At least, that's what the new trespassing law suggests.

It's a political winner, though, that new law. According to a 2018 poll by the provincial government, two-thirds of Saskatchewan residents supported requiring people to ask for permission before going onto private land.[15] However, as Doug Cuthand argues, tightening access to private property violates First Nations treaty rights to hunt, fish, and gather on the land. "It's obvious that the Sask. Party government is more interested [in] pandering to its rural base; in the process, there is no respect for First Nations treaty rights to hunt for food," he writes. "This is a party that has written off 25 per cent of the province's population." For Cuthand, the changes to the province's trespassing laws are rooted in racism against Indigenous Peoples. "It's time for a change in race relations in Saskatchewan," he concludes.[16]

Because of the restrictive trespassing laws and the lack of any right of responsible access, walking outside the city in Saskatchewan almost inevitably means walking on the grid roads laid out by bureaucrats working for the Dominion Land Survey in the late nineteenth century: one road running east to west every two miles, another running north to south every mile. The title of one history of the Dominion Land Survey demonstrates its ideological purpose: *Vision of an Ordered Land*, a phrase which suggests that prior to the arrival of surveyors, the land was in chaos, a situation settlement would cure.[17] The authors of an article on the making of the prairie landscape in Canada describe the survey's "mechanistic" qualities: its lines, they observe, "cut across the land with mathematical precision, oblivious to the demands of topography or vegetation." The "rigid symmetry" of those lines, and the roads, ditches, and barbed-wire fences that followed them, "bisected sloughs, lakes, and rivers, cut through aspen groves and slashed through the boreal forest."[18] The scope and inflexibility of the survey was "almost inhuman," they assert, and its lines "determined the size of prairie farms and the placement of the road transportation network" while also deepening "the sense of isolation and alienation experienced by many immigrants carving out homesteads on the vast sweep of the prairies."[19]

Tim Ingold notes that as imperial powers have occupied the world, they have thrown "a network of connections" across what they see as its blank surface: straight and regular "lines of occupation" that facilitate the processes of settlement and extraction, blindly running over the "lines of habitation" that are woven into the land, cutting them the way a highway cuts across the paths followed by both animals and humans.[20] Such lines of occupation divide as well as connect, disrupting the lives of those who were present before the arrival of the colonizers by restricting their movements.[21] Saskatchewan's grid roads are paradigmatic examples of Ingold's lines of occupation. They obliterate the trails that existed before the arrival of settlers; they ignore topographical features; they facilitate certain kinds of movement but prohibit others. They are part of the colonial project, its expression in gravel across the face of the land.

The roads in Saskatchewan make tangible the Dominion Land Survey's imaginary lines, but some of those roads were never built, leaving strips of public land, called *road allowances*, where pedestrians ought to be able to walk—in theory. In practice, though, road allowances are as off limits as the fields next to them. You need to know where they are, and while farmers are supposed to get permission before cultivating them, they don't always bother. Besides, rural municipalities are unlikely to refuse if a farmer asks for that permission, and so the road allowances often disappear into the fields of barley and canola. With them goes another way to walk on the land. So, without access to fields or pastures, I almost always end up on the grid roads when I walk outside the city. Being confined to those roads, being separated from the land by legislation and farming practices, might be the hardest thing about walking in rural Saskatchewan—harder even than the gravel beneath my feet.

I stop to watch a long train of covered hopper cars trundle west, carrying potash to Vancouver where it will be loaded onto freighters and sent overseas. Not every walker is like Thoreau, preferring footpaths to roadways. The early twentieth-century English historian George Macaulay Trevelyan, for instance, sees some merit in both forms of walking, although in the end he shares Thoreau's preference. "There are many schools of Walking and none of them orthodox," Trevelyan writes.[22] Some travel on roads, "the Puritans of the religion"; they have learned that "[t]he road is invaluable for pace and swing, and the ideal walk permits or even requires a smooth surface for some considerable portion of the way."[23] However, Trevelyan prefers to walk elsewhere: "twenty-five or thirty miles of moor and mountain, of wood and field-path, is better in every way than five-and-thirty or even forty hammered out on the road."[24] For him, "[t]he secret beauties of Nature are unveiled only to the cross-country walker."[25] Trevelyan doesn't deny the role of "the hard road" in getting pedestrians to and from those "secret" natural spaces, but he praises what he calls "the 'soft' road"—in other words, the footpath—as a happy medium between gravelled roads and fields that brings together "the speed and smooth surface of the harder road with much at least of the softness to the foot, the romance and the beauty of cross-country routes.[26] Trevelyan advises searching for "as much variety as is possible in twelve hours"—the time span of the walking he seems to recommend: "Road and track, field and wood, mountain, hill, and plain should follow each other in shifting vision."[27] The length of Trevelyan's journeys—in both time and distance—suggests something about the differences between walking now and a century ago, and no doubt Trevelyan would criticize the walks I make as too short, too monotonous, too road-bound. He walked in a place where pedestrians were often permitted to access private land, though, because the notion of a commons—land where landless tenant farmers had the shared right to graze their animals and collect wood for fuel—had not entirely disappeared, despite the enclosure laws passed by the British Parliament during the eighteenth and nineteenth centuries.[28] Such access is rare in Saskatchewan. I know there are footpaths across private land not far from here, but I'd have to drive at least half an hour to get to them, and I'm trying to avoid travelling by car as part of this walking project. I'll call for a ride home if I can't manage to walk back by myself, but I'm going to walk to my destination. That's the rule I've set for myself.

Other walkers celebrate roads rather than footpaths or fields or forests. Take Walt Whitman, for instance. His poem "Song of the Open Road" begins with these words:

> Afoot and light-hearted I take to the open road,
> Healthy, free, the world before me,
> The long brown path before me leading wherever I choose.[29]

Part of what excites Whitman about that "long brown path" is the variety of other people he meets—almost every kind of person, so long as they are able to walk. But people-watching isn't the only benefit Whitman discovers on the open road. Walking there becomes a form of self-expansion; as he inhales "great draughts of space," he seems to become larger and better than he initially thought: "I did not know I held so much goodness."[30] Whitman is attracted to Nature, it's true; Nature is, like the earth itself, "rude and incomprehensible at first," but with perseverance, the "divine things well envelop'd" it contains will reveal themselves to the pedestrian, "divine things more beautiful than words can tell."[31] However, it's human connection that Whitman craves, even more than interactions with the natural world—particularly the person reading the poem, whom Whitman invites to walk with him, to participate in the experience he extols, if only vicariously. Whitman addresses the reader in intimate terms at the end of his poem, suggesting how important the companionship of other walkers is to him:

> Camerado, I give you my hand!
> I give you my love more precious than money,
> I give you myself before preaching or law;
> Will you give me yourself? will you come travel with me?
> Shall we stick by each other as long as we live?[32]

Like Trevelyan, Whitman would be disappointed by my walks, I think, but for a different reason. Where Trevelyan would think they are monotonous and without enough direct experiences of nature, Whitman would be disappointed by their solitary quality, by the absence of other people. But 2020 is a very different time, and Saskatchewan a very different place, than the times and places in which those men walked. I could blame the pandemic, but even before COVID-19 walking wasn't the common, shared experience here that it was for them. In fact, geographers tell us that North

Americans consider any distance longer than a quarter of a mile too long to be walkable.[33] Almost no one would find Thoreau's daily journeys imaginable today, let alone Trevelyan's epic weekend rambles. Including me.

I carry on along the pedestrian path beside Wascana Creek. The red-winged blackbirds and grackles have returned to nest. I love red-winged blackbirds: the flashes of colour on the wings of the male birds, their happy trilling call, the way their return announces that spring is here to stay. Some people complain that they're too aggressive, but I envy their assertiveness. I end up on 13th Avenue, west of Lewvan Drive, a divided highway built on an abandoned rail right-of-way. I stop to take a photograph and disturb a pair of grey partridges, game birds introduced from Europe. They fly off, complaining. Across the road, beside the railway tracks, a small area of grass has burned, leaving a smell of ashes in the air. Meadowlarks sing. When I cross the border between the city and the Rural Municipality of Sherwood, the road surface changes; it's been recently graded, but last night's rain has left it soft and muddy. At Pinkie Road, I head south. The grain-drying facility across the road smells like propane. White cumulus clouds fill the sky.

I turn west again and cross the Bypass on the new overpass. I stop, look down at the highway, and take a photograph, worrying about lighting and focus. There doesn't seem to be much traffic; perhaps that's an effect of the pandemic, or because the warehouse park at the GTH is mostly empty and struggling to find tenants, or because it makes little sense to drive all the way around Regina on the Bypass to meet up with the highway to Saskatoon when there are shorter ways to get there. I don't know. I keep walking. The pavement beyond the overpass becomes a gravel grid road. I listen to the meadowlarks and the quiet hum of traffic behind me.

The spaces where I'm walking—grid roads, busy streets, and eventually the shoulder of a four-lane highway that partially encircles a small, provincial capital—are what Marc Augé would call non-places, "the real measure of our time."[34] While places are about the possibility of stories, about human action, non-places are spaces of passive spectatorship, of looking—perhaps through the windshield of a car travelling at 110 kilometres per hour or faster—rather than doing.[35] Non-places have no stories, no relationships, no connections. Instead, we interact with various institutions through the prescriptive, prohibitive, or informational signs posted in them for us to read: TURN RIGHT, NO SMOKING, SASKATOON 205 KM.[36] They are spaces with which most of us are familiar, even if we usually hurry through them, paying little attention. They are more or less the same no matter where we are, and they define much of our contemporary reality: highways, airports, shopping malls. As Zygmunt Bauman suggests, non-places "colonize ever larger chunks of public space and refashion them in their own likeness," reducing our opportunities to interact with each other in a sophisticated, even civil fashion.[37] Think about road rage, or how we act when we're lining up at a departure gate. In spaces without relationships, we behave as if we have no relationships, either.

By choosing to walk on the edges of highways, in these untrodden but often well-travelled non-places, I am working against their imperatives, becoming one of the "bad subjects" Louis Althusser describes, one of those who resists as much as possible the ideological interpellations non-places impose on us.[38] Althusser predicts that such bad subjects will "provoke the intervention of one of the detachments of the (repressive) State apparatus"—like the Mounties who occasionally roar past me when I walk outside the city limits.[39] That prediction is overblown in my case; if the police notice my presence, they've never stopped to ask what I'm up to. Not so far, anyway.

My attempt at resisting the demands of non-places is subtle, but it still exists. When I photograph the signs I see next to the road, I'm disobeying their injunctions: I'm walking, not driving, using the highway for something other than its intended purpose. Maybe describing the things I see and hear and smell and feel here will make these non-places into places again. Maybe imagining what was here before settlers arrived armed with John Deere plows, Red Fife and Marquis wheat, and the *Dominion Lands Act* will return these non-places to story. Who knows? Maybe I could start to develop a relationship with these non-places, with all their gravel and roadside garbage, or even come to understand why the late Métis painter Bob Boyer insisted that the land—all the land, not just the parts that are nice to look at—is sacred.

///

Boyer was on a panel of writers and artists who were discussing the spiritual qualities of the Qu'Appelle Valley in southern Saskatchewan, the subject of Trevor Herriot's first book, *River in a Dry Land: A Prairie Passage*. Herriot was on that panel, too. Boyer looked at Herriot and told him that he didn't understand why he'd chosen to write about that valley. "It's no more important than any other place," he said, bluntly. "It's all sacred ground. All of it."[40] Since I read the book in which Herriot recounts that uncomfortable conversation, I haven't been able to forget Boyer's insistent words. They reflect an interconnected epistemology and ontology of relationality, along with an understanding of the sacred, that are all part of Indigenous ways of knowing the world. I'm certain we settlers could learn a lot from that way of thinking. That would mean changing our attitudes towards the places where we live. After all, if the land is sacred, we ought to treat it that way. The problem, of course, is where, or how, to begin. What would be the first step?

I remember something I once learned from the accomplished nêhiyaw poet and Elder Sky Dancer Louise Bernice Halfe. We were walking together down a gravel grid road during a walk on the route of a historic trail in Saskatchewan organized by our friend Hugh Henry. I told her that walking alone, as I often find myself doing, sometimes leaves me feeling separated from community. Oh, she said, even when you're walking alone, you're still part of a community, because walking involves developing relationships with everything around us: plants, animals, the land, the sky. That's the meaning of the nêhiyawêwin expression—it's a prayer, really—*kahkiyaw niwâhkômâkinak*, "all my relations." According to this way of thinking, our relationships aren't only with other humans; they are with the more-than-human as well. More importantly, those relationships are sacred. This belief reflects one of the foundational principles of nêhiyaw law: *wâhkôhtowin*, or "relationship." That principle applies equally both to relationships between people and to relationships between people and the land.[41] According to Anishinaabe legal scholar John Borrows, wâhkôhtowin "is viewed as the overarching law governing all relations," originating "from the Creator who placed all life on earth."[42] The nêhiyaw writer and lawyer Harold R. Johnson tells us that wâhkôhtowin is more than just a legal or familial relationship; it's "a powerful spiritual connection" and a "love so immense that a mere human is incapable of enduring it all." It's a sense of being "plugged in to the neural networks, the mycelia, the root systems of the forest"—or, here, of the grassland: "You experience and can translate energy and frequencies. You are repeatedly told by the spirits of the plants and animals and insects, 'you are a beautiful human being.'" wâhkôhtowin, Johnson argues, is a form of constant communication between humans, the world around us, and the Creator, and it is sacred.[43]

This idea, especially as it's evoked by Johnson, is powerful: wâhkôhtowin is the kind of connection I'd like to experience as I'm walking here. It's the actual goal of the walks I am making, one that goes far beyond merely turning non-place into place. It feels so ambitious, and so difficult to achieve for someone like me who, since childhood, has learned a different way of being and knowing, that I hesitate to admit to myself that wâhkôhtowin is what I'm actually after. I take a deep breath and say the word out loud: *wâhkôhtowin*. It feels so big, this word, but maybe it doesn't have to be. Relationships, Ariel Gordon reminds us, aren't necessarily built through "grand gestures"; sometimes, she writes, all that's required is "a willingness to ask and answer."[44] I can do that, I tell myself. I can converse with this place, ask it questions, listen for its answers. That's a place to start.

But that realization doesn't dispel all of my discomfort with wâhkôhtowin. Part of the reason is that I find it hard to see the sacred in the stubble. When I walk on one of the remnants of grassland that remain, I do feel I'm in a sacred place, even though I'm not a spiritual person, and I sense my connection to the plants, the animals, the sky. But when I'm walking on a grid road or a highway next to a field of canola, in a place where the ecosystem is fragmented and impoverished, it's harder to sense that connection. Perhaps, as Niitsitapi philosopher and Elder Leroy Little Bear suggests, some places are more sacred than others, more connected to the energies of the spirit. "That's the reason why there's certain locations, whether they be medicine wheels or locations like Milk River, Chief Mountain and the Sweetgrass Hills; they're all connected," Little Bear, a professor emeritus at the University of Lethbridge, told Don Hill. "It seems that's where all these energies come together. It's not that it can't happen elsewhere. But there are certain places that act as amplifiers of energy waves that flow through you and me and everyone else."[45] Maybe the land where I'm walking was never one of those places, or maybe some of its sacred qualities were stripped away along with the grassland, notions Boyer would likely have rejected out of hand. If he was right, if the land remains sacred even when it's a field of stubble or a warehouse park, then some hint of that numinous quality should still be perceptible. Maybe by walking here I'll find a way to recognize it.

///

A light snow was falling at the end of October 2019 when Saskatchewan's premier, Scott Moe, climbed into the cab of a semi for a run along the brand-new Regina Bypass as part of the ceremony marking its completion. "Today is a glorious day," he told reporters. The province had completed the largest infrastructure project in its history, and it had done so "on time and on budget."[46] The project would make driving on the Trans-Canada Highway east of Regina much safer, he said, because it replaced the old hair-raising at-grade intersections, where motorists had to make left turns into oncoming traffic travelling at more than 110 kilometres per hour, with overpasses and cloverleafs. I remember the frequent news stories about yet another horrific accident, yet another death, at one of those intersections. Nobody could complain about making them less dangerous.

But opposition politicians weren't happy about the Bypass. They pointed out that the budget had increased dramatically as the scope of the project had grown, and that the cost was an astonishing amount for a province of one million people. In the provincial legislature, New Democratic Party (NDP) MLA Yens Pedersen compared the Bypass to the Coquihalla Highway, built through the mountains near Kamloops, British Columbia: "the Coquihalla had 26 more overpasses than this project. The Coquihalla had 18 more interchanges, had 19 more underpasses, 8 more avalanche dams—because we know we don't need any avalanche dams in Saskatchewan—19 containment basins, and over 270 more kilometres of pavement than the bypass project," and yet it still cost $200 million less than the Bypass, which he described as "60 kilometres of road on the flattest, wide openest chunk of dirt in the continent."[47] NDP MLA Cathy Sproule, the party's official critic of the project, said that the ceremony was "a lot of fanfare for one of the most expensive pieces of roadwork on flat ground that this country's ever seen."[48] She was particularly scathing about the western portion of the Bypass, calling the notion that it was necessary to support the increased traffic coming out of the GTH "a fallacy or a fantasy."[49] Yes, the project had led to improvements in safety, Sproule acknowledged, but she disagreed with the government's decision to give the $600 million contract for building and maintaining the project to a French company, VINCI, and accused the government of "grossly mishandling the land-buying process."[50]

The land is at the centre of this dispute over the new highway. It's at the centre of the GTH scandal. It's also at the centre of the colonial thinking that led to the deaths of the children buried in the cemetery at the Regina Indian Industrial School. Who gets to own the land? Who gets to profit from it? Who gets to say how it will be used? Those seem to be the basic questions that have shaped this place, ever since settlers began arriving with the railway in 1882. I doubt they were important questions before then, when Indigenous Peoples looked after the land for millennia, but settlers have different ways of thinking about the land, which preclude the notion of relationship.

Behind me, to the east, I can see the city's downtown and the legislature's copper dome. I look down at the Bypass. Sooner or later, I'm going to walk around the city on that highway. I'll have to carry food and water, sleep overnight in ditches or fields. It won't be easy, but I know there's no way to avoid that highway: if I'm going to learn about it, to write about it, I'll have to walk on it.

That'll come later. Right now, I'm just trudging west, away from the overpass above that highway. I decide to keep going until I reach the tiny bedroom community of Grande Coulee, where I'll call for a ride home. I smile at the name. There's nothing but flat farmland in Grand Coulee. The closest things to coulees there are the roadside ditches. I wonder where that name came from. I need to look it up—to do my homework, the way Iain Sinclair would.[51]

There's little sign of human presence on this road, not even much litter—just a pair of rubber gloves and a couple of empty vodka bottles, possibly evidence of some rural pandemic disinfection ceremony—and yet this space is entirely shaped by settler activity: the roads and fields of stubble tell a story of a landscape that has been almost completely reshaped for settlement and agriculture. It is, as William Least Heat-Moon says about a corner of Chase County, Kansas, "a forlorn place filled with the evidence of mankind but mostly empty of men: a dried-up water hole on the veldt where you find only tracks of its inhabitants."[52] Almost none of the original grassland remains near Regina, because the heavy clay soil is good for growing grain. When that grassland was destroyed, the animals and birds it supported were displaced. The bison that grazed here now live mostly behind fences, in parks and paddocks and on ranches. Perhaps they're lucky: populations of grassland birds are in freefall, with many species heading for extinction.[53] The land's original human inhabitants were confined to reserves by government policies of deliberate starvation before most settlers even arrived.[54] All of that history is written on the stubble I'm walking beside. Today only about 10 percent of the grassland that once covered southern Saskatchewan still exists.[55] The rest is gone, destroyed, never to return; restoring a prairie, as I've discovered on a tiny scale in our front yard, is extremely difficult. Saskatchewan's grasslands have become the most threatened ecosystem on the planet.[56] That ecosystem is important, not just as habitat for birds and animals, grasses and forbs, but also as a carbon sink: the roots of grassland plants extend many metres below the soil, so that each hectare stores as much as 180 tonnes of carbon, equivalent to the annual emissions of thirty-nine cars.[57] And it's disappearing faster than the Amazon rainforest.

The clouds move east. The wind is unceasing. A car stops; the driver asks if I need help. I smile and tell him I'm fine. What my friend Matthew Anderson has written is true: if you're walking in rural Saskatchewan, everyone who sees you will assume you're in trouble because your vehicle has broken down. Nobody walks here by choice.[58] After all, walking in rural Saskatchewan makes little sense: the distances between towns and villages are long, places which offer water and food and shelter are rare, and the land has been so thoroughly, even brutally industrialized that it allows for few of the pleasures that pedestrians like Trevelyan sought in the picturesque English countryside. The pleasures of walking do exist here, as I've learned through experience, but they're not always obvious.

Not everyone has equal access to those pleasures, of course; we don't all get to move through space in the same way. Some

of us—usually those whose skin is read as "white," or who are male and cisgendered and clearly middle class, like me—have more freedom of movement than others. In December 2014, for instance, nêhiyaw actor Simon Ash-Moccasin was beaten by Regina police officers for what he describes as the crime of "walking while Indigenous."[59] Four years later, the Regina Police Service apologized to Ash-Moccasin and paid him an undisclosed amount of money in compensation.[60] But police aren't the only danger to Indigenous pedestrians. In 2018, a Métis woman from Saskatchewan was threatened by a rifle-toting farmer while walking down a grid road in Alberta. When she called the RCMP, they refused to lay charges.[61] No doubt other racialized pedestrians have had similar experiences; think of Garnette Cadogan's moving essay about what it's like for a Black man to walk in the United States, or J. Drew Lanham's bitterly ironic "9 Rules for the Black Birdwatcher."[62] Such encounters can be deadly: in 2017, Barbara Kentner, a thirty-four-year-old Anishinaabe woman from Wabigoon Lake Ojibway Nation, was walking down McKenzie Street in Thunder Bay, Ontario, when she was struck by a heavy trailer hitch thrown from a passing car; she later died of her injuries. The young white man responsible for the attack, Brayden Bushby, was found guilty of manslaughter and sentenced to eight years in prison.[63] Women who aren't racialized also feel unsafe when they walk; because the possibility of sexual harassment or assault is always present, all women must be constantly vigilant.[64] The freedom to move through space isn't shared equally, and my ability to walk without those anxieties is the product of my immense, unearned privilege.

I stop and stretch my tired, sore legs. In the distance, the car that stopped to help me disappears in a pale cloud of dust.

I look back towards the overpass I've just walked across. What does the settler civilization that has tried so hard to displace Boyer's and Little Bear's Indigenous civilizations hold dear? The Bypass suggests we care about speed. We believe that time is money, and money is all that matters. We value what we can extract from the land, not what it gives freely. We alter the land in profound ways to make these principles a reality. Our language works against any notion of connection with the land: the pronoun "it" tends to make the land and its more-than-human inhabitants into things, not beings.[65] That might be one of the reasons the grasslands of Saskatchewan continue to be plowed under: if a section of land is more profitable as canola rather than as June grass and smooth blue beardtongue and songbirds, then the June grass and beardtongue will be destroyed and the birds left to find another home.

They have no value in themselves for us—or perhaps we just can't apprehend their worth.

I know the word *we* isn't fair; some settlers do try to resist consumer capitalism and settler colonialism. That resistance can seem inconsequential, though, even compromised, since most of us live inside those ways of thinking and being, even if we long for something different. I take in the fields of stubble on both sides of the road. How can settlers find an ethical way to live here—one that respects the rightful claims of First Nations and Métis peoples to the land, along with the rightful claims of the land itself? How can we decolonize ourselves? Those questions suddenly feel overwhelming. I keep walking west into the afternoon sunlight.

TWO

EAST/ SÂKÂSTÊNOHK

MAY 2, 2020

It's early in the afternoon. I'm walking east along 15th Avenue, in Regina's hipster neighbourhood, the two or three blocks near the General Hospital that boast a craft brewery, punningly named Malty National; a coffee shop; a vegetarian restaurant; and a store that sells hemp clothing. My goal today is the point where the Bypass crosses Arcola Avenue, at the city's southeastern edge. I could walk directly east, to the complicated interchange where the Bypass connects with Highway 1 east of the city, but when I walk around the Bypass, I'll see that interchange then. Besides, that's probably a rather boring walk, since it would take me in a straight line through the city's big-box retail suburbs. My path today will be more varied, I figure, and for that reason more interesting.

A northern flicker searching for insects in the bark of an elm tree enjoys the sunshine with me. At Winnipeg Street, I turn south and trudge through Broder's Annex, a neighbourhood of wide streets lined with stucco bungalows in need of paint. The city's latest economic boom, which ended five years ago when global commodity prices crashed, never reached the people living in these houses. Maybe the next one will be more fairly distributed—if we're granted another.

I had intended to avoid Wascana Centre, because it tends to be thronged with people taking their pandemic mental-health strolls these days, but I'm wondering whether the American pelicans have returned to Wascana Lake, so I put on my mask and turn in that direction. I don't see any pelicans, though, just mallards, gulls, and geese. Young men have knocked over the sign warning that the skateboard park is temporarily closed, and they're hanging out together as if the pandemic weren't happening. Their sense of indestructability is understandable—I would've been the same at their age—and besides, since our premier announced that some businesses would be allowed to reopen as lockdown restrictions ease, people seem less cautious about COVID-19. The first wave of the virus hasn't made many people ill here; we've been lucky. Nothing like the death and chaos in places like New York or Italy has happened in Saskatchewan. But I'm afraid a second wave is inevitable. Then what? More illness, more deaths. And after that? How many waves will we endure?

I cross the old Ring Road—built between the 1950s and the 1970s, it's the precursor to the Regina Bypass—on an overpass and continue along the gravel path that runs alongside Assiniboine Avenue. It's one of my favourite places to walk in this city, because it reminds me of roadside paths, called *sendas*, in Spain. There's smoke in the air; someone is burning leaves left from last fall. Kids are everywhere, cycling on the sidewalks, enjoying the warm spring sunshine. I pass a young woman walking a beagle. The pair reminds me of my father, who loved his beagle, Rexie. Every night, after supper, he'd walk her to the corner store and buy a cigar for himself and some gummy bears for the dog. The candy didn't do the dog any good; she got fat and her teeth rotted. The cigars weren't good for Dad, either. They likely contributed to the heart attack that killed him ten years ago.

My father wasn't an easy man to love. I know he was only behaving the way his father did. As a child, I supposed all children were treated that way, although my father was always careful to lose his temper only when the windows were closed, so that none of the neighbours could hear him. Anyone I've talked to about his rages has assured me that they weren't normal. Even in the 1960s and 1970s, every kid wasn't regularly grabbed by their shirt and slammed against the wall, or struck with a belt, screamed at and ridiculed, or told to pack a bag and prepare to be dropped off at the Children's Aid Society. I remember that incident vividly: my father's red, swollen face; the loud ringing in my ears, something like feedback; the sensation of floating up to the corner of the bedroom ceiling and looking down, watching the pair of us, a shouting man and a crying child. Even though I knew he wouldn't deliver on that threat, if only because he would've been ashamed to tell his church friends where I'd gone, I was still terrified. I imagined some Dickensian orphanage where the other kids would beat the hell out of me when our keeper's back was turned. I could picture the dingy dormitory, the rows of grey steel bunkbeds, the smeared light coming from a single yellow bulb. Sobbing, I begged him not to send me away.

I've tried to forgive him. I wept at his funeral, mourning the relationship we never had and, worse, never would have. But I carry the effects of his behaviour with me: a reservoir of anger and depression and shame that must be watched, constantly, in case it overflows its banks. As it sometimes does.

I enter Wascana View, a neighbourhood where every street is named after Wascana Creek, which flows along its southern edge.

All the houses here are two-storey pink or buff stucco boxes. The city's Mormon temple sits at the neighbourhood's entrance; its golden statue of the Angel Moroni and his trumpet is a landmark standing against the clear, blue sky. I can smell paint. A merlin screeches. The sounds of two lawnmowers converge, a harmony of lawn care.

I follow Wascana Circle to the McKell Wascana Conservation Park. The park used to be a farm owned by the McKell family, who homesteaded this land in the 1880s. Wascana Creek meanders in curves and oxbows here, and the land is marshy: perfect habitat for ducks. Rather than see the land become yet another subdivision, the McKells signed a conservation easement with Ducks Unlimited, preserving it for waterfowl. All the walking paths are named after corporate sponsors; that's how the fundraising that sustains organizations like Ducks Unlimited works. I cross the creek on a footbridge and follow a path into what I think is a tame pasture, although when I see a winter-bleached stand of little bluestem, one of my favourite prairie grasses, I realize I could be wrong. I can see the Bypass in the distance. It looks surprisingly busy, but the traffic is too far away to be heard. Instead, I listen to the wind and the red-winged blackbirds and meadowlarks. I cross a line of fence posts without wire. A blank sign tells me nothing.

The McKells could've made a killing by selling their property to a developer. They chose not to. That tells me they must've had a connection with this place; they must've cared for it, even loved it, if they wanted it preserved. Or so I imagine. That's not strange. Many settlers love the places where they live. In *Yardwork: A Biography of an Urban Place*, for instance, Daniel Coleman displays his love for his backyard in Hamilton, Ontario. After a rootless early life as the child of Canadian missionaries in Africa, he became a professor of Canadian literature at McMaster University and found himself putting down roots in that "soot-stained, gritty city."[1] Coleman's understanding of his connection to that place was transformed by what he learned from his Indigenous colleagues, particularly Haudenosaunee and Anishinaabe sociologist Vanessa Watts, who uses the term "Place-Thought" to describe the idea that the land is alive and thinking, that it gives us what we need to survive and tries to teach us how to live alongside it. Coleman began asking himself if he could begin to learn "some place-thinking," if he might start "reading the relationships that constitute a place."[2] Watts is clear that Place-Thought isn't the same as feeling love or affection for a particular location; its focus on the way that more-than-human beings contribute to the development and maintenance of human society is different from the way settlers think about the land.[3] Place-Thought is about being in relationship with the land, which, since it is "full of thought, desire, contemplation and will," chooses how it will relate to its human inhabitants.[4] Watts explains that Indigenous creation stories establish a cosmology where Indigenous people are extensions of the land they walk upon, and where they have an obligation to maintain communication and kinship relations with that land.[5] In contrast, the cosmology established by the creation story European settlers carried with them to this place—our expulsion from the Garden of Eden, our exile, our restless search for the Promised Land, the idea that we have been given "dominion" over the more-than-human creatures around us[6]—leads to an inability to recognize our kinship with the world. Our restless movement, our sense that this world is not our home, our belief that we have sovereign authority over the land and its inhabitants, that we are called to govern and control them,[7] all make that recognition impossible.[8] Or, at least, very difficult. The results can be seen everywhere around us.

Without a sense of relationship to the land, settlers tend to see it as something that can be used and manipulated for our own benefit, from which profit can be extracted, instead of a living entity to which we are connected. The McKells, though, didn't think that way, or at least not entirely. Somehow, the land—the very place

where I'm standing—taught them something profound about its value. If it hadn't, this park wouldn't exist.

Like Coleman, like the McKells, I want to become one of the land's students. I've been teaching for some thirty years. I've discovered that when teaching and learning are going on, a conversation is happening. An exchange is taking place, a relationship being created. That's my goal, what I want to come out of this walking: learning, connection, relationship.

The path I'm on peters out in the middle of the pasture. I see farm buildings in the distance, probably on Old 16, the road Trevor Herriot followed when he walked to his family's cottage on Cherry Lake while researching his book *The Road Is How*, one I've walked on before as well.[9] I decide not to go that far. I don't want to encounter a farmer's angry dog—getting bitten would mean hours waiting for a tetanus shot in an emergency ward half closed due to pandemic restrictions—so I turn back. Twittering swallows are flying overhead. Bluebird nesting boxes are fastened to the fence posts. I cross back over the creek and follow its winding course southeast. There's a row of mansions on my left: huge houses backing onto the park and the creek. The view is an amenity, the creek a spectacle. A jackrabbit—a white-tailed hare, to be specific—bolts out of the tall grass. I wonder if its young are hidden there and decide to walk closer to the houses, where the grass is mown short, so I won't disturb them.

No doubt a great gulf exists between the cosmology that shaped the McKells—and me—and Place-Thought. And I'm keenly aware of the dangers of *môniyâwak* like me idealizing Indigenous forms of knowing and wanting to participate in them. Those desires can easily become just another colonizing gesture. At the same time, Place-Thought and wâhkôhtowin are powerful ways of understanding our relationship with the land that sustains us, and I want to get close to them—if I can. Some settlers have written about living in relationship with the land, even if that relationship might not be quite what Watts is talking about. Herriot's essay "A Way Home" is one example. There, he suggests that "if enough people would discover all that is good and holy" in grassland songbirds, "we might be able to turn things around"—that is, stop destroying the remaining grassland and its inhabitants—"before it's too late."[10] That language—"all that is good and holy in these birds"—speaks to Herriot's sense that this ecosystem, which exists only in fragments, if that, where I'm walking, is sacred. That sense of the sacred is connected to identity. Herriot invites his readers to visit a patch of wild grass and lie down in it, allowing "the exhalations of the soil enter your body breath by breath." The birds singing in the sky above "will tell you where you are and, if you listen long enough, they may tell you who you are in the bargain."[11] Although Herriot was born and raised in Saskatchewan, he discovered himself and his connection to this province by learning about the birds that need grassland to survive. He got to know the names of their species; he taught himself to recognize their behaviour, their songs. That learning matters: not as a way of turning those more-than-human creatures into possessions, but because it enables him "to call things forth from generality into a particularity that allowed for admiration, familiarity, even wonder."[12] That learning gave Herriot a sense that he belongs here. "The influence of beings as unprepossessing and elusive as grassland birds is something like gravity, a weak though persistent mystery that holds us in place," he concludes. "The heart recognizes such a gentle force, knows that in simply becoming aware of its pull we take a small step towards belonging here ourselves."[13] This sense of relationship and belonging is different from Place-Thought, but it's something to build on. I bet it's close to the way the McKells felt about their patch of ground.

I see a gate in the steel fence separating the houses from the park and walk through into a vacant lot: one more mansion is required to complete the set. I'm in a newer neighbourhood now, called The Creeks. The streets here are strangely silent. No one is outside. Sparrows and my own footsteps are the only sounds. Then I hear two women chatting behind me as they walk their dog. Their voices seem to bring the sounds of the city—traffic, power washers, lawn mowers, hits from past decades being played on a radio in someone's garage—back to my ears. The houses in this new neighbourhood are crowded closely together. Developers are still following Dewdney's example and maximizing their profits. Kids skateboard in the park. The young trees give no shade.

I walk through the subdivision to the main road, Arcola Avenue. I can hear frogs, meadowlarks, and blackbirds singing during lulls in the traffic. I turn to walk southeast on Arcola. The overpass where the Bypass crosses Arcola is ahead of me; new neighbourhoods of houses and apartments stand on my left. In the distance, across the Bypass, I can see an intermodal terminal, its tall gantries surrounded by stacks of containers. Intermobil, the sign says. It's a competitor of the Global Transportation Hub, linked to the Canadian National Railway line rather than the Canadian Pacific. Jackrabbits run along the fence separating the houses from Arcola Avenue. Despite the rain we've had, Chuka Creek, which runs through a culvert underneath the highway and then between the houses to the west and the Bypass, is nearly dry. No frogs are singing, and only one red-winged blackbird trills from its perch on one of last summer's dry, brown cattails, but the infinite sky is more present, more immense, than it was in The Creeks and Wascana View. A hawk roosts on a glowing streetlight, and trucks thunder southwest on the overpass.

Like Herriot, Jeffrey A. Lockwood, who teaches insect ecology at the University of Wyoming, sees the grassland—in his case, the shortgrass prairie of the American high plains—as a sacred space that exerts a powerful effect on his life. Lockwood is a scientist, but he believes that the grassland manifests God's transcendence and immanence.[14] He also talks to the grasshoppers he studies and the wider ecosystem of which they are a part. "I have learned to converse not only with the grasshoppers but the soil, grasses, and birds," Lockwood writes. "I speak to the prairie and God answers."[15] This dialogue is something like prayer, and he calls his work "prayerful science."[16] Lockwood acknowledges that few of us are able to see the land in this way; many of his students cannot imagine a parcel of land having any value except as real estate, as an asset with a monetary value.[17] They are far from alone in that belief; it is the foundation of our economy. I'm reminded of the shady real-estate bargains that were part of the development of the Regina Bypass. The land had no intrinsic value in those deals; it was only worth what its owners could get for it.

Surely Lockwood's connection to the grassland is a kind of relationship. Could it be as close as settlers can get to seeing the land as kin? I could learn from Lockwood and Herriot, adopt their way of thinking about the land, even if I'm nowhere near a patch of remnant grassland where it might be easier to converse with the land as they do. Instead, I'm walking down the gravel shoulder of a busy road. Is it possible to be in a relationship with this non-place? If all the land is sacred, as Boyer said it is, then such a relationship ought to be possible—even if it might be easier to recognize in a less abject location.

That desire to come into a relationship with the land and to learn from Indigenous cosmologies, however, might turn out to be completely wrongheaded. Stó:lō musicologist and art historian Dylan Robinson argues that all settler attempts at learning—about the land, about Indigenous Peoples—are necessarily extractive. The Stó:lō word for settler, he points out, is *xwelítem*, meaning "starving person": not only starving for food, but for gold as well.[18] That hunger for resources has been joined by new forms of hunger: the hunger to be good, to fit Indigenous Peoples into the multicultural mosaic, "to understand and make accessible Indigenous 'issues' through settler logics."[19] Robinson's argument applies to anything settlers do, from walking on the land to learning an Indigenous language—two things I've done. The bottomless appetite implied by the word *xwelítem* reminds me of the insatiable hunger that animates the cannibal monster in nêhiyaw sacred narratives, the *wîhtikow*. That monster is often associated with settlers: Indigenous poet, scholar, and activist Jack D. Forbes argues that Christopher Columbus was a wîhtikow, as are the systems of economic and colonial exploitation established on Turtle Island by the settlers who followed him,[20] and Potawatomi biologist and writer Robin Wall Kimmerer sees the wîhtikow's footprints in environmental degradation and the "insatiable consumption" that is its cause.[21]

The wîhtikow behaves the way it does because it has no relationships to anything. That's one of the lessons taught by "Wesakaychak and the Cannibal," one of the sacred stories, or *âtayôhkêwina*, that nêhiyaw writer Edward Ahenakew learned from Chief Thunderchild during the winter of 1923 and published six years later.[22] In that story, the nêhiyaw culture hero, *wîsahkêcâhk*—also called *ostêsimâw*, the Elder Brother, when there's no snow on the ground—encounters a wîhtikow while walking through a forest. Despite being "frozen with terror," wîsahkêcâhk gathers his wits and addresses the monster as a close relation.[23] "My dear little brother, I have long been looking for you," wîsahkêcâhk begins, going on to suggest that they share the same mother.[24] The wîhtikow interrupts wîsahkêcâhk, utterly repudiating any sense of kinship and demanding that the Elder Brother prepare to be cooked and eaten in a futile attempt at satisfying its appetite: "Hurry up! Make a fire! I have no brothers and I am hungry. I am glad I met you."[25] wîsahkêcâhk is saved by an ermine, which takes pity on him and jumps down the wîhtikow's throat, biting and tearing at its heart until it dies.[26] The ermine is given a new white coat by wîsahkêcâhk in gratitude.[27] Where the wîhtikow denies any form of relationality, the ermine sees its connection to wîsahkêcâhk, and risks its life to save him from the monster. The story suggests that recognizing our kinship with others is the antidote to the wîhtikow's insatiable emptiness.

Settlers aren't raised to see our kinship with the rest of the earth, though. I certainly wasn't. When I was twelve years old, family friends visited our cottage in Muskoka, north of Toronto. Their son, Greg, who was a year older than me, brought along his air rifle. My parents frowned when they saw it; I knew they were imagining a high-speed drive on narrow, twisting highways to the nearest hospital with a blinded child bleeding all over the back seat. They took me aside, warning me to be careful. I thought they were overreacting, as usual. Nothing bad is going to happen, I thought.

On the second afternoon of their visit, Greg and I paddled the canoe over to the other side of the lake. I wanted to show him the swamp, one of the places I liked to go. A team of scientists from the provincial Ministry of Natural Resources was studying the effect cottages have on lakes, and they had built a concrete dam across the mouth of the swamp, with instruments that measured the flow of water into the lake kept inside a tiny, attached shed. There once was a beaver dam here, but beavers had become rare as more cottages were built. Greg's air rifle came with us. Beneath the shade of the trees around the swamp, it was damp, chilly, and I wished I'd thought to bring a jacket. I slapped at a mosquito. Dozens, hundreds of shiny green frogs rested on lily pads and rocks all around us, watching, wary, ready to disappear into the black water if we came too close.

One of us took the first shot. The target: one of the frogs. A miss. Reload, pump air, try again. This time the frog's head exploded, silently, and its corpse sank into the water. We kept shooting, laughing, passing the air rifle back and forth between us. The frogs didn't move. They either didn't hear the gun's muffled, metallic crack, or they didn't understand this kind of long-distance danger. Another shot, another frog, and another, and another. Dead and dying frogs lay all around us. When I realized the enormity of what we had done, I felt sick. I handed the air rifle back to Greg. He looked at me. "I think we should stop," I said. He nodded. We paddled silently back across the water.

We didn't tell anybody about the slaughter. I worried that someone would see the devastation we'd left behind and tell my parents, but nobody ever said anything. Maybe raccoons fattened themselves on our cruelty, hiding the evidence of it. I don't know; I didn't go to the swamp for a long time.

I wasn't the first child to act so brutally, so thoughtlessly. So many of us, boys especially, snuff out the lives of other creatures as if we are gods administering senseless punishments. Herriot's proposed solution to this problem is to recognize that "killing without rituals of sacrifice, respect and forbearance is the path to an empty belly, an empty spirit, and an empty land."[28] Such rituals, like leaving tobacco to honour the sacrifice of other creatures for our needs, remind us to express gratitude for their deaths.[29] They also remind us that we are tied to those creatures through webs of kinship, networks of relationship. Decades ago, standing beside that swamp's black, peaty water, I knew nothing about such connections. My friend and I behaved like junior *wîhtikowak*, killing for no reason, not even to fill our bellies. Not much separated our actions from those of corporations that clearcut the boreal forest or strip-mine a peat bog or plow under a section of grassland for profit. Scale, perhaps, but little else.

Recognizing our kinship with the more-than-human world might be the antidote to the poisonous thinking that drives such destruction, and it requires settlers to learn from Indigenous Peoples. But, if Robinson is right, there may be no learning about Indigenous ways of thinking for settlers that is not born out of the emptiness, the desire to consume everything, that characterizes the wîhtikow, and therefore no way that settlers might affirm Indigenous values of reciprocity, responsibility, and accountability.[30] No possibility of relationship with anything, in other words. Just insatiable emptiness and greed. I hope that isn't true. I am certain that if settlers can't begin to see themselves in relationship with the land, if we can't recognize that the land is our kin, our family, and see that it always has been, then we will end up devouring our home, leaving only bones and ashes behind.

So I'm going to try to recognize that relationship, even if the attempt might be ill-conceived, even if it might fail. Not for the first time, I think of Rebecca Solnit's words about hope. "Hope locates itself in the premises that we don't know what will happen and that in the spaciousness of uncertainty is room to act," she writes. "When you recognize uncertainty, you recognize that you may be able to influence the outcomes—you alone or you in concert with a few dozen or several million others. Hope is an embrace of the unknown and the unknowable, an alternative to the certainty of both optimists and pessimists."[31] I don't know for sure what's going to happen, whether I'll be able to come to feel my kinship to the land in my bones, but in that uncertainty I can find space to make the attempt.

I walk beneath the Bypass and then a crackling, humming high-tension line. Arcola Avenue narrows to two lanes here and becomes Highway 33, a straight line of pavement heading southeast. There is more traffic here than on the grid road I walked west of the city, and more traffic always means more trash: beer cans, Tim Hortons cups, cigarette packages, and shards of metal and plastic debris shed by passing vehicles—the kind of junk the wîhtikow leaves behind. Frogs are singing in the wet ditch. I experience a strange illusion: I see someone sitting in the passenger seat of a junked car rusting away behind a windbreak, along with farm equipment and a pickup truck. Who is it? What is he doing? I look again: no one's there. A fire burns in the far distance, sending a column of dirty smoke into the air, a dark smudge on the endless blue sky.

I turn to look back at the overpass that carries the Bypass above this highway. I've been researching its history, beginning with a visit to its website. That website tells me that the idea for a new highway around Regina goes back more than twenty years. "Since the 90's, traffic congestion along Victoria Avenue and Highway 1 East has been a major safety concern," it says. "The at-grade intersections are not adapted to the growing commuter traffic between Balgonie and Regina."[32] Fewer than 2,000 people live in Balgonie, though. Can they really generate that much traffic? Perhaps the website refers to the traffic coming from all the communities east of Regina, including Pilot Butte, Emerald Park, and White City. That's maybe 10,000 people. Do they all commute to Regina? If that's the purpose of the Bypass, why does it also loop around the west side of Regina, up to what used to be Highway 11? This explanation doesn't makes sense. There has to be more to the story.

Widening Victoria Avenue in 2004 did little to ease the congestion, but that shouldn't have been a surprise: since the 1960s, traffic engineers have known about the concept of induced demand—the term used to describe what happens when increasing the supply of something, like roads, makes people want that thing even more.[33] Induced demand means that the more roads you build, the more people will drive. A 2009 study of highway growth in American cities by two economists, Gilles Duranton and Matthew Turner, noted that however much a city increased its road capacity between 1980 and 1990, the amount of driving in that city went up by the same amount, as if the two figures were moving together in lockstep. For Duranton and Turner, this phenomenon is explained by what they call "the fundamental law of road congestion": new roads create new drivers, and the intensity of traffic ends up remaining the same.[34] I wonder if the Regina Bypass will become an example of induced demand. It seems unlikely: from what I've seen, the highway is mostly empty of traffic. Maybe induced demand only happens if a road goes somewhere people want to travel.

Because the Bypass website seems to be mostly spin, I start reading newspaper articles about the highway. I learn that political pressure encouraged the provincial government to develop the Regina Bypass southeast of the city. Back in 2010, for example, councillor Michael Fougere—later Regina's mayor—spoke about the need for a bypass on the east end of the city. "We wouldn't be doing our job as a council if we're not asking the province to move forward on this one," he told the *Leader-Post*'s Joe Couture.[35] Planning for a southeastern bypass around the city had already started, but actually building it would depend on the amount of growth in the area. A road west of the city—one linking the planned Global Transportation Hub, a warehouse park, to the Trans-Canada Highway—was then considered a higher priority. At the time, that highway, the one linking the GTH to the

Trans-Canada, was expected to cost between $150 and $200 million. Nobody was talking about what the southeastern bypass would cost. Maybe nobody knew.

Construction on what was then called the West Regina Bypass began in 2010. Given the cost of the new highway, I thought there would've been a ground-breaking ceremony, where Regina's mayor and the premier and other dignitaries posed for photographs, smiling, holding a shiny, gold-painted shovel. Strangely, though, I can't find any evidence of any kind of ceremony at all. Instead, the construction project just seemed to happen, slowly, in pieces, first west of the city, to provide access to the Global Transportation Hub, and then spreading south and east. Doug Wakabayashi, a spokesman for the Ministry of Highways and Infrastructure, told the *Leader-Post* that the first stage of the highway's construction was the building of temporary two-lane roads leading to the GTH. The second stage would be a four-lane divided road from Highway 1 west of the city up to Dewdney Avenue, where an interchange would direct truck traffic to the GTH, and the third the construction of another four-lane divided road from Dewdney Avenue to 9th Avenue North, along with a two-lane road from there to Highway 11.[36] Expanding that two-lane road to a four-lane divided highway, and building an interchange at Highway 11, would be the project's fourth stage, but that would depend on the volume of traffic generated by the Global Transportation Hub.[37] The province seems to have abandoned that caution as the project continued to develop. According to the *Leader-Post*'s Bruce Johnstone, the West Regina Bypass was supposed to cost $100 million.[38] That cost was later folded into the larger Regina Bypass project. Nobody outside the provincial government knows how much the western part of the highway cost. In 2018, Highways minister Lori Carr stated, "The bypass was tendered as a project as a whole, the entire project, so we don't break it out by west, east, south."[39] Because we don't know what it cost, there's no way to tell if the traffic to and from the GTH has justified the expense. According to a 2018 *Leader-Post* report, the volume of traffic on that highway was "wildly off" the provincial government's projections,[40] but it's possible that the highway is busier now than it was then. If traffic volume hasn't made the West Regina Bypass necessary, however, I doubt that the government would acknowledge its costly error. No votes would be gained by such a confession; it would be more prudent to keep pretending everything is working out as planned.

I can see the Cowessess gas station in the distance. That looks like a good place to stop after this afternoon's long walk—almost twenty kilometres. The Cowessess First Nation bought the land and started the business with Treaty Land Entitlement money some time ago. Back in the nineteenth century, when First Nations made treaties with the Crown, they were supposed to get a certain amount of reserve land. Some First Nations never did get the full amount, or else land was taken from them and given to others. So the already tiny reserves—the nêhiyawêwin word for reserve is *iskonikan*, meaning "leftover," as in leftover food—got smaller.

In *Treaty Promises, Indian Reality: Life on a Reserve*, Anihšināpē Elder Harold Lerat explains what happened to the land that Cowessess First Nation lost at the beginning of the twentieth century. Although the people at Cowessess had become excellent farmers by the 1890s, or perhaps because of their success, their settler neighbours complained that the reserve was too close to the village of Broadview and curbing its growth, and that the First Nations people had too much land, anyway.[41] Those complaints led to the federal government's demand that the First Nation surrender 95,000 acres of land in 1907.[42] Other land was surrendered to the Canadian Pacific Railway[43] and the Oblate Fathers.[44] After the First World War, the federal government forced Cowessess to surrender additional land to accommodate returning veterans.[45] All those surrenders. Saskatchewan is a big place. You'd think there'd be land enough for everyone, but if anybody needed more, it was taken from First Nations. For every one of these surrenders, the people of Cowessess received less money in compensation than the land was actually worth. And every one of those surrenders was a violation of the treaty between Indigenous Peoples and settlers, which guaranteed that while most of the land would be shared, reserve lands would be kept for First Nations alone.

In the 1990s, some twenty-five First Nations signed agreements with the federal government and Saskatchewan to remedy these injustices. They received $440 million in Treaty Land Entitlement (TLE) funds to buy land to make up for the land they never received, or which had been wrongfully taken away.[46] The TLE money that Cowessess received was supposed to make up for these historic wrongs. Was it enough? The gas station is just part of what Cowessess is planning; they also manage a large farming operation and a golf course, and they are building a 10-megawatt solar farm on land east of Regina, which will produce power enough for 2,500 homes.[47] Cowessess is developing a large wind-power project, too; once it's operating, it will generate enough electricity for 100,000 homes.[48] Other First Nations have purchased land around Regina and are waiting for opportunities to develop it. The Zagimē Anishnabēk First Nation is developing an office park on Pinkie Road, south of the Regina Indian Industrial School cemetery; they own a gas station and a Tim Hortons on the edge of that site. The prairie grasses and buffalo might be gone from the Wascana Plains, but the land still provides for its first human inhabitants.

I've walked to the Cowessess gas station and back before. The convenience store used to sell bags of bannock, but the last time I was there, the fellow behind the counter told me the baker had closed his business and moved away. I'm too tired to walk back into the city this afternoon, so I call home for a ride. I buy an iced tea and a small bag of peanuts and sit at a picnic table outside in the warm sunshine. It's been a good walk, even if my legs and my feet are sore, and I sense that I'm starting to learn something important about this place—something I need to know—by walking here. Maybe the land itself is teaching me. That idea makes me happy. I sip my iced tea and look up at the sky, smiling.

THREE

SOUTH/SÂWANOHK

MAY 4, 2020

The sun is shining brightly this morning. It rained briefly last night; the lawns have turned green and the buds on the elm trees are beginning to open. I recall Robert Frost's words: "Nature's first green is gold."[1] I pass a crew of city workers standing around an open sewer hatch. Crossing the creek, I stop to watch the birds: grackles, red-winged blackbirds, mallards. I saw a pelican yesterday, gliding overhead. Spring is definitely here. I walk along side streets and alleys as long as I can before I have to turn onto Albert Street, Regina's main north-south artery. I'll walk south from there along Highway 6 until I reach the Bypass at what used to be the village of Rowatt. Then I'll walk back to the city. That's my plan for today.

The streets and alleys are quiet, empty of people. Someone has spilled wheat on the pavement next to a garage. Crows are eating soggy bread in a vacant lot; they fly away when I try to take their picture. In a silent park, the swings are wrapped in yellow caution tape; children can't play on them because of fears that they'll pick up the COVID-19 virus from the seats or chains. I think about the new pandemic vocabulary, words like *fomites*: surfaces on which viruses linger, waiting to infect the unwary. I've never experienced this neighbourhood—Lakeview, it's called—so intensely, even though, or perhaps because, I'm completely alone.

It's almost noon when I get to the strip of fast-food restaurants on the south end of Albert. Only their drive-thrus are open—the dining rooms are closed because of the pandemic—and there are long lines of idling cars, their drivers waiting for bags of food. The pandemic seems to have left us all more isolated and car-addicted than ever. Something as simple as sitting in a restaurant, sharing in the act of eating with others, is now impossible. The sidewalks, like the park I passed, are empty. This street has never been a pedestrian paradise, but it's rare not to see others occasionally sharing the public space of the sidewalk. I'm hungry and bite into the apple I'd planned to eat when I got to the Bypass.

Just before the Ring Road, the point where the city ends and Albert Street becomes Highway 6, frogs sing in the ditches at the side of the road. Their companionable music follows me all day, along with the songs of red-winged blackbirds and meadowlarks; whenever there is a pause in the traffic, I hear them. Such pauses are rare; Highway 6 is busy with cars and trucks heading into and out of Regina. Just south of the Ring Road, I conduct an informal survey of the roadside litter. Over 100 metres, I see a ten-metre-long piece of blue binder twine, pieces of wire, broken sunglasses, tire rubber, steel straps, straws, a shattered tail light, a work glove, a juice bottle and a beer can, a zip-lock bag, a piece of a Venetian blind, and a scrap of plastic sheeting—and that's just what I can make out from the shoulder. So much garbage, and only those who pass by on foot are likely to notice it. David Sedaris, one of my favourite humourists, used to walk twenty-five miles a day around his home in southern England, picking up trash. The local council ended up naming a garbage truck after him.[2] I ought to follow his example and return with gloves and garbage bags to start cleaning up this mess.

I pass a running shoe lying on the shoulder. I'm always surprised when I see shoes beside a highway—especially when there's just one. It happens more often than you'd think. Who throws one shoe out of a speeding car? Why keep one and fling the other into the ditch? I have a hard time understanding how that happens, what the motivations of the shoe's owner might be. It's a mystery.

How much of the garbage I see has come from the semis thundering past? I think about Walter Bond, the cyclist Charles Wilkins met while he was walking from Thunder Bay to New York City. Bond had cycled across North America half a dozen times over the years—to Vancouver, Florida, Alaska. Wilkins says that Bond told him that whenever he saw garbage on the highway, he stopped, picked it up, and tossed it into the ditch.[3] During his cycling journeys, he had been hit many times by nails, broken glass, bolts, screws, parts of mufflers. Once a length of industrial wire cut right through his lip and broke one of his teeth.[4] Another time he was blown off a bridge into a creek when a semi-trailer's tire exploded a metre away from him on a Québec highway. Because of those experiences, he'd made a commitment not to leave debris lying in the road. Wilkins was impressed by that story and started following Bond's example.[5] Maybe I should do the same. Not here, though, on busy Highway 6. I'm not venturing off the shoulder into this traffic for any reason.

The sign in front of an evangelical church across the road, housed in a building that resembles an equipment shed, states its mission: "Picture / Plan / Pursue / Prosper." Prosper? I ask myself. Is prosperity a sign of godliness? The Baptist church my parents took me to when I was a kid was an odd place, its theology crabbed and confining, but it didn't claim that prosperity was a sign of godliness—at least, not explicitly. Perhaps that idea was implicit in the suits and dresses the congregants wore. It was a resolutely middle-class congregation, a place where owners of small businesses and their families gathered to worship. The church I'm looking at isn't subtle: it loudly proclaims that God wants his followers to prosper. It's advocating something called *prosperity theology*, common in Pentecostal and other evangelical churches, which equates religious faith with financial success. Prosperity theology, Tara Isabella Burton suggests, represents "the worst of the conflation of American-style capitalism, religion, and Republican party politics."[6] The evangelical ministers who support Donald Trump are advocates of prosperity theology.[7] Who's surprised?

A piece of gravel in my boot feels like a boulder, but when I look, it turns out to be a tiny stone. The blast of air generated by a passing semi-trailer flings grit in my face and sucks my hat off my head. I step off the paved shoulder to retrieve it and sink into deep, soft mud. Swallows chatter overhead. I can see the Bypass in the distance. I startle a flock of pigeons, which rise up from a freshly plowed field. At first, I can't see any evidence of the drive-in movie theatre that used to be around here. Then, farther south than I remember, I see the sign board that used to announce what was playing standing blankly in a field. The screen is gone, as is the sign that said CINEMA 6. I remember my friend Mike Rollo's film *The Broken Altar*, a study of abandoned drive-ins.[8] So much has changed, and so quickly. "Nought may endure but mutability," the poet Percy Bysshe Shelley wrote.[9] If that was true 200 years ago, it's even more true now.

Seven years ago, I knew this highway better. I often walked south from the university on a grid road, until I hit another grid road that took me west to what used to be the village of Rowatt. Then I would plod back to the city on Highway 6. The whole loop was maybe thirty-four or thirty-five kilometres. Sometimes I walked that route in reverse. Those walks were preparation for the Camino de Santiago. It was hot that summer, and I found the route exhausting. I usually stopped in Rowatt, sat on the edge of the railway tracks, and ate my sandwiches. I always listened to podcasts then as I trudged along the gravel. I wasn't thinking about where I was; I didn't care. Now, because I'm trying to pay attention to my surroundings, to recognize my relationship with this place, I walk more consciously. It's a different experience: richer, more thoughtful. Slower. I regret the way I used to separate myself from where I walked. I won't do that again.

Because I'm wearing hiking boots—grey Salomons, like the ones I wore in Spain—and confined to roads, Jeffrey Lockwood might suggest I'm not making "intimate contact" with the prairie.[10] He recommends walking barefoot on grassland, something almost nobody does, and with good reason: "Walking barefoot amidst the prickly grasses, ragged rocks, needle-leafed thistles, and low-lying cacti seems hazardous, even foolhardy. Nudity and thorns just don't seem to be a good match."[11] But being barefoot is an intimate way of encountering the land, since it requires moving at a snail's pace. "You can move faster for a brief time, but soon you'll need to stop, balance on one foot or carefully sit down and remove a spine or thorn," Lockwood notes.[12] In addition, "barefoot prairie walking dramatically shifts your visual perspective." You have to look very closely at where you're walking, and that careful attention makes such walking more intimate. "Each patch of prairie becomes a new encounter, demanding its own terms, striking up its own dialogue," he suggests. "Naked feet transform the prairie from a homogenous expanse of anonymity into a unique series of personal encounters."[13] The encounter barefoot walking provides isn't only about the risk to the walker's own flesh, though. "This is also the moment at which you damage the prairie," Lockwood explains. "Your weight snaps stems, crushes insects, and collapses burrows. Most of the time, a mindful step does little harm, but your presence is not without consequence and meaning to the prairie."[14] Such walking is truly a dialogue, one that affects both sides in the exchange. It requires the pedestrian to be mindful, to pay attention, but the prairie isn't the only place where we could have such an experience. "Perhaps with practice," Lockwood offers, "we can walk through our neighborhoods, our downtown streets, and our shopping malls with such awareness."[15] My camera and my notepad are helping me become more aware of my surroundings, but perhaps I ought to take off my boots as well. I consider the idea. With my flattish feet, which require me to use orthotics, my podiatrist would recommend against it. Looking down at the metal fragments and broken glass that litter the highway's shoulder, I'm grateful for my Salomons.

I pass under silent high-tension lines. A large fabric Quonset hut stands on the east side of the road, and I wonder what its purpose is. I recall seeing a llama farm around here, but now there's only a garden centre. A goose and a killdeer wade in a flooded ditch, and a drake mallard warns its mate of my presence. This highway is the kind of place—or non-place—that Bettina Stoetzer calls "ruderal." Ruderal places are defined by disturbance; they are "environments usually considered hostile to life: the cracks of sidewalks, the spaces alongside train tracks and roads, industrial sites, waste disposal areas, or rubble fields."[16] Stoetzer is thinking about urban locations, and I'm outside the city, but these roads and fields, the weeds growing in the ditches, the garbage beside the highway, are signs of the immense changes that have taken place here. Stoetzer argues that "human-nonhuman relations" can "emerge spontaneously in inhospitable environments" like this one, and her use of the word *relations* tells me that walking here could be a form of dialogue with place.[17] Even here, in this unpromising, ruderal location, the conversations wâhkôhtowin depends on can happen.

Attention, dialogue, relations: these ideas have me wondering, again, about how settlers can experience the land as kin. David Abram, who coined the term "more-than-human world," contends that people, whether they know it or not, are always already in relationship with a living land, because our consciousness is in our bodies as well as our minds. "It is as visible, animate bodies that other selves or subjects make themselves evidence in my subjective experience, and it is only as a body that I am visible and sensible to others," Abram states. "The body is precisely my insertion in the common, or intersubjective, field of experience."[18] His emphasis on the importance of the body shows the way his ideas are rooted in phenomenology. But the intersubjectivity he's describing doesn't only involve other humans; he uses words like *presences* to include more-than-human entities.[19] Acknowledging the life of the body requires us to acknowledge that we are one of the Earth's animals.[20] And the life of the body, because it's rooted in our senses, involves touching as well as being touched by everything around us.[21] That touching is a form of communication.

Even here, where I'm touching the earth through layers of pavement, attention, dialogue, connection, and relationship are still possible. I can feel it.

On the horizon, I see a line of traffic on the Bypass: trucks floating over the fields of stubble. Perhaps their drivers are simply trying to avoid stopping in Regina, or getting entangled by the traffic in the city's east end. That's the point of an expressway: unceasing movement. It won't be long before there's a gas station at this overpass; travellers need fuel and food. But those trucks could also be headed to the GTH. Either way, the government's predictions about the need for the Bypass, about the volume of traffic it will carry, might turn out to be correct. It's also possible they'll be dead wrong.

Finally, I arrive at the bridge carrying Highway 6 over the Bypass. Last fall's annual sunflowers—a native species which often seeds itself in disturbed spaces—stand stiff and brown beside the road at the top of the embankment. On the other side of the overpass is Rowatt, or what's left of it. The grain elevators that stood here twenty years ago are gone, and the railway siding that served them, where I used to eat my lunch, has been torn up. The old railway ties are piled beside the gravel rail bed. There's a large farm chemical supply depot here now, owned by the American transnational behemoth Cargill: shining steel bins filled with fertilizer and herbicides. How are the chemicals delivered without a railway siding? A sign beside the stack of ties gives no clues. There's a smell of creosote hanging in the air. I eat a stale energy bar while pondering this question. Later, my friend Hugh Henry explains that farm chemicals are transported by truck these days, not by rail, so there's no need for the tracks—another reason to build more highways.

Not much remains of Rowatt: one or two inhabited houses and a Roman Catholic church that was deconsecrated a few years ago. The village, named after some official of the Grand Trunk Railway,[22] was settled by German immigrants and more or less abandoned by the early 1990s, even though its grain elevators remained standing for another decade.[23] Without those elevators, there's no reason for Rowatt to exist: farmers truck their grain to the inland terminals east of Regina now. Maybe they take their loads along the Regina Bypass. The quiet purpose of the chemical depot, and the strange humming sound it produces, contrasts with the general air of abandonment. Something is happening inside the depot; nothing is happening outside of it.

I cross Highway 6 during a lull in the traffic and turn north, back towards the city, gathering imaginary string, like Theseus, as I retrace my way through the world's simplest labyrinth. A flock of red-winged blackbirds fly up from the grass beside the highway. I walk back across the overpass. In the distance, I can see the city and the traffic crawling along the Ring Road. The Ring Road has acted as a barrier to Regina's southern sprawl, but elsewhere highways and railway lines have been no barrier to development. Is that bad planning or inevitable suburban growth? "The direction of postwar residential growth in Regina was determined not so much by geography as by the city's manmade features," Bill Brennan writes in his history of the city.[24] The airport and the sewage treatment plant, for instance, have prevented residential growth on Regina's western edges.[25] But nothing—except the Ring Road and the municipal boundary—stands in the way of development to the south.

Highways have not deterred the city's expansion in other directions, though. In 1973, for instance, Regina's city council approved a new subdivision south of the airport, on the other side of what's now Lewvan Drive, then a Canadian National Railway spur. The provincial government believed that the land's proximity to the airport made it unsuitable for residential purposes, however, and refused to allow the city to proceed.[26] Thirty years later, a similar development was approved by the city, and construction of what's now Harbour Landing began.[27] Neighbourhoods north, northwest, and southeast of the city have also leapt beyond the barriers of highways—the Ring Road and 9th Avenue North—as well.

Perhaps the barrier is the municipal boundary. South of the Ring Road, the land is part of the Rural Municipality of Sherwood. The City of Regina has annexed land before—including the land on which the Global Transportation Hub is located—so why not do the same south of the Ring Road? There's no reason it couldn't—or that the rural municipality couldn't create its own development there. Several years ago, in fact, the RM announced a plan to create a large subdivision called Wascana Village south of the university, right where I used to walk on my way south to Rowatt. It was supposed to house 15,000 people, and it was controversial, in part because Sherwood's reeve, Kevin Eberle, owned land where it was supposed to go. An inquiry led by Justice Ron Barclay found "horrendous" conflict-of-interest issues at the rural municipality, and Eberle was removed from his position.[28] Eberle's land speculation wasn't that much different from Dewdney's, but he wasn't powerful enough to get away with it. Partly because of the conflict-of-interest scandal, Wascana Village wasn't approved by the province, and the project didn't proceed.[29] But since Harbour Landing waited for three decades before construction began, Wascana Village could be resurrected someday.

I trudge along the highway's shoulder. The city has changed so much over the past fifty or sixty years. Even in the two decades I've been here, I've witnessed its growth: Harbour Landing; Westerra; the Coopertown development in the northwest, apparently stalled because of the economy; and the new subdivisions in the city's southeast. And it's not just this city, either. Everywhere I've lived has been transformed in the same way. Our civilization is premised on constant growth, constant expansion: an infinite economy on a planet with finite resources. It makes no sense. There are almost eight billion people living on this planet now, and we'd need four Earths if every one of those people were to enjoy the lifestyle I take for granted—if every one of us were to live in a house like the one I live in, driving to work, buying books and cups of coffee, doing all the things I do every day without reflecting on my privilege.[30]

Indigenous ways of thinking suggest that there is another way to live, one that's not premised on extracting everything we can from our planetary home. What would happen if we saw ourselves as in a relationship with the land where we live? What if we all saw the Earth and the other beings we share it with as animate? That's a question I've been thinking about since I read Robin Wall Kimmerer's essay on learning the Potawatomi language, "Speaking of Nature." Kimmerer's grandfather lost his ability to speak Potawatomi when he was sent to the Carlisle Indian Industrial School in Pennsylvania, and she writes about trying to learn that language as an adult. One of the aspects of that language she finds striking is its division of nouns—and the verbs associated with them—into the categories of animate and inanimate. "You hear a blue jay with a different verb than you hear an airplane, distinguishing that which possesses the quality of life from that which is merely an object," Kimmerer explains.[31] That aspect of Potawatomi and some other Indigenous languages—it's a feature of nêhiyawêwin, too, the Plains Cree language I've studied at First Nations University of Canada—strikes Kimmerer as being incredibly important. "It's no wonder that our language was forbidden," she argues. "The language we speak is an affront to the ears of the colonist in every way, because it is a language that challenges the fundamental tenets of Western thinking—that humans alone are possessed of rights and all the rest of the living world exists for human use."[32] Instead of calling the rest of the world's inhabitants relatives, Kimmerer points out, settlers see them as natural resources.[33] Kimmerer believes that if our language were different, our way of thinking would be different, too. After consulting with an Elder, Stewart King, she concludes that we could get rid of the pronoun *it* from the English language when talking about living things, substituting instead *ki* (singular) and *kin* (plural), pronouns derived from the Potawatomi noun *aakibmaadiziiwin*, meaning "a being of the earth."[34] It is, she says, a way to expand what we recognize as a person to the world around us, the way that the Whanganui River in New Zealand was granted legal personhood in 2017, for example.[35] That suggestion might be worth trying. Why not?[36]

I can now see individual buildings on the horizon: to the north, the dome of the Legislative Building and City Hall; to the east, Saskatchewan Polytechnic; and to the west, apartment buildings at Harbour Landing. A meadowlark on a power pole sings the same phrase, over and over. An RCMP vehicle turns west down a township road, past a sign warning against littering. A killdeer complains that I'm too close to her nest. As I slowly approach the city, I can recognize more buildings: the Saskatchewan Government Insurance head office, the three Hill Towers, the university. A southbound cyclist passes me; he nods curtly. My feet are sore, and I'm tired. Not long ago, I could walk this far before lunch, and the same distance again before supper. How was I able to I do that? It feels impossible now. To the west, a field is filled with bales of hay. Some are wrapped in plastic; others are left open to the elements. Two startled ducks take to the air. Frogs sing in a flooded field.

When I started making these walks, I hadn't expected to see and hear so many birds and frogs. The edges of the city, the ditches beside the highways, are full of life. I've been especially surprised by the meadowlarks, birds I associate with farm fields and pastures. Trevor Herriot calls the western meadowlark "the most recognized prairie bird"[37] and contends that settlers see it as "an icon of agrarian rootedness and loyalty to the farm."[38] They're a nostalgic bird for settlers, a reminder of a way of life that lasted only a few decades.[39] Rural Saskatchewan has been losing population since the 1930s; fewer and fewer people remain to hear the meadowlark's song.

Other peoples understand the meadowlark differently. Dakota scholar Kim Tallbear notes that Indigenous stories don't consider more-than-human creatures as animals, separate from humans. Instead, those stories "feature relationships in which human and nonhuman persons, and nonhuman persons between themselves, harass and trick one another; save one another from injury or death; prey on, kill, and sometimes eat one another; or collaborate with one another."[40] In one of the Dakota stories collected by Yankton Dakota ethnographer Ella Deloria, for instance, a meadowlark tricks a rattlesnake that has encircled her nest by sending her children off to borrow a kettle with which to cook the snake a special meal.[41] Tallbear tells us that such stories "avoid the hierarchical nature-culture and animal-human split that has enabled domineering human management, naming, controlling, and 'saving' of nature."[42] That kind of management is characteristic of settler colonialism and its way of relating to the land by managing nonhuman others.[43] Tallbear is right. Perhaps if we lived in relationship with other creatures, rather than trying to manage them, we wouldn't take so much from the planet to sustain ourselves—turning the boreal forest into toilet paper, plowing under what's left of the grassland ecosystem, or dumping so much carbon into the atmosphere that we create a climate catastrophe that threatens every living thing, ourselves included.

Herriot also tells me that I'm wrong about the meadowlarks. I've been seeing those birds and their haunting song as a sign of the tenacity of natural things, as an indication of how ecosystems find ways to coexist alongside extractive human activity. That's the wrong lesson to take from their apparent ubiquity. "Though it is still one of the most abundant of our prairie songbirds," Herriot writes, "the western meadowlark is now declining at a steady 2 percent per year," mostly because even the scraps of habitat it needs—the grassy edges of fields—are disappearing as farmers cultivate the land more intensely.[44] At that rate of loss, there are about 20 percent fewer meadowlarks today than when Herriot published those words in 2009. What I've been considering a success story is anything but. Meadowlarks, like every grassland creature, are vanishing, and the ways that settlers use the land is the reason why.

I reach the Ring Road overpass and walk into the city. It's late afternoon and traffic is heavy. I'm exhausted, but it's still going to take at least another hour to get home. The sky is beginning to cloud over. Tonight it's supposed to rain.

///

In February 2013, the province announced a new project, related to the West Regina Bypass: the South Regina Bypass. This new highway, the *Leader-Post*'s Vanessa Brown reported, would divert heavy truck traffic off Victoria Avenue East at Tower Road and then extend south of the city "before connecting into the Trans-Canada Highway at the future West Regina Bypass near Pinkie Road."[45] The project's budget was $400 million. Residents of the city's east end were adamant that the new South Regina Bypass needed to be built. "This is sorely needed and long overdue," one resident told Brown. "It's gotten to the point now that the amount of traffic is ludicrous."[46] It's true that the eight lanes of traffic on the eastern section of Victoria Avenue, between the Ring Road and the city's edge, are constantly busy. I've always wondered why the city didn't consider the effect that the combination of people driving to shop in the big-box retail developments in the east end and others trying to get to the Ring Road around Regina would have on the flow of traffic—never mind the principle of induced demand. The car reigns on Vic East, but nobody seems to have prepared for it, even though we are all its subjects. And, of course, nobody who finds themselves stuck in traffic imagines they're part of the problem.

A month after the South Regina Bypass was announced, the province revealed that it was considering using a public-private partnership to fund the new highway. According to the Organisation for Economic Co-operation and Development, public-private partnerships are agreements between governments and one or more private-sector partners, which might operate or finance the project. In those agreements, the private-sector partners deliver a government service while making a profit. According to the report, the effectiveness of these agreements depends on a sufficient transfer of risk to the private-sector partners.[47] "Sufficient transfer of risk," the report contends, means that the risks involved in P3 deals ought to be shared fifty-fifty between governments and their private-sector partners; that way, those partners are more likely to operate efficiently.[48] Otherwise, they won't make any money.

Perhaps because they don't think governments can be efficient, conservative politicians like the idea of P3s for all kinds of projects.

It wasn't surprising, then, that in June 2013 the province decided that the South Regina Bypass, as well as several new schools and a hospital in North Battleford, would be built through P3 arrangements. The project to upgrade Regina's wastewater treatment plant would also be a P3,[49] along with Mosaic Stadium, where the Saskatchewan Roughriders play.[50] "If we continue to do things in the conventional way of approving, designing and building infrastructure, quite frankly, we're not going to get there, or if we get there, it won't be on a timely basis," Brian Manning, a former senior bureaucrat in the Alberta government who had been appointed as the president and CEO of SaskBuilds, the province's new Crown corporation in charge of constructing infrastructure, told Bruce Johnstone.[51] Manning believed the private sector is inherently better than the public sector when it comes to building infrastructure, and the provincial government clearly agreed. Don McMorris, for example, then the Saskatchewan minister of Highways and Infrastructure, told Brown that new highways built in Alberta were cheaper when built as P3s.[52]

Not everyone likes the use of P3s, though, or agrees that they are cheaper and more efficient than having governments build things and deliver services. For one thing, a provincial government can borrow money for an infrastructure project more cheaply than a private corporation could, and taxpayers end up paying for those higher interest rates. And claims that P3s are cheap and efficient, Université Laval business professor Pierre-André Hudon argues, are hard to verify, either because financial data are unavailable or "because of political manipulation of accounting procedures."[53] What Hudon says about government accounting procedures might be especially true if the government involved is defending a decision to spend money on a particular project. P3s also lock governments into "long-term contracts and remove decision-making power from elected officials," amplifying the governance problems involved in traditional ways of constructing infrastructure, Hudon contends.[54] Perhaps the preference for P3s is simply an ideological one: if you believe that the private sector can solve every problem better than governments can, and that the public sector is inherently inefficient, you might turn to the private sector to build and manage public infrastructure, even if that means losing democratic control over those projects. You might decide that trade-off is worthwhile.

I think about the P3s I've walked past in Regina—the new Connaught School building on Elphinstone Street, for instance. I honestly don't understand how a corporation can make money building and operating a school building while passing savings on to taxpayers. Why build a school that way? According to Johnstone, some projects—Mosaic Stadium and the wastewater treatment plant—are good candidates for P3s. "First of all, P3s work best for large-scale ($100 million to $200 million projects or more) and ones that require specialized skills, state-of-the-art technology and a proven track record of delivering projects of similar size and type on time and on budget," he writes. "Do you want contractors learning on the job, while they're building a stadium or a waste water treatment plant for the first time? No. You want companies of sufficient scale and competence to build large projects that are technically challenging and financially daunting."[55] However, Johnstone does question the wisdom of the province's decision to award one contractor a bid to build nine schools in Saskatchewan. "Most large or even medium-sized contractors in the province can build a school," he notes.[56] Besides, why did all those schools have to be built by the same contractor? The province argued that this approach saved money, but according to Johnstone, "there's also ample evidence that the 'cookie cutter' approach to building P3 schools, while cost-effective, may not be the best model for the schools' users—local communities."[57]

The track record on P3s in Saskatchewan is mixed at best. On one hand, the upgrades to Regina's wastewater treatment plant came in substantially under budget, and the city's mayor, Michael Fougere, credited the P3 process for those savings.[58] On the other hand, the new hospital in North Battleford has been a disaster. The roof had to be replaced, as did the exterior walls, and there have been many problems with the building's plumbing, including toilets flushing with hot water instead of cold.[59] Could a project managed by the government, instead of a private company, have gone so wrong? Of course. But the question of whether that hospital was built badly because of, not in spite of, the P3 arrangement needs to be answered. Similar questions have been asked about the Regina Bypass. A few years ago, farmers complained that one of the new overpasses, near the village of Balgonie, east of the city, was too narrow for their equipment, a surprising oversight in a province defined by its endless fields of wheat, and demanded that the problem be corrected.[60] Would a different funding and ownership model have avoided such mistakes? We need to know.

Whatever the benefits or drawbacks of P3 arrangements might be, Prime Minister Stephen Harper's Conservative government, which contributed $200 million to the Regina Bypass project, strongly believed they were the way to go, and the provincial Saskatchewan Party government agreed. In May 2014, McMorris announced that not only would the Regina Bypass be designed and built by a private company, but it would be operated and maintained by one, too, for thirty years after the day it opened.[61] A year later, a French conglomerate, VINCI, won the contract to build and operate the Regina Bypass. According to VINCI's website, the company operates in 110 countries, where its more than 100,000 employees design and build all kinds of things, ranging from urban-development projects to nuclear engineering.[62] It was also accused of violating the human rights of migrant workers who were building the stadium for the 2022 FIFA World Cup in Qatar.[63] Will VINCI be more efficient than the provincial highways department at plowing snow and patching potholes on the Bypass? Has

VINCI taken on sufficient risk to ensure it will operate the highway effectively? Citizens of Saskatchewan have no idea; the terms of VINCI's contract with the province are confidential, as David Marit, then the minister of Highways and Infrastructure, told the Legislative Assembly of Saskatchewan's Standing Committee on the Economy in 2017.[64] We'll have the next three decades to decide if the deal with VINCI makes sense.

Questions about the highway's cost were also being raised. By June 2013, the price tag for the project was estimated at between $700 and $800 million, with the southeast leg contributing $300 million to the total cost. McMorris told the *Leader-Post*'s Craig Slater that it could be the largest infrastructure investment in Saskatchewan's history. Construction on the south part of the Bypass would begin in two years' time, McMorris continued, noting that more planning would be required to construct interchanges east of Regina at Pilot Butte, White City and/or Emerald Park, and Balgonie.[65] Ten months later, when the route was finalized, the project was expected to cost $1.2 billion, a significant increase over the previous estimate; by August 2015, the price tag had grown to $1.88 billion, not including purchasing the land.[66] The government wouldn't say what the final cost would be.[67] Perhaps it didn't know.

The government's apparently careless approach to spending on the Regina Bypass didn't sit well with some observers. *Leader-Post* columnist Murray Mandryk wrote that a combination of public indifference and poor government accounting had produced "some rather bad results," including the Regina Bypass. The province, he complained, was "hurriedly and carelessly overspending on a $2 billion-plus project that's likely being built in the wrong place for the wrong reason."[68] The government's defence was that the details of the Regina Bypass contract couldn't be released for competitive reasons—the governance problem Hudon identifies. Nobody knows if the $680 million that the province is paying

VINCI to operate and maintain the highway is the right amount. That fee includes the transfer of risk, which in this case refers to the cost of replacing or restoring the highway once VINCI's thirty-year contract is up. Some accountants don't like the concept of transfer of risk. Ontario's provincial auditor, Bonnie Lysyk, who used to be Saskatchewan's provincial auditor, criticized its use in her assessment of Ontario P3s, concluding that it "didn't apply to any accounting reality." "But it is a good way for a government to hide cost overruns and thus prove its philosophical case that P3s are less expensive than the traditional method of private companies bidding and then building an infrastructure project without taking any long-term ownership of it," Mandryk pointed out. At the same time, he argued, "it would also be a very good way of government claiming that a P3 project came in under budget if there were no cost overruns, or only modest ones."[69]

None of the controversy about the Regina Bypass hurt the governing Saskatchewan Party or Premier Brad Wall. The public protests about the cost of the highway were small, and few people seemed to care about the P3 arrangement, perhaps because it was the only way to get funding from the federal government. There were petitions and demonstrations against the P3 deal to upgrade Regina's wastewater plant, however, even though that was the only way to get federal funding for the project. It's hard to understand why the reaction to the Bypass was so different from the reaction to the wastewater treatment plant project, or why the criticisms of the highway had no effect on the government's popularity. Maybe people stop paying attention when the sums under discussion seem astronomical; maybe they care more about sewage treatment than highways. In any case, the Saskatchewan Party government easily defeated the NDP in the April 2016 provincial election.

Some people remained critical of the Bypass even after it was finished. Early in 2020 Mandryk suggested that the high cost of the Bypass was due to "the impossibly complex financial arrangement of a public-private partnership with its excessively expensive maintenance agreements."[70] The government's insistence that the four-fold increase in the Bypass's total distance was "due to an expanded vision with additional overpasses on the west side to link into the Global Transportation Hub," Mandryk continued, was itself a problem, given the GTH's own failings.[71] But even if the highway and the GTH were expensive failures, even if all Saskatchewan is left with are two costly white elephants, nobody has paid a political price. Certainly not the Saskatchewan Party government: during the October 2020 election, the NDP hardly mentioned either project, and Wall's successor, Premier Scott Moe, returned to power in a landslide, with more than 60 percent of the votes cast.[72]

Perhaps none of the debate and disagreement and controversy about the Regina Bypass matters now. The contracts were signed. The land was bought. The highway was built. Even if the decisions were wrong, we're stuck with the results. People are driving along the Bypass as I write these words— not many, perhaps, but a few. I imagine the sound of trucks and, in the gaps between vehicles, the wind and the songs of birds.

FOUR

NORTH/ KÎWÊTINOHK

MAY 11, 2020

It's a chilly morning, and I wait to set off until the temperature is well above zero. My plan is to walk north on the shoulder of Highway 11 to the northern terminus of the Bypass. I'm anxious about this excursion, because I'll be on the shoulder of a busy highway, and busy highways are dangerous for pedestrians. I've walked on that shoulder before; seven years ago, I trudged thirty-five kilometres north on that road to Lumsden as part of getting ready for the Camino de Santiago. It wasn't a pleasant journey, with traffic roaring past just a few feet away from me, and I've never done it again. So I spend part of the morning checking maps, trying to see if there's another way I could get close to the Bypass's northern extremity. There isn't. Only one route makes sense: Highway 11. Or what used to be called

Highway 11. Since the western leg of the Bypass took that name, the highway where I'll be walking seems to be anonymous. That makes it an obvious non-place.

I'm not happy about this idea, but I can't see an alternative. The notion of trucks and cars speeding by so close that I could almost reach out and touch them bothers me. Maybe it's the pandemic, or being almost sixty years old, but I've been more conscious of my mortality this spring, more aware of life's fragility, and I'd rather not end my time on this planet by getting hit by a truck beside a busy highway. But I'm also not going to let that anxiety dictate where I walk. I've made a commitment to myself: I'm going to learn about the Bypass by walking. I'm not going to back out because I'm afraid of traffic.

It's late morning by the time the temperature crawls into the positive single digits. I walk up Albert Street. North of downtown, the vacant lots and empty storefronts tell a story about the neighbourhood's fortunes. There are few pedestrians. The sidewalks have been cleared of litter and grit, though, and a flotilla of street sweepers passes me, removing the winter's debris. I stop under a small basswood tree and drink some water. The farther I get from the city centre, the more activity I see: people, traffic, shops. My stomach tells me it's lunch time, but I don't feel like downloading an app and entering my credit card information with frigid fingers just so I can eat a disappointing hamburger while standing in the cold. I try a gas station. The sandwiches there look unappetizing, and the pandemic means no coffee. There are too many fomites infected people might touch: the handle of the coffee pot, paper cups, stir sticks. I decide to skip lunch. I should've thought ahead, tossed a sandwich into my backpack, but I didn't.

As I walk, I continue to think about how settlers might bring themselves into a relationship with the land—and if that's even possible. One branch of philosophy that supports the idea that we can be—or even already are—in a relationship with the more-than-human world goes under the name "object-oriented ontology." Object-oriented ontologists believe in a flat ontological hierarchy—that is, that there are no essential differences between humans and the objects in the world around them. Jane Bennett, for instance, argues against the "habit of parsing the world into dull matter (it, things) and vibrant life (us, beings)."[1] Instead, she believes, we should "encourage more intelligent and sustainable engagements with vibrant matter and lively things," and "articulate a vibrant materiality that runs alongside and inside humans to see how analyses of political events might change if we gave the force of things more due."[2] Bennett sees everything as participating in this "vibrant materiality," not just aspects of the natural world. Trash, road signs, fences, bottles of soda—they're all "lively things," objects that are strangely vital; she detects vibrations in what might appear to be inert matter—in debris that has collected over a storm drain, for instance, which she describes as rapidly shifting from "dead stuff" to "live presence."[3]

Living things are just as complex, Bennett argues, but in a slightly different way. Our bodies are themselves collections of organisms and things, including bacteria of various kinds, without which we could not survive. "In a world of vibrant matter, it is thus not enough to say that we are 'embodied,'" she contends. "We are, rather, *an array of bodies*, many different kinds of them in a nested set of microbiomes."[4] Recognizing this fact might cause us to reconsider our relationships with other sentient forms of life, since we humans are not separate from the world around us. We're part of it. It's part of us.

I carry on north to the bridge over the Ring Road. A Richardson's ground squirrel whistles. Jackrabbits hide in a copse of trees encircled by the off-ramp. They bolt when they hear my footsteps crunching on the gravel shoulder. At the overpass, Albert Street becomes Highway 6, the way it does on the opposite end of the city. Plastic trash has blown up against the bushes next to the road.

If Bennett is right, I share my "vibrant materiality" with that trash, with the concrete, with the trees and ground squirrels and jackrabbits. We're all connected, related in different ways. There are houses to the left, and from one of them comes a sound of hammering. Somewhere a small dog yips. The wind is cold. A grackle creaks. In the distance, I can see a new neighbourhood on the other side of Highway 11. To the left, new houses have been built right up against that highway. Across the flooded ditch, a man is walking next to the fence separating their backyards from the road. I wonder what he's doing. Maybe he wonders what I'm doing. He's carrying a shopping bag. Perhaps he's collecting bottles and cans to return for the deposit, or like David Sedaris he's tidying up. A dead squirrel lies on the gravel shoulder. There is so much death beside a busy highway, so many lives ended by speeding traffic, but since the process of decomposition involves living organisms consuming dead flesh, eating the bodies of the deceased, the roadkill hosts life, even if it is no longer alive itself.[5] That's the only consolation I can take from the corpses lying in the ditches and on the shoulders of these roads. They're all part of Bennett's "vibrant matter."

I'm approaching the Highway 11 off-ramp. The Evraz steel mill, which makes pipe for the petroleum industry out of scrap metal, looms across the highway, looking dark and Satanic, to paraphrase William Blake.[6] The sky is a massive blue vault. Tumbleweeds blow across the highway into the path of a truck. I walk up the ramp onto Highway 11. To the left are the city's most northwestern neighbourhoods, where I've walked many times. The ditch is full of garbage: rusty steel, shards of plastic, shredded tires, cables, tarps, part of a wooden crate—another place where I could follow Sedaris's example and pick up trash.

Another thinker linked to object-oriented ontology, Bruno Latour, focuses on the natural world and, in particular, climate change, which he sees as the key to understanding the political history of the last fifty years. Latour argues that we need to shift away from our preoccupations with the Global (as in the global economy) and the Local (various kinds of parochialisms and nationalisms) to the Terrestrial, which he defines as the natural world understood as our territory, our home. For Latour, the Terrestrial, as an agent, is alive, and we need to recognize its vitality; but, even more importantly, it possesses us. We belong to it, but it belongs to no one.[7]

One way of coming to terms with the Terrestrial, Latour suggests, is to investigate, from the bottom up, our dwelling places—the things we, as terrestrial beings, depend on for our survival, along with other beings—by making an inventory.[8] This inventorying is difficult, because the animate beings that compose it "all have their own trajectories and interests."[9] Nevertheless, Latour argues that such inventories would account for the way the Terrestrial engenders us. The walks I'm making around Regina might be the beginning of my own inventory, an exploration of the history and geography and geology of the place where I live and the use (or misuse) made of it by settlers, a recognition of how the Terrestrial makes my life here possible. The descriptions of the non-places where I'm walking might become the record of my inventory.

Object-oriented ontology is exciting, like David Abram's phenomenology, because it suggests a way that I might enter into a relationship with the land around me, but I need to be careful. In her critique of Latour, Métis anthropologist Zoe Todd argues that "the appropriation of Indigenous thinking in European contexts without Indigenous interlocutors present to hold the use of Indigenous stories and laws to account flattens, distorts and erases the embodied, legal-governance and spiritual aspects of Indigenous thinking."[10] Latour, Todd contends, doesn't recognize that Indigenous Peoples all around the world have understood notions like the Terrestrial for thousands of years. One could say the same thing about Abram: he relies on non-Indigenous anthropologists to explain Indigenous world views, rather than turning directly to the words of Indigenous people. Vanessa Watts, on the other hand, thinks that Latour and other object-oriented ontologists don't go far enough; they don't understand that because all things have spirit, all things have agency and are capable of intentionality and, therefore, are sacred.[11] At least you're considering Indigenous thinkers like Todd and Watts, I tell myself. Give yourself some credit.

Still, their critiques leave me thinking about how hard it would be for settlers to rework our way of thinking about the world from the ground up. Indeed, Leanne Betasamosake Simpson describes her fifteen-year relationship with Elder Doug Williams from Curve Lake First Nation, during which they have "hunted, fished, trapped, picked medicines, conducted ceremonies, harvested birch bark, made maple syrup, canoed ancient routes and harvested wild rice"—an ongoing connection she describes as the most profound educational experience of her life.[12] Williams has also taught Simpson the history of the Michi Saagiig Nishnaabeg, their political traditions, ceremonies, philosophies, and values, and has taken her to visit sacred sites. "It is this relationship, more than any other, that has made me Michi Saagiig Nishnaabeg," she writes. "Doug has invested more time in my spiritual, emotional and intellectual education than anyone else in my life."[13] Compared to that protracted learning process, my walking might seem like nothing at all.

Or, perhaps, not nothing. In his essay "We Need a New Story: Walking and the *wâhkôhtowin* Imagination," nêhiyaw education scholar Dwayne Donald explains how he's inspired by the concept of wâhkôhtowin, "which refers to enmeshment within kinship relations that connect all forms of life"—the kind of relationships that are denied by settler colonialism.[14] "When human beings undertake walking as a life practice, the wâhkôhtowin imagination can be activated, wherein the networks of human and more than human relations that enmesh us become vivified and apparent," Donald writes. "From this confluence of walking and the *wâhkôhtowin* imagination emerges the possibility of a new story that can give good guidance on how to live life in accordance with kinship relationality."[15]

Donald recalls a walk he completed just before the summer solstice in 2008. His destination on that walk was the Viking Ribstones, a sacred site dedicated to the spirit of the buffalo; it is one of the few remaining places on the prairies that still has buffalo stones in their original location, and it is sacred for nêhiyawak and others.[16] Donald's walk was "an intentional act of relational renewal":

> I walked to honour the spirit of the buffalo. I walked to step in the footprints of my ancestors and approach the site as they once did. However, attempting to renew these relations when so much has changed proved to be difficult. Instead of natural prairie, I walked on a gravel road. Instead of free-ranging herds of buffalo, I saw cattle behind barbed wire fences. Instead of the rich diversity of flora and fauna my ancestors knew, I saw monocrops, dugout sloughs and the occasional bird.[17]

Donald walked for five hours before he saw the hill where the Viking Ribstones are located. He squeezed through a barbed-wire fence and crossed a meadow, trespassing on private land, then climbed that hill and made an offering. "I had visited this site several times before, but the act of walking to the site deepened my relationship to the place," he writes. "I felt like the stones recognized me as a long-lost relative who had finally returned home."[18]

Donald leads mixed groups of Indigenous people and settlers on walks beside the North Saskatchewan River in Edmonton, experiences that "wake up something important inside of people that was put to sleep as they became educated. By walking and listening, people begin to perceive the world around themselves differently." They come to feel themselves to be "enmeshed in relationships," walking themselves into kinship with the land."[19] These walks, he argues, are the most important contributions that he can make to "the complex task of repairing Indigenous-Canadian relations and renewing them on more ethical terms."[20] That task cannot be accomplished by Canadians learning about Indigenous Peoples; it requires a different form of engagement, one walking can facilitate.[21] Walking won't solve all of our problems, Donald concludes, but it's "a fundamental way that human beings perceive the world and come to story their place in it."[22]

No doubt Donald and Simpson are describing relationships to land which possess different degrees of knowledge and intimacy, and their essays confirm that there's no one "Indigenous" approach to kinship relationality. However, Donald sees his practice of leading group walks as something not unlike the nêhiyaw writer Willie Ermine's notion of an "ethical space of engagement," a space which can function as a neutral zone between cultures, "a venue to step out of our allegiances, to detach from the cages of our mental worlds and assume a position where human-to-human dialogue can occur."[23] Given the genocide of Indigenous Peoples attempted by settlers ever since Columbus stepped ashore, we shouldn't expect anything like an "ethical space of engagement," however much we might need one. Ermine's suggestion that such a space exists, and Donald's creation of one, are astonishing acts of generosity.

Their generosity reminds me of nêhiyaw poet Beth Cuthand's "For All the Settlers Who Secretly Sing," a poem dedicated to the settler writer Sharon Butala. In *The Perfection of the Morning: An Apprenticeship in Nature*, Butala describes her attempt to develop a relationship with the Old Man on His Back plateau in southwestern Saskatchewan. Towards the end of that book, she describes having a vision while walking on the ranch she and her husband operated on native grassland there: she sees an Indigenous "shaman," his "arms raised in an attitude of prayer or invocation," and immediately she feels unworthy, as if she's trespassing on a sacred site.[24] For Métis writer and critic Warren Cariou, Butala's sense of unworthiness is "a condemnation of the entire settler tradition": no redress or reconciliation is possible because Indigenous people have been expelled from the land.[25] Cuthand responds to Butala's visions and her desire to connect with the land in a different way. Her poem suggests that when the land's song "rises" in Butala, and when the land hears her singing that song "secretly" back to it, the land realizes that she "belong[s] here too."[26] Note the relationship between Butala and the land implied by the poem; the land provides Butala with a song, and then listens to her singing that music, as if they were engaged in a dialogue with each other, or as if Butala were the land's student. The use of the plural noun "Settlers" in the poem's title extends the possibility of this kind of learning and belonging to other settlers who, like Butala, are able to apprehend and sing the land's music. Cuthand's generous and open-hearted poem, like Donald's and Ermine's essays, is both humbling and inspiring, given the ongoing reality of colonialism in this country. It gives me hope that I might learn the land's songs as well—that I too might find a way of connecting to the land.

To sing to the land, or even talk with it, one would need a detailed language for describing it. "This is a book about the power of language—strong style, single words—to shape our sense of place," Robert Macfarlane's *Landmarks* begins.[27] Macfarlane collected place-words from all over the United Kingdom for a decade, discovering them in a variety of sources, in order to gather together "terms for the land and its specificities—terms used by fishermen, farmers, sailors, scientists, crofters, mountaineers, soldiers, shepherds, walkers and unrecorded ordinary others for whom specialized ways of indicating aspects of place have been vital to everyday practice and perception" and, by "assembling some of this fine-grained and fabulously diverse vocabulary," to release its poetry into "imaginative circulation."[28] Some of these terms describe things Macfarlane has seen but never before been able to name, such as *smeuse*, a word in Sussex dialect that means "the gap in the base of a hedge made by the regular passage of a small animal."[29] Now that he knows that word, Macfarlane tells us, he "will notice these signs of creaturely movement more often."[30]

Macfarlane is careful to note that he isn't advocating "a tyranny of the nominal—a taxonomic need to point and name, with the intent of citing and owning"—since he perceives "no opposition between precision and mystery, or between naming and not-knowing."[31] When I read those words, I find myself thinking about Trevor Herriot's insistence that knowing what things are called helps us to experience their presence,[32] and Robin Wall Kimmerer's argument that "[n]ames are the way we humans build relationship, not only with each other but with the living world."[33] And yet, knowing what things are called always happens within a context that exceeds those names. "There are experiences of landscape that will always resist articulation, and of which words offer only a remote echo—or to which silence is the best response," Macfarlane writes. "Nature does not name itself. Granite does not self-identify as igneous. Light has no grammar. Language is always late for its subject."[34]

What words are specific to aspects of the land in southern Saskatchewan? A handful—*grid road, coulee, road allowance, bin yard, shelterbelt, correction line*—come to mind, and then I struggle to find words that aren't in common use elsewhere, like *drumlin* or *glacial erratic*, or that aren't a by-product of industrial agriculture, like *chem-fallow*. Almost every word I can come up with is in English, the language of the colonizer, the language of settlement. Coulee is the outlier—and its origins are in the language spoken by French trappers, if the *Oxford English Dictionary*'s etymology is correct. I find myself wondering about words in nêhiyawêwin that might denote qualities of the land that perhaps I haven't noticed—or that might've been erased when the grassland was destroyed by the plow or when the children were sent to residential schools: words that are equivalent to the ones that drew Macfarlane's attention to aspects of the land he'd never considered. The dictionary I bought for the nêhiyawêwin courses I've taken helps, as does the online dictionary I can access with my phone. We learned a basic land vocabulary in those courses—*sîpîy* (river), *sâkahikan* (lake), *waciy* (a big hill or a mountain)—along with some terms related to weather—*kisinâw* (it is bitterly cold), *yîkwaskwan* (it is cloudy), *kimiwan* (it is raining)—and a few words that refer to specific places, notably *oskana kâ-asastêki*, "where the bones are gathered together," the word for Regina, and *mînisihk*, "at the berry," which in popular speech means Saskatoon (the city, not the fruit). My nêhiyawêwin dictionary, though, is filled with words related to places and landforms—many of them verbs. A valley, for instance, is a noun: *wâyahcâw*.[35] A long, narrow valley is also a noun: *posiskahcâw*.[36] But to be an area with valleys is a verb: *wâyatinâw*, "it is an area with valleys."[37] *tawatinâw* is also a verb: "it is a valley."[38] The Qu'Appelle River is *kâ-têpwêwisîpîy*: "The River That Calls," a reference to a nêhiyaw story, or group of stories, about that river.[39] That word has an English echo in "Katepwa," which names a lake, resort community, and provincial park near Fort Qu'Appelle. The town of Fort Qu'Appelle, however, is known by a word that calls to mind a different kind of story: *kipahikanihk*, "at the jail" or "at the enclosure."[40]

I love these words, the way they sound, the way they feel in my mouth when I say them, and I wonder how this province might be different if we hadn't turned our backs on the languages that were spoken here before settlers arrived. "Turned our backs"—well, we did more than that: we tried to silence those languages. That's what residential schools were intended to do, in part: to make those words unspeakable, as if we had nothing to learn from them—a reflection of the arrogance of settlers who thought they knew everything worth knowing. Where the echoes of those words continue to exist, they can be hard to hear. In *River in a Dry Land*, Herriot writes about the Aiktow Valley, the place where the Qu'Appelle River flowed east from the springs that mark its source towards its destination, the Assiniboine River in Manitoba, but where, in wet years, it also flowed west, into the Saskatchewan River. The English word for this unusual phenomenon is "inosculation," but Aiktow, Herriot writes, comes from a nêhiyawêwin word that means "the River That Turns."[41] I'm fascinated by that word and search my dictionary for it with little luck. The orthography used when some settler wrote that word down must be different from the orthography used today—or else that settler misheard it. I finally locate the actual word in a new online nêhiyawêwin dictionary: *ayîtaw*, "at both ends, on both sides."[42] I like that. I try to shape my clumsy tongue around its syllables, smiling.

The Aiktow Valley, and the massive, sacred buffalo stone that once sat there, were destroyed by the Gardiner Dam and the Qu'Appelle Dam projects in the 1960s—the valley drowned beneath Lake Diefenbaker, the reservoir created by those two dams, and the stone dynamited rather than allowing it to meet the same fate.[43] I hate the idea that such sacred places were destroyed in the 1960s, during my lifetime and so not part of a distant history of colonialism, but I also have to acknowledge that the city water I drink comes from Lake Diefenbaker, and that I've therefore benefited from that destruction. Every time I turn on the kitchen tap, I'm reminded of that fact.

Even though some place names in Saskatchewan do echo nêhiyawêwin words—the province's name itself comes to mind—nêhiyawêwin itself remains endangered. Many people—including my nêhiyawêwin teachers—are working hard to keep it alive. And yet, without the power afforded to English as a language of business and government, nêhiyawêwin, like other Indigenous languages, will continue to struggle. Would it make any difference if nêhiyawêwin were one of the province's official languages? It might—but what provincial government would take on that project? Imagine the complaints about expense and difficulty—all covers for an underlying colonial belief that Indigenous languages aren't important or worthy—that would be expressed by many settlers here. Those settlers vote, and their opinions, however misinformed or racist, get taken into account. Democracy fails when it becomes a tool for the majority to oppress others; it's failing in this province for that reason.

The passing traffic is deafening, but when there's a lull, I can hear the wind. I suddenly recall the nêhiyawêwin word for highway, *kihci-mêskanaw*, or "big road." Then the blast of a passing semi-trailer showers me with sand and dirt. One of my walking friends, Sky Dancer Louise Bernice Halfe, is a fluent speaker of her language; she can explain the etymology of words in a way I can't. I do my best, using the online dictionary as I trudge along the highway's shoulder. A faint smell of skunk hangs in the air. Skunk is *sikâk*, which is almost the same word as *sihkâk*, "they bother him or her," although the two words probably aren't related; nêhiyawêwin is full of what my French teachers in high school called *faux amis*, false friends. I make up a childish sentence—*sikâk wîhcêkihcikêw*: the skunk makes things stink—and chuckle.

Across the highway a meadowlark, *pîscêwâciwasôs*, is singing. A child's wading pool—at least, I think that's what it is—lies beside the highway. The word *mahkahk*, "wash tub," is the nearest I can get to the thing I'm looking at. Adding *pimâtakâ-* in front of *mahkahk* would make a compound word: "wading wash tub." That's better. I hear a train horn behind me: *iskotêwitâpân* is the word for a locomotive. I can parse that one; *iskotêw* is the word for fire, and *pân* has to do with a vehicle that carries things. The word for a toboggan or sled, or a wagon, or a car—any vehicle, really—is *otâpânâsk*. So a locomotive is literally something like "fire wagon." That makes sense—the first locomotives nêhiyaw people encountered would've been steam engines burning wood or coal—but it's about as far as I can get, etymologically.

Not for the first time, I envy my friend Louise's knowledge of the language and wonder how she kept it when she was sent to residential school. I wonder the same thing about one of my nêhiyawêwin teachers, Solomon Ratt, who was taken from his family and compelled to attend the residential school in Prince Albert. He has written books about learning the language, as well as books that tell stories in nêhiyawêwin and English. He's working on a memoir; I'm looking forward to reading it.[44] The wind—*yôtin*, "it is windy"—shakes the grass—*maskosiya*—beside the shoulder of the road. Farm equipment has left trails through barley stubble in an adjacent field. *kistikêw* means "he or she farms the land." The highway curves north, and I can see the Bypass in the far distance. A curving road is a verb, *ka-wâwâkamok*, "there are curves"; "north" itself is *kîwêtinohk*, a word related to the verb that means "he or she goes home," *kîwêw*. A Swainson's hawk on a power pole—a "large hawk" is *sâkwàhtamow*—sees me and flies off, complaining. Another hawk is smashed on the highway. Perhaps it was that Swainson's mate.

An SUV veers towards me and the ditch, then changes course. I need to put my phone away, stop looking at the online dictionary, and pay attention to the traffic passing a couple of feet to my right, or I could easily join that hawk. I pass the sign welcoming travellers to Regina, the one that uses the old city logo: a silhouette of the two Hill Towers at the intersection of Scarth Street and 12th Avenue. The new logo, a looping "R" in rainbow colours, is less specific to this city—and yet, when a third Hill Tower was built, the old one suddenly became outmoded. When I walked on this highway seven years ago, I sat in the shade of that sign and ate a sandwich. Even though it's still too cold to stop and rest, I once again wish I'd brought some food along.

On the horizon, I can see vehicles on the Bypass. It's getting closer; I can almost read the sign announcing the exit southwest towards Highway 1. I pass under a crackling, buzzing high-tension line and step over a discarded USB cable. A man's shoe is lying on the shoulder. Two mallards—once this spring I saw a pair of canvasbacks, but otherwise I've only seen mallards—fly up from the highway's flooded median strip. I walk beneath the overpass where the Regina Bypass crosses this highway: my goal for the day. The overpass is silhouetted against the sky. The Bypass itself seems empty. There's little traffic there, compared to the nameless highway where I'm walking. The noise of passing vehicles echoes off the overpass behind me. A yellow-headed blackbird rests on a dry, brown cattail in a slough beside the highway. Frogs are singing in the Condie Reservoir and Boggy Creek. A table leg lies on the shoulder. Surveillance cameras are trained on the highway, and an electronic billboard refers motorists to the provincial government's website for information on COVID-19. A black baseball cap sits in the ditch near a truck's rubber mudflap.

I can see the Condie Nature Refuge on my left, on the other side of a fence. That'll be a good place to stop. Birds are singing in a row of trees and shrubs. Signs warn against trespassing and hunting. The fence is broken and tire tracks lead from the highway into the refuge. Has someone been poaching deer? I look behind me. I can still see the steel mill on the hazy horizon. I turn west onto Highway 734. There is more traffic here, on this minor road, than I saw on the Bypass. There's no shoulder, and I keep climbing down into the steep-sided ditch to avoid oncoming vehicles. I see an old flip phone, smashed, on the shoulder. Maybe someone made a grand gesture. Grand gestures always look good in movies, or in one's imagination, but they're often quite different in real life. Grand gesture: throw your cell phone out of the car window. Reality: now you have no phone. It's just a flip phone, though, so maybe it doesn't matter. It's been superseded by a newer, shinier model, which will be junked in turn when the next version hits the market. So many rare minerals extracted, used, and then thrown away. Or else it was a disposable phone, a burner, meant to be tossed.

I remember making a grand gesture in my Grade 11 French class. I hated that class: not because I objected to learning French, but because every time the teacher left the room, I was bullied by one of my fellow students, who saw her absence as an opportunity to punch me. He's gone on to become the president of a company that makes body armour. Since the teacher was constantly in the hallway talking to another teacher—perhaps they were having an affair, since her stern demeanour always softened, became almost flirtatious, when she saw him at the classroom door—this happened in almost every class. I'm not sure why my bully chose me.

Maybe I was still as awkward as I'd been in elementary school, where I'd been burdened with braces to correct an overbite and ugly, dark-framed glasses, wearing double-knit trousers and off-brand canvas sneakers when the other kids were wearing Levi's and Adidas. I always lost my temper when other kids teased me, giving them lots of entertainment and encouraging them to continue—a way of expressing anger that I had learned from my father. By Grade 11 I thought I was past all that. I wasn't. I knew better than to punch back; I wouldn't win the resulting fight, and I'd be blamed for starting it. That had been my experience since kindergarten. No one intervened; the rest of the class just laughed. That had been my experience since kindergarten, too. So I just tried to ignore the bully, as my parents and teachers had always advised me to do. That didn't work. It never did. I wonder if it ever does.

On the last day of class, we found out whose marks were high enough to merit being excused from the final examination. I made the cut. The teacher disappeared into the hallway. I decided to make a grand gesture of contempt for what I'd experienced in that classroom over the previous ten months. I took my notes out of my binder, walked over to the open third-floor window, and threw them out. The pages scattered all over the lawn below. In less than three minutes the vice-principal was at the door. "Who threw that paper out of the window?" he barked. Someone pointed at me. "Get out there and clean up the mess you made," he growled. I followed him down the stairs to the lawn outside and started picking up paper. The windows above were lined with laughing faces. The vice-principal stood watching while I worked. He didn't ask why I'd done such a thing. I probably wouldn't have told the truth if he had. I remember feeling trapped and defeated, ashamed, a failure. I'd always felt that way. I still do, much of the time, all these decades later. I'm trying to change that.

I turn south onto the range road that leads to the entrance to Condie. Robins and mourning doves and red-winged blackbirds call from the shelterbelt of the farm across the road. I hear a rooster crow. Then I'm at the entrance to the park. The reservoir was constructed when the Canadian Pacific Railway dammed Boggy Creek in 1885 to provide water for its locomotives.[45] A village stood nearby, named after homesteaders who settled there in 1882, and a Canadian National Railway siding existed there until the 1980s.[46] Now the land is set aside for waterfowl and other birds. Someone told me years ago that there's little native grassland here, so I've never visited—I'm not interested in tame pastureland; maybe I'm a plant snob—but Tourism Saskatchewan's web page suggests that later in the summer wild roses, western red lilies, and gaillardia will be in bloom.[47] I'll have to come back to see if that's true. I've never seen western red lilies—the provincial flower—growing this close to Regina. I did once order seeds from a company in Manitoba, and while they germinated—never a sure thing when it comes to native plants—slugs ate the tiny seedlings. Maybe I should try again.

I walk past horses grazing in a pasture to my left. To my right, Boggy Creek winds its way along. I look for a place to sit down. My legs are tired; I've been on the road for hours without a break. I see a sign with a large sculpture of a flying crane and sit on the base. The sculpture and the sign must have been centennial projects: the sculpture's aesthetic, and the font used for the sign, belong to the mid 1960s. I call home and ask for a ride. I listen to the birds and the wind and the distant traffic. After the deafening noise of the highway, it's quiet. A bird in the tree behind me repeats the same questioning phrase, over and over. I wonder what it's asking me. When I turn to look, it flies away.

FIVE

THE GLOBAL TRANSPORTATION HUB

MAY 14, 2020

M*y goal today is to walk to the Global Transportation Hub—* the warehouse park that's the reason the Regina Bypass was built in the first place. Let's take a look at this thing, I tell myself as I tie my boots. Let's see what all the fuss has been about.

It's a good thing I'm walking this morning. I woke up grumpy, down in the dumps, and I'm hoping that a walk will improve my mood. I check Google Maps to see how far I'll be going. Not only does it tell me the distance, but it directs me to a route I would never have thought of: across Lewvan Drive, along a sidewalk that runs beneath the CPR tracks, and then through McNab, a neighbourhood where I've never walked. I didn't even know it existed, which surprises me: Regina isn't a big city, and I thought I knew it better. I decide to follow Google's suggested directions instead of following my usual practice: heading in what feels like the right direction and hoping I find my way.

After the past week's cold weather, this morning's warm spring sunshine is a revelation, and over the next couple of kilometres, I take in all the details the city has to offer. The elm trees are leafing out; a scrim of green covers their branches. An old woman rakes straw at the vegetable garden in front of St. Mary the Virgin Anglican Church, and a bumblebee is fumbling dandelions on somebody's lawn. A train horn sounds at the level crossing over on Elphinstone. A spindly shrub next to the sidewalk is starting to open into fragrant pink blossoms, and a robin watches me warily from its nest above a garage door. On the next corner, three men are tearing down an old wooden fence and loading the rotten boards onto a truck. Grackles are making their rusty hinge sound. A house sparrow rests on a purple martin house. A letter carrier climbs into his van and drives away. Dogs bark. I see a pair of winter gloves left on the sidewalk and hear a Bobcat digging behind someone's garage. I wait to cross Lewvan Drive, then follow the sidewalk north under the railway tracks, stopping under a poplar to inhale its sweetness. A cyclist passes. Later, I'll see the same cyclist come up off the Bypass and wonder if he rode all the way around the city.

At the corner of 11th Avenue, a portable sign directs people to a COVID-19 testing site. A woman standing in an alley blows her nose. Three men are hammering shingles on the roof of a garage. A sign warns of slow-moving equipment, and as if on cue, another Bobcat trundles towards me. A robin scuttles past a NO TRESPASSING sign; it doesn't apply to him. He can walk or fly wherever he likes; I'm limited to the ground, hemmed in by rules and fences. For a moment I envy his freedom, and then I think about cats, merlins, windows—all the ways his life can come to a sudden end. A jogger runs by with a border collie on a leash. A playing field across the street from a high school glows yellow with dandelions.

I turn west on Dewdney and start the long, straight plod towards the Global Transportation Hub. I cross Wascana Creek. Red-winged blackbirds sing in the willows on its banks, and a single Canada goose floats on the still water. When the sidewalk ends, I continue on the greening lawn. In the ditch, a crow pecks at something bloody; when I reach for my camera, it flies off to join another, complaining. At Courtney Street, the grass ends and I continue walking on the paved shoulder. In a park to the left, a man is practising his golf swing. A sign announces that the city has received an application to turn the land into a "mixed use neighbourhood." Does that mean the park is only temporary? More red-winged blackbirds are calling, and a family cycles on a path through an empty field between the park and the new Westerra development. A sign invites me to build my freedom: not the robin's freedom to go where it likes, but the freedom of having a mortgage instead of a landlord. My consideration of that trade-off is interrupted by someone throwing dirt over a fence into the ditch. I mistake the flying clods of earth for birds landing on the grass. The flattened remains of a rabbit lie in the road. Ducks fly past. Another cyclist is heading west.

That windowless bunker I saw when I walked here a month ago is still howling. I can see the Bypass now: the traffic on the horizon and the overpass west of Pinkie Road in the distance. A sign announces the Saulteaux Crossing Business Park, being developed by Zagimē Anishinabēk First Nation. A liquid petroleum gas storage terminal sits on the other side of Dewdney Avenue; lines of tank cars are parked beside it. Meadowlarks are singing; their song accompanies me for the rest of the walk. That music is so different from the mechanical wailing of the bunker or the sounds of trains at level crossings. Jane Bennett argues that everything is alive and sentient, but are the life and sentience of machines the same as those of a meadowlark?

From the top of the overpass, I see that an interchange has been built to funnel trucks right into the GTH along Rotary Avenue, instead of expecting their drivers to use Dewdney. In fact, there's only a partial interchange on Dewdney; getting traffic into the GTH from the Bypass is more important than getting traffic into Regina. The two projects, warehouse park and highway, are impossible to separate; they will stand or fall together, and if the GTH isn't a success, the Bypass will share in its failure. In the distance, I can see the massive Loblaws warehouse facility in the GTH, too—the biggest building there. I hear frogs singing beside the Bypass. I look down at the highway before I start walking again. There's more traffic on Dewdney Avenue than there is on the Bypass. A raven croaks.

Finally, I arrive at the Global Transportation Hub. There's a lot of vacant land here. In fact, it's mostly empty. I realize I've never liked the use of the adjective *Global* to describe this project. There's a naive Babbittry in that word, a foolish boosterism, even a kind of hubris. Doreen Massey argues that we need to be aware of the ways that places connect to the wider world, the way they integrate the global and the local.[1] In a world where every place is connected to every other place, no one location is more global than another: all are global, connected to each other on multiple levels. A gopher whistles. Some politician came up with that name, someone who imagined that the word *Global* has some kind of talismanic power. But it doesn't. Not to me, anyhow.

I consider Jane Jacobs's description of "depot cities," which "begin mainly as trading centers or depots, convenient sites where merchants establish themselves and deal in goods that are not necessarily produced or processed in the settlement itself or destined for buyers in the settlement."[2] Many cities started out that way, but as their economies developed and matured, they started to make things, creating economic growth through the export-multiplier effect.[3] Regina has always been a depot city, taking things made elsewhere off trains and putting them in warehouses before loading them on trucks and shipping them somewhere else. It's never really developed beyond that stage, which might explain its tendency to economic stagnation, despite the presence of the provincial government and its civil service, the headquarters of Crown corporations, the university, and the technical college. There's some manufacturing, it's true; I've passed a factory that makes farm equipment many times on these walks. Still, if Regina is a depot city, how is the GTH an improvement? If the provincial government wanted to invest more than $2 billion on economic development in this city, were a highway and a warehouse park the best option?

It's not just a question of economic development, either. There's a transience built into the idea of a depot: things come, things go. The way of life settlers brought here, imposed here, is designed around that transience. Farms were established, worked, abandoned, then bought by bigger landowners who tore down the houses where people tried to make lives for themselves. Schools were opened, then closed; villages built, then deserted. Maybe those small farms and the communities they were part of aren't worth feeling nostalgic about; earning a living on a section of land, or less, is a hard life. Still, that churning transience prevents us from rooting ourselves, from connecting with the land. Sometimes I find myself wondering if Regina will be any more permanent. What happens when climate change melts the Rocky Mountain glaciers that feed the Saskatchewan River and Lake Diefenbaker?[4] The reservoirs that provide water to Cape Town, South Africa, a city of some four million people, almost ran dry a couple of years ago.[5] Could something like that happen here? The provincial government's plans to use Lake Diefenbaker to irrigate half a million acres of land will see us guzzling even more of that precious water.[6] Is any of this sustainable? The way we consume the earth, including the construction of the Lake Diefenbaker reservoir itself, is completely different from the way the Indigenous societies that flourished here before settlers arrived lived. They have maintained an ongoing relationship with the rivers and grasses for tens of thousands of years. Will our settler society last that long?

Jacobs became famous for stopping highways: first, planning czar Robert Moses's vision of an expressway across lower Manhattan, connecting the Holland Tunnel to the bridges to Long Island, a project that would have meant the destruction of Greenwich Village and SoHo; and then, after she moved to Toronto, the Spadina Expressway, which would have destroyed historical neighbourhoods in the city's centre, including Kensington Market and the Annex. I wonder what she would've made of the Regina Bypass. She loved prewar cities, their functional chaos, as her first and perhaps most important book, *The Death and Life of Great American Cities*, makes clear.[7] Would she have been upset over a highway that paved over farmland without damaging the centre of Regina? The city's centre is in enough trouble. Heritage buildings continue to be torn down, replaced by parking lots. More transience: the landfill swells with the rubble of the city's past. Perhaps Jacobs would've been concerned about that, rather than the Bypass.

A sculpture of sorts marks the entrance to the Global Transportation Hub: a tan shipping container stacked on top of a white one, its plinth. It proclaims the purpose of this place more eloquently than the sign, which announces "Canada's Premier Inland Port." I take a closer look at the sign. It includes a map of the development. Empty lots are coloured in to make it look like they're occupied. Anyone looking at the GTH can see that the warehouses this sign identifies are empty lots. It looks like a childish attempt at bending the truth. Not the first such attempt, either: three years ago, the government was criticized for trying to lure Chinese investors to the GTH by using a map of the site featuring businesses that didn't exist. The government's defence: the map was "an artist's rendering," a depiction of what the development could look like.[8] In other words, a fantasy. So much about the GTH is a politician's bedtime story: endless development leading to electoral success.

I look around at the reality of the GTH. The warehouses here are featureless boxes without windows. They look temporary. Perhaps they are: structures that are bolted together can be unbolted again, leaving behind the concrete pads they were erected on. When warehouses were built in downtown Regina before the First World War, they were sturdy buildings made of brick and stone. They made a statement: we are here to stay. We are solid, dependable, reliable. Now that kind of architectural branding is unnecessary. The point is to keep construction costs low. Besides, few people will ever see these buildings. Who's going to come all the way out here to take a look?

Outside the Global Trade Exhibition Centre, a worker takes a handcart out of a van. Dozens of trailers are parked in the loading bays at the Loblaw Distribution Centre, and a row of white semis waits by the road. That building seems to house the only going concern here. Occasional trucks pass. It's quiet, maybe because of the pandemic. A killdeer tries to lure me away from her nest. On the other side of the Canadian Pacific intermodal terminal, a long train loaded with containers is heading west. Geese rest in the empty lots. Unlike the Intermobil terminal on the east side of Regina, the Canadian Pacific intermodal facility has no gantries. Instead, large tractors—like forklifts, except that they grab containers from the top with a giant claw—are moving containers around. Perhaps there isn't enough traffic here to justify building gantries. The road ends. A tall fence surrounds the yard. Signs warn against trespassing. I imagine robins, killdeer, meadowlarks, perching on those signs. The wind blows past signs and fences. The sun shines on them, the rain and snow fall on them.

I turn back north. A Canada goose lies on the shoulder of the road. At first, I think it's dead, struck by a vehicle, but as I get closer, it lifts its head and glares at me. I want to be fair to this place. Maybe I caught it on a slow day. I'll have to come back again, see if it's always this quiet. Like any other place, or non-place, there's more here than one quick visit can uncover. There must be.

I head east on Dewdney Ave, back towards the city. Grackles are poking around on a recently seeded field. A dead jackrabbit, wearing its white winter coat, has been thrown into the ditch. The meadowlarks are still singing.

When did the idea for the Global Transportation Hub begin? Suggestions that an inland port in a place like Regina could take some of the pressure off the busy Port of Vancouver were being floated in 2006.[9] Inland container ports in the United States had become hubs for manufacturing and warehousing.[10] Why couldn't Regina follow that example? In December 2007, the Canadian Pacific Railway announced it would move its existing downtown Regina intermodal facility to a new site west of the city, a $93 million infrastructure project which was to be supported by a $27 million grant from the federal government.[11] Six months later, Loblaws announced it would construct a one-million-square-foot, $350 million warehouse and distribution facility nearby.[12] Premier Brad Wall held a news conference in front of a field of yellow canola. Within two years, he said, that field would become a massive building, "equivalent to five-and-a-half football fields," the precursor to a facility twice as large.[13] Loblaws was the CPR's biggest customer, so it made sense to be located near the intermodal facility; the new warehouse and distribution centre would serve all of Western Canada. "Soon we will be part of feeding Western Canada though the transportation of 80 semi-loads of groceries each and every day," Wall told Johnstone.[14] Regina's mayor, Pat Fiacco, predicted that the project would be the first of many, that Regina would become one of those inland ports.[15] Larry Hiles, the president and CEO of Regina Regional Economic Development Authority, said that within five years a billion dollars would have been invested in the area—only half of what the city could expect.[16] The Canadian Pacific Railway completed construction of its new intermodal terminal in 2013; the Loblaw Distribution Centre opened in 2012.

By January 2009, the provincial government had given the project a new identity: it would be a "global transportation hub."[17] That month, the city paid the Rural Municipality of Sherwood $1.5 million to annex the land where the GTH would be located.[18] The city would provide water and sewer lines for the GTH; Mayor Fiacco promised that investment would pay for itself through increased property tax revenue within ten years.[19] It was a heady vision in the middle of a global recession. The economic activity the GTH promised would fuel the city's growth; in 2013 city council unanimously approved a plan that imagined an eventual population of 500,000.[20] The GTH and the Regina Bypass would be the keys to the city's future.

///

June 3, 2020

I'm trying a different route west to the Global Transportation Hub today, walking south of the airport rather than north. In an alley, a bold male robin issues a challenge, scolding me. I murmur calming words, but they have no effect. South of Wascana Creek, drifts of elm seeds lie beside the curb. The sound of hammering echoes from both sides of the street; the pandemic is a time to renovate. A girl wearing a red bikini pulls the cord to start a lawn mower. Behind Lakeview School, children are playing a game together, cheered on by a single adult.

In the front yard of a house, someone has built a small dirt track for BMX bikes with banked curves and moguls—another pandemic project. I hear more hammering; an addition is being built onto the back of this house. A Bobcat waits silently in the backyard. I walk down an alley. A family cycles by. A pair of yellow warblers flash past me. A plastic fence is broken, and a ruffled crow perches on a telephone line. A lawn is covered in dandelions, their seed heads white in the sun. Next door, I notice a curious homemade trailer, built around an upturned rowboat, in somebody's driveway, as if inspired by the Peggottys' house in *David Copperfield*. It has a flat tire. A man passes, smelling like hand sanitizer. A grey partridge scuttles across a lawn, and a flock of grackles scolds a crow. Down the street, a pink pool noodle is wrapped around the trunk of an ash tree. The sidewalk ends, and I continue on the edge of the road, past empty playing fields and beach volleyball courts at the Regina Rugby Club. Beside Lewvan Drive, a meadowlark is singing.

It was calm earlier this morning, but now the wind is stronger and I'm walking right into it. Billboards, damaged by the wind, speak gibberish: "Now selling the final PhD." Members of Unifor, locked out at the Federated Co-operatives' heavy oil upgrader, are picketing outside the new Co-op supermarket, and I stop to chat with one of them. I ask how long the lockout has been going on: six months. "I'll never shop there again," I say. "It's no longer a coop-erative," he replies. "It's just another corporation." I wish him luck and keep walking. A rabbit runs across the street, dodging traffic; in a vacant lot, it stops to examine a stack of plastic sewer pipes and then hops away. The sidewalk ends and I turn north on Campbell Street, a gravel road at the western edge of Harbour Landing. On the horizon, a red semi glides silently along the Regina Bypass. I pass a farm. The road has been sprayed with oil to cut down on the dust from passing vehicles, and there's a strong smell of tar. A rooster crows. A barn swallow flies low across the road. One of the native sage species—*artemisia ludoviciana*, prairie sage—is growing in the ditch: a surprise. How did it get here? Gophers whistle; a killdeer cries. Birds sing in the windbreak around the farm. I smell lilacs but don't see any. How long will it be until the city leaps past Campbell Street and paves over this place?

The road makes a hard left turn to skirt the south side of the airport. A city worker is sleeping in her idling truck. Another meadowlark flutes beyond the airport fence, and a tiny plane rises into the air. I stop to look at a roadside memorial: a stone cross; plastic flowers, animals, and birds; a beer glass; one boot. Who does it honour? North of the airport, a train sounds its horn: a long line of containers, heading west. At Courtney Street, the airport ends. The city ends. To the south, Courtney Street becomes a dirt road; a sign reads IMPASSIBLE WHEN WET. The fields on either side of the road have been seeded. I hear an angry dog barking outside the farmhouse up ahead. Is it tied up? I hope so. Large signs by the driveway issue a warning: BEWARE OF DOG. Shrubs in the shelterbelt around the farmhouse are in bloom; I look at their pink and white blossoms and wonder what they are.

I'm getting closer to the Regina Bypass. The Westerra development sits on the northern horizon. Beyond the Bypass, I can see the big white Loblaws warehouse at the GTH. I pause to drink some water. Over the rushing wind, I can hear trucks on the highway. To the north, an eastbound train is hauling covered hopper cars filled with potash.

I cross the Bypass. To the north, stacks of containers are piled in the Canadian Pacific Railway's intermodal facility. Ashes lie beside the road—a strange place for a campfire. I turn north at Range Road 2210—otherwise known as Fleming Road—a line of dirt that'll become mud when it rains. A dusty robin hops around. "*tânisi, pihpihcêw*," I say. "Hello, robin." He looks lost. "Go back to the city," I tell him, "where there are trees." At the intermodal yard, two large tractors—they're called *container handlers* or *reach stackers*, depending on how they grab the container, according to a quick Google search—are jockeying steel boxes around.[21] A truck honks its horn, and the container handlers beep loudly as they carry their burdens from one place to another. They are tall, ungainly looking machines. Their constant beeping must annoy their operators. Maybe they wear earplugs. Without gantries, the Canadian Pacific intermodal terminal looks temporary, even fly-by-night, compared to the solidity of the Intermobil terminal across town. Containers are stacked three high in a long line beside the railway tracks. Empty flatcars sit on a siding. A fence at the end of the road deters but doesn't block access to the yard; I could easily walk around it, cross the tracks, and wander inside. A sign on the fence warns of video surveillance. I sit on a concrete barrier dropped in the road to discourage drivers from getting too close to the yard and eat the apple I've brought along. White cumulus clouds scud east. A red-winged blackbird trills, and I hear another meadowlark. One of the machines drops a container onto a truck trailer with a screeching noise. What's in those containers? Are they full or empty, coming or going? There's no way to tell, nobody around I could ask. Everyone in the yard is inside a vehicle of some kind. Trucks pick up loads, then drive off. The container handlers move to a different part of the yard, and it becomes surprisingly quiet; the sound of the machinery blends in with the wind and the birds. The sun is warm on my upturned face. It's peaceful.

Then the container handlers return, and the spell is broken. I open my eyes, drink more water, stand up, and turn to retrace my steps. My legs are stiff after my rest, as always, and I stamp my feet, trying to wake them up. Discarded bottles of coloured dye lying in the dirt suggest there's been some kind of Easter egg party here. To the south, silent traffic moves along Highway 1. I turn east. The only sounds are the wind and my feet crunching on the gravel road. The city sits on the horizon, with the Bypass in the foreground. A raven hovers, and two pairs of mourning doves fly up from the ditch, their wing feathers squeaking, followed by several more grey partridges. I walk back across the overpass. A police car speeds by, lights flashing and siren wailing. A flock of red-winged blackbirds is singing in an overgrown dugout. There are so many of them; every slough and dugout has its own population. I surprise a pair of ducks, which splash into the air. I cross the Canadian Pacific Railway tracks. A Towmotor grumbles in the yard at Brandt Industries. I pick up a quartz crystal from the shoulder—discarded, perhaps, because its curative powers were exaggerated. An abandoned shoe lies next to the road. A plastic bag in a dry slough moves in the wind like a wounded bird.

///

By 2015, some people had begun to question whether the government's ambitions for the GTH hadn't been too grand. Some 1,800 acres of canola had been transformed into Canada's only autonomous and self-governing inland port. It was supposed to "transform Saskatchewan's transportation industry, drive substantial population growth and increase private-sector investment in the province," the *Leader-Post*'s Rattra Y. Taylor recalled.[22] But had the investment in the GTH by multiple levels of government paid off? The project had only ten clients. Had it stalled? The fact that the project was attracting Crown corporations rather than private companies was an issue, too. "It's got very narrowly defined uses. It's not just an industrial park. So that narrow definition may be limiting some people that would otherwise want to be there," Colliers International's Michael Kelsey told Taylor.[23] The GTH only wanted transportation and logistics companies, and those firms had to buy a minimum of five acres of land. That rule was supposed to make the GTH different from other industrial parks in Regina, which often include smaller businesses, like welding or autobody shops. Bryan Richards, the president and CEO of the Global Transportation Hub, defended the restrictions. "We want it to be an addition to the infrastructure and a collaboration (with) the region of Regina, not a competitor for some of the other opportunities," he told Taylor.[24] Richards suggested that once the Regina Bypass was open to traffic, more companies would locate in the GTH. People would have to be patient, he told Taylor; it could take twenty years for the project to mature.[25]

Doubts about the wisdom of the GTH were joined by stories about irregularities in the process of acquiring the land, which may have cost taxpayers more than it was worth. In 2016, CBC Saskatchewan investigative reporter Geoff Leo began reporting on strange land deals that had occurred as part of the GTH project—deals that ended up costing the government some $21 million. In 2013, for instance, 139 Land Corporation, a company belonging to an Alberta businessman named Robert Tappauf, bought 204 acres of land next to the GTH site from a Regina company, McNally Enterprises, for $45,000 per acre, and from the Sisters of Our Lady of the Missions, an order of Roman Catholic nuns, for $55,000 per acre.[26] Tappauf has been described as a "land baron"; his company owns some 100,000 acres of land in Saskatchewan and Alberta.[27] Tappauf told Leo that he was planning to develop an industrial subdivision on the site. "While Tappauf was negotiating his land deals, the Ministry of Highways was drawing up plans that involved this very land," Leo writes. "Both parcels sit in the path of the planned West Regina Bypass and as early as 2011 the ministry was considering building an interchange that would swallow up large pieces of the land."[28] Meanwhile the government had been buying neighbouring pieces of land from McNally Enterprises and the Sisters of Our Lady of the Missions for much less money—just $9,000 to $11,000 per acre—under threat of expropriation, claiming that it needed the land for the West Regina Bypass.[29]

The day that land deal was concluded, Tappauf's company sold the land to a numbered company owned by Regina developers Anthony Marquart and Harold Rotstien for between $71,000 and $84,000 per acre—even though 139 Land Corporation doesn't show up as either the buyer or the seller in Saskatchewan's land titles system.[30] In that one day, Tappauf made almost $6 million, although the land titles record makes it appear that the land was sold directly to Marquart and Rotstien, without Tappauf acting as the middleman.[31] Ruth Eisworth, the president of McNally Enterprises, said she didn't know about the second sale until she received a "terrifying" letter from City of Regina officials accusing her of receiving $6.3 million for the land when she'd actually been paid $3.9 million. She was afraid the difference would cause her tax problems. There's no clear explanation about why Tappauf's name doesn't appear on the record of the sale; he says he was just trying to avoid paying extra legal fees.[32]

In October 2013, an appraisal conducted for the Ministry of Highways concluded that both Tappauf's and Marquart's companies had overpaid for the land—that it was only worth $30,000 to

$35,000 per acre. In fact, the appraisal company said it had asked six Regina land developers if they would pay what Marquart had paid for the land, and none said it was worth that much, even if it had been fully accessible for development—which it wasn't, since the government was planning to build an interchange for the West Regina Bypass there.[33]

Nevertheless, in 2014, one year after Marquart's company purchased that land, the GTH bought it for $103,000 an acre, three times what the government's own appraisal said it was worth. Marquart's profit was a tidy $5 million.[34] Bill Boyd, the cabinet minister responsible for the GTH and the chair of its board, stated that land prices in the area were on the rise and that property was needed for the interchange, which had been promised to the companies located there. The money the GTH paid for the land came from a last-minute deal with SaskPower, which paid $25 million for a large parcel of land at the GTH.[35] The land SaskPower purchased is still empty. University of Regina professor Ken Rasmussen, who teaches at the Johnson-Shoyama Graduate School of Public Policy, told Leo that the transaction was an obvious transfer of funds from one Crown corporation, SaskPower, to another, the Global Transportation Hub. The deal, he continued, was done at the expense of Saskatchewan taxpayers, who could have gotten that money from SaskPower as a dividend instead.[36]

Why didn't the government expropriate Marquart's land, as it did with properties elsewhere along the path of the Bypass? Nobody seems to know. Adam Ailsby, a Regina lawyer with expertise in expropriations who had represented or advised several landowners along the Bypass route, told Leo that throughout the process of assembling land for the Bypass, the message from the Ministry of Highways had been clear and consistent: "We have an appraisal. That is the price. If you don't like it you have recourse through the courts."[37] The government was "grinding landowners" to keep the price of land low, Ailsby continued, but then for some reason it decided to treat other landowners differently.[38] Ailsby couldn't understand why. "It's inappropriate to be doing it for one and not for all," he said.[39]

The story continued. In March 2014, the Ministry of Highways bought fifty-eight acres of the land in question from the GTH for just $50,000 per acre, less than half what the Crown corporation had paid just a few days earlier. Why would the GTH sell that land at a loss? Why didn't the Ministry of Highways just expropriate it in the first place? For Ailsby, only two things could explain the government's behaviour. Either "the guys that are buying the land are just really, really stupid," he said, or else "there's something else going on behind the scenes that I don't know about."[40] Eisworth was less diplomatic. "It just stinks to me," she told Leo. "The whole thing just stinks."[41]

Boyd defended himself from suggestions that he had used his influence to help Tappauf. "I have never met Robert Tappauf," he stated. "At no time did I ever speak to Robert Tappauf about anything regarding the Global Transportation Hub or any land pertaining to that project." Boyd also refused to discuss any aspects of the land deals.[42] Tappauf denied knowing Boyd as well.[43] However, Boyd was renting six quarter sections of farmland from members of the Tappauf family or its companies.[44] Is it really possible that he didn't know his landlord?

As Leo continued investigating the land deals around the Global Transportation Hub, the government responded to his reporting. Within days, the provincial auditor, Judy Ferguson, stated that the land transactions looked strange, and that her office would take a look at them.[45] Opposition politicians called for a judicial inquiry.[46] The government fought back, charging the CBC $180,000 in access-to-information fees for documents related to the land deal, an amount that Michel Drapeau, University of Ottawa professor who is an expert on the law related to access-to-information requests, called "unthinkable."[47] The GTH also refused to release one of the appraisals at the heart of the land deals, saying that it would hurt the appraiser's reputation and harm the provincial government.[48] Saskatchewan's information and privacy commissioner, Ron Kruzeniski, criticized the Ministry of Highways for "excessive delays" in responding to freedom of information requests by the CBC for documents related to the GTH. Ministry officials, Kruzeniski stated, had violated *The Freedom of Information and Protection of Privacy Act*, which is supposed to ensure transparency and accountability of public officials.[49] Kruzeniski told the ministry to refund some of the money it had charged the CBC for those requests. It refused. By the end of January 2017, Kruzeniski had condemned the government's handling of freedom of information requests related to the GTH land deals three times. After reviewing the reports on the issue prepared by the Information and Privacy Commissioner's office, Drapeau said that a disrespect for the commissioner and the law appeared to be a systemic problem in the Saskatchewan government.[50]

Other problems with the way the development of the Global Transportation Hub had been managed came to light. A confidential contract between the provincial government and the Canadian Pacific Railway revealed that the CPR had been given 300 acres of serviced land at the GTH for free. Most of the land had been expropriated from farmers for $4,000 per acre in 2008, and providing water and sewer services to that land cost about $10 million.[51] Why did the railway get it for nothing? And why did SaskPower pay $25 million for less than half that much land a few years later?

In her audit, Ferguson found that the way the government had obtained land for the Global Transportation Hub was financially irresponsible. In addition, the report revealed that the GTH had no business plan and hadn't kept important documents or conducted due diligence.[52] However, the report also said there was no evidence of fraud, wrongdoing—by which Ferguson seemed to mean criminal wrongdoing, since lots of things were done incorrectly during the land purchases—or conflict of interest among the GTH's board of directors or management. Premier Wall acknowledged that mistakes had been made, but he argued that the GTH would end up being such a success that the province would recoup the overpayment from land sales.[53] However, because no forensic audit was conducted, we don't really know whether those mistakes were the result of mismanagement, conflict of interest, or worse. Marc Tasse, a forensic accountant, told Leo that only a forensic audit could "clear up all kinds of allegations or suspicions that people might have."[54]

At the end of November 2016, Ferguson announced that the RCMP were investigating the GTH land deals. Until they finished, her office could not conduct a forensic audit. She also backtracked on her statements about the conclusions of the earlier audit, telling the Public Accounts Committee of the legislature that it "did not conclusively state that there was no conflict of interest, fraud or wrongdoing with respect to these land transactions related to GTH."[55] The RCMP investigation lasted nine months. Some 1,000 days of police labour were devoted to the investigation; officers interviewed over forty people and examined thousands of pages of documents. Finally, in July 2018, RCMP superintendent Paul Saganski announced that no criminal charges would be laid.[56] Justice Minister Don Morgan acknowledged that the government had made mistakes: it had moved too slowly to assemble the land, which had allowed "speculators to move in, buy the land and resell it at a much higher cost to taxpayers than we would have paid had we acted sooner."[57] "The GTH is an important project that has created hundreds of jobs and improved market access in Saskatchewan," he said. "In retrospect, it's probably not a business that government should have been involved in. But we are, and we have to deal with it."[58]

And that was that. Opposition politicians and the Canadian Taxpayers Federation continued to demand answers, but when the RCMP declined to lay charges, the scandal died. Without a trial at which those involved would've been called to testify under oath, no one knows why the government apparently decided to enrich three already wealthy men. The results of the October 2020 election—another majority for the governing Saskatchewan Party—suggested that stories of scandals and incompetence had no more effect on the government's popularity than the wind has on the grass growing in the empty lots at the GTH.

///

June 12, 2020

When I started making these walks in April, the trees were bare, the grass brown after the long winter. Now the wild roses in our yard are in bloom, and our bur oak tree—always the last to leaf out—is bright green. I notice a tiny bur oak seedling—probably the result of an acorn buried and forgotten by a squirrel—growing among the western Canada violet and Solomon's seal in the shade of the mature spruce tree in our front yard. Should I transplant it, or leave it where it is? Will it get enough sun? I walk south under the lush canopy of elms through a neighbourhood that smells like freshly mown grass. A man is whistling happily and tunelessly. On Hill Avenue, a city truck is watering the pavement, leaving behind a fresh scent: petrichor but with an overlay of chlorine. A older man is sitting on the curb, looking uncomfortable. "Do you need a hand?" I ask. Yes, he answers. He sat down to wait for a bus and can't get back on his feet. I help him up. He's grateful.

I hear a bird singing happily and loudly in a tree. It's not a song I recognize, and I take out my camera, hoping it might be a Baltimore oriole. We put out cut oranges in our yard to attract orioles, but none have visited. Perhaps the robins drove them away. I approach slowly, trying to see who is singing. Despite my caution, I frighten the bird, and I catch a flash of reddish brown and a long tail as it flies to a distant tree. A brown thrasher, I decide.

I wait for the light to change so I can cross Lewvan Drive. I walked this way just a week ago. The billboards advertising the Harbour Landing development have not been repaired and continue to speak nonsense, but there are no picketers outside the Co-op supermarket today. Grasshoppers whir in the dry grass. I surprise two large jackrabbits, as big as dogs. Another lies dead next to the sidewalk—killed crossing the road. It's clearly been there for a while, but I don't remember seeing it the last time I was here. A gopher whistles. Four more jackrabbits watch me, warily, from a field that's about to disappear, if the heavy equipment parked on its edge is any indication. A grackle complains in a boulevard tree.

On Campbell Street, another rabbit suns itself in a greening field. Red-winged blackbirds trill in a slough, and lights flash atop two adjacent cell towers. A Bobcat idles in the driveway of the farmhouse I passed a week ago. The rooster is still crowing. I ask myself what it means to be here again. For years Nan Shepherd walked repeatedly through the Cairngorms, a mountain range north of Edinburgh, Scotland, and through that repetition, she came to know that place intimately—to the extent that such knowledge is possible. Could walking on these grid roads become the focus of something similar to Shepherd's desire, never quite realized despite her repeated efforts, to know the "essential nature" of a place?[59] The Cairngorms are a natural marvel, the largest national park in the United Kingdom: a sublime gathering of mountains and plateaus, burns and lakes and valleys, apparently unscarred by the extractive economic imperatives of contemporary civilization. This edge of Regina, though, is devoted to those imperatives: on one side of the road, industrial agriculture; on the other, the airport; and, in the distance, trucks moving along the Bypass and Highway 1. It's as far from a national park as you can imagine, but it still has its rewards: the immense cloudless sky, the meadowlarks singing joyfully on the other side of the airport fence. I wonder what repeated encounters with this place might reveal, and whether they'd be worth the effort they'd require. To find out, I'd have to walk here over and over again.

It's quiet: only the sound of my feet on the gravel, the birds, and the wind. Occasionally a vehicle passes. I notice a golf ball at the side of the road, standing out from the usual coffee cups and beer cans. What's it doing here? I kick a rusted pair of locking pliers into the ditch, mindful of the damage they might do if they were thrown up at a pedestrian by a passing truck. Not that many pedestrians come here; I'm alone, as usual. A killdeer tries to decoy me away from her nest in a field of stubble. A dog barks at me from a farm just up the road—the same dog I heard the last time I was here. Today the farmer is riding a quad around the yard. We wave to each other. I can hear the Bypass now, a faint howl in the distance. A steady line of traffic is heading south. Maybe the Bypass won't be an exception to the principle of induced demand after all. On the other side of the overpass, a constellation of shiny steel washers lies next to the road. Then I trudge down the off-ramp onto the shoulder of the highway.

I hadn't planned to come this way today, but it feels inevitable, walking here. The highway is empty now; the earlier traffic may have been an anomaly. The wind is getting stronger, and the sun is hot. Grackles creak. I pick up a heavy galvanized nut belonging to a large bolt as a souvenir. Meadowlarks sing above the wind. I stop to drink some water. The smell of a manure pile in a pasture next to the highway fills the air. A flock of red-winged blackbirds rests on the fence surrounding that patch of grass. Three cyclists are slowly climbing the incline up to the bridge over the Canadian Pacific tracks, the only hill for miles. A grey partridge lies dead on the shoulder, its feathers softly ruffled by the wind.

I leave the highway at the on-ramp to Rotary Avenue, the main east-west street at the Global Transportation Hub. The street is empty. Stubs of roads, blocked by concrete barriers, lead nowhere.

To the south, a locomotive shunts a few flatcars carrying containers onto a siding. The fields here, empty but for dry grass and dandelions, are crossed by deep drainage ditches. A temporary sign announces that half of the land in the GTH has already been sold. I pass the Loblaws warehouse and cross Fleming Road. A sea of trash surrounds the Emterra waste transfer station, where Regina's recyclables are sorted. Much of this city's waste paper and plastic and aluminum are shipped overseas to be recycled; we don't do that work here in Canada.[60] A row of concrete barriers blocks Rotary Avenue. I pass them and walk to the end of the road. I'm surprised at the size of the GTH. The map on my phone tells me that Rotary Avenue is three and a half kilometres long. It's taken me forty-five minutes to walk this far, and it's clear that the GTH's

land goes even farther: it seems to carry on to the horizon. I turn back and sit on one of the barriers to rest. The GTH website says that the development covers 1,800 acres, and I'm beginning to understand how big that is.

On my way out of the GTH, I study the map on the sign at its entrance. The last time I was here, I thought that map exaggerated where companies were located, making them look closer together than they actually are. Now, after walking the length of Rotary Avenue, I realize that it only indicates where companies have bought land. There's no sign of the SaskPower warehouses that supposedly sit where Rotary Avenue and Sharp Bay meet, nor is there any sign of Morguard's building across from the Loblaw Distribution Centre. Is the map supposed to identify the land that's already been sold, or is it a directory of who the occupants are and where to find them? If it's the latter, then it's a worse attempt at deception than I previously thought.

I walk east along Dewdney Avenue. There are so many meadowlarks singing today, perched on wires or power poles. A hawk—likely a Swainson's, although I can't say for sure—is hunting gophers in a field next to the LNG storage facility. A cyclist rides by, heading towards the city. I see a jackrabbit, its body desiccated as if it's been dead since last summer, on the shoulder. It must've been killed trying to cross the road. It's not the same dead jackrabbit I saw the last time I walked here; this one's a different colour, in a different place. How did I not notice it then? The importance of repetition in learning about a place comes to mind again, and I realize that I am learning about these roads by walking on them. Each time I come here I see new things.

My legs are tired and my feet are starting to blister, so I head for the Tim Hortons in the gas station at Saulteaux Crossing. I order an iced cappuccino—too sweet, as always, more like ice cream than iced coffee—and call home for a ride. I wait outside under the Esso sign. My friends Mark and Wanda stop to say hello; they're buying gas and then driving south to Ogema to get one of the pizzas that village is famous for. A road trip: what a good idea.

///

In July 2018, on the same day that the RCMP announced it wouldn't be laying charges related to the land deals at the Global Transportation Hub, the provincial government announced the development was for sale. Morgan, the minister responsible for the GTH, said the private sector should own and operate the warehouse park; the government shouldn't have been involved in it. "Private sector companies are in the business of property management," he said. "Private sector companies are in the business of selling real estate and we think that is the best way of going forward."[61] The government claimed that selling the project's last 700 acres would bring in more money than it had already spent; the opposition argued this prediction was a fantasy, since the GTH was in debt and unable to pay more than the interest on its outstanding loans.[62]

University of Regina business professor Paul Sinclair disagreed with Morgan. Similar projects all over the world—*freight villages*, they're called—have required "centralized management, long-term planning, carefully staged investment, robust governance and thoughtful environmental regulation," all things which could only be provided by the public sector, he wrote.[63] To Sinclair, the GTH was an example of what sophisticated, intelligent governments are supposed to do: anticipating potential opportunities, such as shipping Saskatchewan peas, beans, and lentils by container to Asia, and thereby facilitating the province's economic development.[64] "Selling off the Global Transportation Hub is the ultimate dashed dream, and a failure from which our province may not readily recover," he concluded.[65] Of course, if you believe that government is incompetent by its very nature, then of course you'd want to limit its involvement in projects like the GTH.

Sinclair was expecting pragmatism from a government apparently driven by an anti-government ideology.

The odour of corruption and failure wafting around the GTH remained. In the summer of 2019, the management and marketing of the facility was taken over by Colliers International, a commercial real-estate developer. Morgan hoped that Colliers would be able to put some distance between potential buyers and the scandals that had tarnished the project. "The controversy is there and if you were a business in Toronto or something you would say, 'Do I want to go in on something that has had this much controversy and discussion?'" he admitted to the *Leader-Post*'s Amanda Short.[66] Nevertheless, he refused to call the project a failure. Others have been less reticent. Early in 2020, Mandryk wondered what the point of the GTH is "if the best we can do is recover some real-estate costs that government bought at inflated cost for highly questionable reasons."[67] The government had grossly mismanaged the project, he argued.[68] Who can say? Perhaps the private sector could've done a better job with the GTH. Or perhaps a different government might've made the project a success. We'll never know. All we can say for sure is that the 2020 annual report for the GTH revealed that it was $46 million in debt, had sold no land in three years, was losing more than $1 million every year despite cutting its costs, and still had 717 acres of unsold and unleased land.[69] Not much of an outcome, given the resources that went into both that warehouse park and the highway that serves it.

The sad thing is that many people, if they think of the GTH at all, will simply shrug and assume that governments never do anything right, that the private sector is always more efficient, effective, and competent. This provincial government certainly thinks that way—that belief is the core of its ideology—and so maybe it's not surprising that it seems to have bungled the GTH project. But, as the COVID-19 pandemic has shown us, the private sector can't solve all our problems. Corporations represent private, short-term interests. That's their nature. They can't look beyond the next quarter's financial reports. We need some way to work together, to come up with long-term plans, to consider what we need as a collective. And the demands by corporations for government bailouts because of financial losses from the pandemic suggest that the private sector is much more fragile than ideological myths suggest. We've required something more than private interest and short-term thinking during this crisis, and government, for better or for worse, seems to be the only option on the table.

There's another way of thinking about the GTH land scandal. Let's pretend the warehouse park and the highway were necessary. And let's put aside our anger at the waste of more money than most of us will see in our entire lives in land deals that don't make sense—of course those millions of dollars could've been better spent. And let's stop wondering about the reasons Boyd seemed to go out of his way to help Tappauf, risking his political career in the process. Instead, let's consider the size of that scandal in the context of the entire project. Suppose the provincial government did waste $20 million buying land at an inflated price. What was the cost of the entire GTH and Bypass project? More than $2 billion, right? Does anybody really think that every dollar spent on an infrastructure project that big is going to be spent well, no matter who's responsible for it? $20 million on a $2 billion project is just 1 percent of the total. If that's all the money that went astray building the highway and the warehouse park, maybe we could call them a success. However, if that $20 million is the tip of a larger iceberg, a sign of widespread corruption, then we should be outraged. Unfortunately, we'll never know whether those land deals really were exceptions. If they were, if the project was otherwise managed carefully, maybe they aren't worth getting upset about.

Of course, that way of thinking still leaves unanswered questions. Did the government really save money by contracting the maintenance and operation of the highway out to VINCI? Could the GTH have been built without the Bypass? Could the intersections on Highway 1 east of Regina not have been upgraded on their own, apart from that highway? Is the Bypass carrying enough traffic to justify its existence? Did we spend $2 billion on a white elephant? Those questions are fundamental to the wisdom of building the Bypass in the first place. They're far more important than a few shady land deals. But since they weren't asked before the project started, it's unlikely they'll be answered now that it's finished.

///

June 14, 2020
The forecast is calling for another hot and windy day, so I start early. Sparrows are chirping, and I hear children playing in a park. On Elphinstone Street, a dead squirrel, a dry, stiff husk of fur, lies in the middle of the sidewalk. How did such an old corpse get here? I didn't see it the last time I walked along this block, just days ago. Where did it come from? At the corner of 13th Avenue, the crosswalk light is broken. Two robins are responding to each others' songs. Are they arguing? Is it a competition of some kind? Or is it a duet?

I wait to cross Lewvan Drive. A kilometre to the south, a digital billboard near the airport glows bright red, then orange. I follow the sidewalk under the Canadian Pacific Railway tracks. Gophers whistle in the dry grass. Summer weeds—sow thistle, Canada thistle, and goat's beard, native to Europe and Asia, brought by settlers as seed contaminants long ago and now naturalized—are everywhere. Outside a pink house with plum-coloured trim, I smell cigarette smoke. Dead cedar trees line a path to another house's door. A rabbit sprints across the road. A kid sitting beside the sidewalk nods hello. Even with the wind it's hot and humid on Dewdney Avenue. I'm sweating even though I'm walking in the partial shade of a row of half-dead Manchurian elms. A crow flies low into traffic and somehow emerges unscathed. At Wascana Creek, a red-winged blackbird clings to his perch in a tree, defying the strong breeze. Two Canada geese and a clutch of goslings are swimming against the current.

I arrive at the RCMP's Depot Division, where recruits are trained. Louis Riel was hanged here on public gallows. I think about a recent incident where Mounties struck an Inuk man with their truck as part of an arrest,[70] and wonder what's being taught inside those buildings. The streetlights click and groan in the wind. A rubber glove lies in the grass—an artifact of an earlier phase of the pandemic—and a magpie perched on a stump beyond the chain-link fence cries or laughs, ignoring the NO TRESPASSING signs. Torn banners announcing homes for sale snap in the gale, which threatens to tear my hat off my head, despite the strap fastened around my chin. I slip it off and stuff it into my backpack. I duck behind the Westerra site office to pee. I'm hidden from the road, but then I realize I'm visible to everyone in the houses across the fence from the office. I hear the whine of a circular saw and catch the burning wood smell that comes from using a dull blade. Tumbleweeds skitter across the asphalt. The strange concrete bunker is finally silent. A baby crow, or perhaps a grackle, lies dead on the shoulder.

I turn north on Pinkie Road. Passing vehicles raise clouds of stinging dust. Finally I reach the Regina Indian Industrial School cemetery. A week ago, I drove here early, before the wind came up, to record the sounds of birds and traffic for another project, but I didn't bring any tobacco and didn't pay my respects. I haven't felt good about that. It was extractive, even though I was only taking away a digital sound file. Settlers need to learn to stop taking without giving back. That's the reason I walked here today, despite the wind: to make amends.

The sign asking visitors to think about the children has fallen over, and I set it back in place. A rabbit leaps out of the ditch and scurries across the gravel road. I kneel on the ground and fish a pouch of tobacco out of my bag. I put some on the ground, and I'm surprised that the wind doesn't carry it away. I think about the children buried here, then sit against a fence post and drink some water. Across the road, a gas flare at the LNG terminal is a horizontal line of flame. The wind whistles in the power lines, but even so, it feels quiet and peaceful here—maybe because I'm sitting down instead of walking.

I stand up, my body stiff after sitting so long, and start for home. Now I'm walking directly into the wind, and it's hard and unpleasant. I've been finding that the constant wind this spring scrapes at my nerves. Other seasonal winds—the Santa Ana in California, the mistral in France, the sirocco in Italy—are said to cause emotional distress. Maybe the wind that's been blowing almost every day this spring is affecting me the same way. I surprise a flock of grackles, which fly up out of the ditch. At the corner of Dewdney Avenue, a man walks past—he's been collecting bottles and cans for the deposit—and we wave at each other. The wind is growing stronger, threatening to blow me off the shoulder into traffic. I decide to take shelter at the Tim Hortons in the Saulteaux Crossing gas station. I order a sandwich and debate my options while I eat. Am I going to keep walking? I call home for a ride, but there's no answer. I can't sit here all afternoon. I decide to keep walking.

I stop taking pictures and notes and concentrate on holding my head so that the wind doesn't tear my glasses off my face. I walk past an industrial waste disposal facility and smell a chemical stench. What am I inhaling? On 13th Avenue, red-winged blackbirds trying to fly into the wind are being blown backwards. A train passes, heading east, hauling a line of double-stacked containers on flatcars. It must be a kilometre long. A truck stops. The driver asks if I need a lift. I'm tempted, but then consider the pandemic, the virus, strangers. I've forgotten my cloth face mask; I'm not sure it offers much protection, anyway. "I'm okay," I tell him.

"But thanks for stopping." I lean into the wind as I stumble up the road. I'm not tired from the walk, or the wind; it's just too unpleasant to be out here.

I can't shake that feeling of unpleasantness. The Global Transportation Hub, the Regina Bypass, the Regina Indian Industrial School—they're all about the land: who owns it, who controls it, who profits from it. That's easy to see when we think about the GTH and the Bypass, but it's also true of the Industrial School. Because it was supposed to eliminate Indigenous cultures and languages, that institution was intended to void the rightful claims of Indigenous people to the land so that settlers could occupy it without considering them. After all, once Indigenous people were no longer Indigenous, once they'd been assimilated, they'd be just like settlers, with no connection to the land that could possibly take precedence over our deeds and land titles. Killing First Nations people wasn't necessary for this process to succeed, although through starvation and disease, Canada did its best to do just that: the numbers of First Nations people living on reserves in Western Canada fell dramatically between the 1870s and the 1890s.[71] Canadian government policies were the reason for this massive loss of life, which fit neatly into the social Darwinist idea, common in the last decades of the nineteenth century in this country, that First Nations people were doomed to extinction because they were not suited for the modern world. It was like telling people they were naturally prone to drowning while forcing their heads under the water, holding them down while they struggled, intoning words of pious sorrow at their unfortunate situation as they fought to stay alive.

Still, the physical death of Indigenous Peoples isn't necessary for settler colonialism to work—just the deaths of their languages, cultures, ceremonies, and ways of looking at the world. That's the argument Patrick Wolfe makes in an influential essay on the genocide of Indigenous Peoples in parts of the world settled by

Europeans. "The question of genocide is never far from discussions of settler colonialism," Wolfe writes. "Land is life—or, at least, land is necessary for life. Thus contests for land can be—indeed, often are—contests for life."[72] Wolfe prefers the term "logic of elimination" to genocide, not because settler colonialism doesn't entail genocide, but because genocide can happen outside of settler-colonial states.[73] The main reason for eliminating Indigenous Peoples, for Wolfe, is simply securing access to their territories.[74] In the process of securing that access, settlers try to destroy Indigenous cultures and social structures and languages in order to replace them with their own versions.[75] That replacement is the point of settler colonialism.

We don't have to take Wolfe's word for it. In 1920, Duncan Campbell Scott, the deputy superintendent of the Department of Indian Affairs between 1913 and 1932, uttered these words before a special House of Commons committee that was studying proposed changes to the *Indian Act*: "Our objective is to continue until there is not a single Indian in Canada that has not been absorbed into the body politic, and there is no Indian question, and no Indian department."[76] The amendments being considered, Scott believed, would help eliminate "the Indian problem."[77] If passed, they would make it illegal for parents to refuse to send their children to residential schools. They would also enable the forcible enfranchisement of First Nations men (at that time, enfranchisement only applied to men), a kind of legal assimilation that took away his Indian status, removing him from his community and granting him twenty hectares of reserve land. When Scott spoke about "the Indian question" in front of that House of Commons committee, he was arguing in favour of the forced assimilation of Indigenous Peoples. That was his primary goal throughout his career as a federal bureaucrat. It is precisely what Wolfe describes in his essay.

I first ran across Scott in a Canadian literature survey course I took almost forty years ago. He wasn't only a civil servant; he was also a poet who wrote about Indigenous Peoples in ways that either suggested they were doomed to disappear, as in his sonnet "The Onondaga Madonna," or that there was something sinister about their cultures and ceremonies, as in "Powassan's Drum."[78] He also wrote sensitively about the landscape of northern Ontario, which as a treaty commissioner he travelled across by canoe during the negotiations of Treaty 9 in 1906. His poem "The Height of Land," for instance, is a lovely evocation of the boreal forest. It also downplays the presence of the First Nations men who guided the party of treaty commissioners so that its speaker, Scott himself, can have what Sarah Krotz calls a "spiritual 'homecoming' in their territory."[79] When I first read those poems, Canadians were beginning to learn about the effects of the policies Scott administered and believed in, and literary scholars were discovering the links between those policies and his poetry. Brian Titley's biography of Scott had just appeared, and I remember my professor's surprise at what he was learning from it. The days of thinking about Scott as just a poet, and not someone playing a key role in the settler-colonial logic of elimination, were coming to an end.

Since then, scholars of Canadian literature have been coming to terms with the legacies of Scott and other settler Canadian writers. That re-examination has often been led by Indigenous writers and academics. One example is the response of Métis poet Marilyn Dumont to "Laurentian Shield," a poem about the boreal forest of northern Québec written by F.R. Scott (no relation to Duncan Campbell). "Laurentian Shield" suggests that before the arrival of settlers, the land and the language it speaks were "Inarticulate, arctic, / Not written on by history, empty as paper."[80] I love those lines, particularly the alliteration and assonance of the pairing of "Inarticulate" and "arctic"—the way those words feel in my mouth when I read them out loud. But the poem's suggestion that the land would only learn to speak through settlement and extractive economic activities is hard to accept. Even though F.R. Scott was one of the founders of the Cooperative Commonwealth Federation, the political forerunner of the New Democratic Party, as well as a professor of constitutional law and an advocate for social democracy in Canada,[81] and despite his sensitivity as a poet, "Laurentian Shield" erases the Indigenous presence from the land even more thoroughly than Duncan Campbell Scott's "The Height of Land."

"Laurentian Shield" incensed Dumont. Her poem "Letter to Sir John A. Macdonald" quotes Scott's poem, aligning his words with Macdonald's transcontinental railway and suggesting that both men, despite their political differences, ignored the effect such projects have had on Indigenous Peoples (specifically the Métis)—in fact, that they ignore the reality of the Indigenous presence in Canada, full stop:

> We're still here
> after Meech Lake and
> one no-good-for-nothin-Indian
> holdin-up-the-train,
> stalling the "Cabin syllables / Nouns of settlement,
> /... steel syntax [and] / The long sentence of its exploitation[.]"[82]

The words inside the quotation marks in Dumont's poem come from the fourth stanza of Scott's "Laurentian Shield," where the land finds its voice only through processes of settlement and extraction. "Letter to Sir John A. Macdonald" merges the processes of settlement and extraction Scott's poem describes together with the national unity debates of the late 1980s and early 1990s and Macdonald's transcontinental railway, which facilitated those processes of settlement and extraction, especially in the west. Its suggestion that Macdonald's railway has been "shut down" likely refers to the cuts to VIA Rail service that were announced in 1990, but those words also say something about the transience of the settler ambitions Scott's poem sees as permanent.[83] The poem sees constitutions and railway construction, and poetry like Scott's, as parts of the same colonizing project. As Jennifer Andrews points out, the "blunt language" of Dumont's poem "powerfully juxtaposes the rhetoric of railway expansion, which becomes a metaphor for the entire Canadian national project; Scott's eloquent depiction of the land that longs to speak; and the brash reality of Métis survival."[84] It ends with these words: "we were railroaded / by some steel tracks that didn't last / and some settlers who wouldn't settle / and it's funny we're still here and callin ourselves halfbreed."[85] "Letter to Sir John A. Macdonald" is a powerful statement of survivance, resistance, and resurgence; it's an important corrective to Scott's blindnesses.

Dumont's poem also evokes Louis Riel, who's dead but "just keeps coming back,"[86] along with the one unnamed "no-good-for-nothin-Indian / holdin-up-the-train." Those words are a nod to Elijah Harper, the Manitoba NDP MLA who refused eight times in June 1990 to give consent to a vote to ratify the Meech Lake Accord in that province's legislature. The reason for Harper's decision was clear: First Nations, Inuit, and Métis Peoples had not been consulted or even recognized in the discussions that led to the agreement. Meech Lake was the first of two failed attempts at amending the Canadian constitution in order to get Québec to sign on to the 1982 *Constitution Act*; the second was the Charlottetown Accord, which was rejected by a 1992 national referendum. In both of those agreements, but particularly in the Meech Lake Accord, the concerns of Indigenous Peoples were considered secondary to those of Québec. First Nations, Inuit, and Métis Peoples were simply expected to wait until some unidentified future time when they, too, might be brought into the Canadian constitution.[87] As if that would ever have happened. Harper's refusal to accept this second-class constitutional status was a tremendous act of resistance—one that reflects the position of Indigenous legal scholars in Canada, who view the relationship between settlers and First Nations, Inuit, and

Métis Peoples as a first-order constitutional matter that takes precedence over anything else, including the *Constitution Act*.[88]

I remember watching Harper on television, shaking his head and quietly saying "no" while holding a sacred eagle feather. I didn't understand the importance of his action then, of his unwillingness to go along with what felt like an inevitability. I have a better idea now. I wonder if his experiences in residential schools in Norway House and Birtle, Manitoba, influenced his decision. Those "schools" would've given him a tangible sense of what the project of Canadian nationhood meant for Indigenous Peoples. So, too, would the poverty he saw on the Red Sucker Lake First Nation where he was born, or the racism he must've experienced as an Indigenous man living in Winnipeg. He knew what he was saying "no" to. His resistance remains remarkable thirty years later. As Jim Coyle suggests, "It was one of the rare occasions in Canadian political history that an Indigenous man or woman was able to thwart the ambitions of those in power."[89]

I stand on the edge of the gravel road for a moment, watching the car of the fellow who offered me a ride disappear into the distance, leaning into the wind. I think about the railway—the nearby Canadian Pacific line where I keep seeing freight trains trundling east and west is the one Macdonald built—and about language. The silence of F.R. Scott's version of the land and the beauty of his evocation of that silence. Dumont's blunt words. The rhetoric of Duncan Campbell Scott's "The Height of Land" and its refusal to accept the reality of First Nations presence on that land. The ugliness of Scott's speech in favour of assimilating Indigenous Peoples. The nêhiyawêwin and Anihšināpēmowin and Nakoda that the Regina Indian Industrial School tried to destroy, and the men and women who are teaching those languages today, writing textbooks and grammars, assembling dictionaries, keeping those languages and the cultures they embody alive—a tremendous work of resistance against colonialism's erasures.

The Indigenous presence on the land here, right where I'm standing, has been replaced—mostly—by farms and highways, by factories and an industrial waste disposal facility and a half-empty warehouse park. The Regina Indian Industrial School attempted to eliminate Indigenous presence in another way: by eradicating the languages and cultures of First Nations people, their spirituality and ceremonies, their connections to the land. It didn't work, of course; the Saulteaux Crossing gas station and the sign announcing that the land belongs to the Zagimē Anishinabēk First Nation are signs of the way Indigenous resistance has slowed the logic of elimination, left it imperfect and incomplete. But it's still operating. Wolfe describes that logic, but he doesn't explain how those of us who are settlers living in settler-colonial states who are repelled by the logic of assimilation can break with that way of thinking. Maybe trying to be in relationship with the land is a way to begin making that change. Maybe learning about our ongoing history of colonialism is another place to start.

Some Indigenous writers demand that settlers do more than just change their thinking. Dylan Robinson calls "the continued ignorance of Indigenous histories and the lack of civic responsibility" of settlers in Canada "*intergenerational perpetration*."[90] He describes the Canadian government's continuing "slow violence" against Indigenous Peoples, including missing and murdered Indigenous women and girls, the lack of drinking water on reserves, and the insufficient support for Indigenous education, as examples of intergenerational perpetration.[91] Responding adequately to intergenerational perpetration requires intergenerational responsibility, he argues. The idea of intergenerational responsibility is bound to raise objections from Canadians who don't feel answerable for their ancestors' actions. And yet, if Wolfe is right and settler colonialism continues as long as settlers occupy Indigenous land, if colonization is a structure and not an event,[92] then Robinson's words, however difficult they might be for us to accept, could shift the conversation about settler-Indigenous relations away from facile notions of reconciliation towards something more meaningful. Something like atonement, a word that Trevor Herriot sees as synonymous with decolonization.[93]

Atonement is a powerful word; it carries with it the idea of intergenerational responsibility, the need to be accountable, to take action to repair past harms, to make amends. Even if I didn't personally steal anyone's land or mistreat children in a place like the Regina Indian Industrial School, I've benefited from the actions of those who did those things, and I need to be accountable for that. Maybe we all do. The notion of intergenerational responsibility might be more than many Canadians can accept, but I'm convinced that if settlers are going to be able to share this land with Indigenous Peoples in a good way, something has to change. Intergenerational responsibility, atonement, decolonization—those words might describe a path forward. I start walking east again, bent crooked against the wind, buffeted by gusts flinging sand and stones, my back to the afternoon sun.

SIX

THE LAY OF THE LAND

AUGUST 29, 2020

It's the last Saturday in August. The sun is just beginning to chase the shadows from the elm trees that line the sidewalk. For the first time since the spring, I'm wearing a sweater against the chill in the air. I'm wearing a fluorescent vest over that. Safety first! I've gathered together a few last-minute bits and pieces, things I might need, and I'm ready to set off. I tie my boots, the same pair I've been wearing all summer. I'll keep buying new pairs of these boots until Salomon stops making them. They fit my feet perfectly.

My plan is to stay with the Regina Bypass until I finish walking around it, a three-day journey. I take out the deerskin pouch I use to hold tobacco. Remembering what Lifespeaker Noel Starblanket, the late nêhiyaw Elder, told me, I put some on the ground and step over it. "That's what you should do before you go on a walk," he said. "And when the walk ends, too—step over some tobacco, just like you are stepping across a finish line." It feels appropriate. I've decided to walk in a clockwise direction, which is the direction that's important to the nêhiyawak; that's the direction that a round dance moves in, the direction in which sacred medicines travel around a circle of people who are smudging—or praying, since the Cree word for smudging, *kakisîmo*, also means to pray, in a traditional sense rather than in a church. I put the pouch back into my pack. Then I start walking under the elm trees towards Albert Street.

For weeks I've been trudging around Regina with a full pack, trying to get ready for this walk, to strengthen my legs and toughen my feet so I don't end up hobbled by blisters. Today, though, my pack is lighter than it was during those walks. When my pack is too heavy, I've learned, I end up focusing on its weight rather than my surroundings. I'm not carrying all the water I'll need—I'll have to call home and arrange for a resupply at some point—and just a little food. I've got Wasa crackers and peanut butter, a dozen cereal bars, some dried blueberries, and a bag of trail mix—not much for a seventy-kilometre walk. My pack is still too heavy, but it's better than it was. If I were a serious hiker, I would've weighed my pack and made tough decisions about its contents, but I don't have a luggage scale, and I'm not that interested in so-called ultralight hiking. After all, the biggest weight I have to get rid of is the spare tire around my middle; that would matter more than losing a few extra grams on my back.

I scribble down what I see, hear, and smell in my notebook, just like I've been doing since April. A sign about a lost cat is taped to a streetlight. East of Albert Street, the sidewalk on College Avenue is cracked and broken. Behind me, lawn sprinklers suddenly come alive. I wait to cross Broad Street. Pigeons on the roof of the apartment building across the street make flapping noises as the green

WALK sign lights up. I pass a row of abandoned stucco bungalows. Two have been demolished, but not the third. I wonder what happened. Was there a fire? Or is this block being redeveloped for some other purpose? What happened to the people who lived in these houses? Their furniture and appliances are still in the ruins. I smell mildew. This city has a shortage of affordable housing, and it's a shame these houses are coming down. Perhaps they were seen by their owners as mere income properties, assets on a balance sheet, rather than dwelling places—as objects, in other words. Things. A couple of blocks farther on, I walk by the Flood Residence, an example of the Prairie School of architecture, which Frank Lloyd Wright made famous. Its first owner, William H. Flood, was a real-estate developer.[1] A plaque next to the sidewalk announces the building's importance. I remember being invited to a Christmas party there many years ago. It's as lovely inside as it is outside. The garden is filled with yellow heliopsis flowers; they're finishing now, turning brown and dropping their petals.

I didn't get much sleep last night. I'm anxious about this walk: not only because I'm not sure I'm ready for it, but also because I worry about wild camping beside the highway. I yawn. I don't expect to sleep well until I'm home again. I cross Winnipeg Street. Morning glories are blooming on a chain-link fence. Next door, calendula flowers have gone to seed. A squirrel inspects a lawn. I hear the sound of talk radio coming through a screen door. I head north, through Broder's Annex. The bungalows here are small, closely spaced, and marked by odd, whimsical architectural details. Behind them, the spire of a church punctures the vast blue dome of the sky.

I watch a squirrel steal a leaf of Swiss chard from someone's front garden. I realize I know the owner: she was the manager of the defunct University Club. I miss eating there. She's lavished care on this place. It has a pristine rock garden, a wooden board walk, and a pair of mature cedars. I hear grackles and a lone cricket.

Around the corner, I peek over the backyard fence at the intimate, tidy backyard. Rain barrels sit beneath every downspout. Our own garden is wilder, less well-groomed, and I gave up on rain barrels after the pair I had split in the winter cold. Maybe I should try again. Midway down the block, I turn north up an alley, past a dead tree. The sun is bright now. I turn north on Reynolds Street. I see another pedestrian several blocks away; I'm not alone on this chilly weekend morning. A FOR SALE sign stands in a front garden filled with yarrow flowers. A single ragweed plant stands tall in the yard next door. I stop to listen to the wind rustling in the poplar leaves and the distant traffic. A tiny house—its interior must be the size of a bachelor apartment—bears a large red BEWARE OF DOG sign. Across the street, two houses share a front-yard potato patch. The tops are dying back now. I realize it's time to harvest our own potatoes. I spot the first discarded mask of this walk; I'm surprised it's taken an hour to find one. Behind me, a newspaper rustles as it's blown across the street.

I turn east on Victoria Avenue. On the other side of the street is a vacant lot, and a row of houses about to become another one, if the signs out front—FOR SALE: REDEVELOPMENT—mean anything. The traffic is loud on this busy street, and I realize I'm going to be accompanied by that noise for the next three days. At Arcola Avenue, I smell frying breakfast bacon. The east wind is cold. I suddenly inhale the scent of cinnamon; it must be coming from the bakery on the other side of Victoria—the one with the bright orange OPEN sign glowing in the window. I'm tempted to stop there for coffee and pastries, but I don't want to turn around and go back to the crosswalk. A raven on top of a billboard barks.

I wait to cross Park Street. I pass a hotel that looks abandoned; perhaps it's a victim of the pandemic or the shutdown in the spring. I plod through the underpass beneath the Ring Road. Trucks bang and thump on the bridge overhead. Garbage, shredded by a lawn mower, covers the lawn. Gophers chirp. A discarded purse and the rear wheel of a bicycle without a tire are lying in the grass. What are they doing here? Were they thrown from the highway above? At a trailer park east of the overpass, fruit on crab-apple trees shines bright red. A horn honks behind me; some-one is impatient at a traffic light. A pedestrian turns to walk up Glencairn Road. An idling Harley Davidson rumbles outside the Motel 6. A pile of human hair—is that what I'm looking at?—lies on the grass. Where did that come from? Outside a funeral home, lawn sprinklers are spraying the sidewalk; they sound just like the vehicle tires passing on Victoria Avenue.

I take a sip of water. Another pedestrian approaches, walking a young German shepherd pulling on its lead. Music is coming from a furniture store, even though it's not yet open. Has it been playing all night? What do its neighbours think about that? The North Service Road ends at Coleman Street, and I cross a condemned temporary bridge over Pilot Butte Creek. Pigeons flap overhead, disturbed in their roosts beneath the bridge's deck by my footsteps. I decide to take a shortcut; rather than following Eastgate Drive on its loop past a mosque and hotels and restaurants, I'll cut a kilometre off my journey and walk through parking lots and lawns until I get to the other side of Prince of Wales Drive. A desire path, faint in the morning sun, crosses the grass here, through the middle of a gopher colony. Robert Macfarlane explains that these unofficial paths are "created by walkers who have abandoned the pavements and roads to take short cuts and make asides."[2] Like other footpaths, they are "acts of consensual making," lines of connection that relate places as well as people.[3] Desire paths can be formed, Charlotte Bates tells us, "with as few as fifteen traversals of an unpaved route."[4] Citing Michel de Certeau, Bates sees these routes as "pedestrian 'tactics' that disrupt and resist the 'strategies' of urban planners and the 'rational plan.'"[5] In Regina, though, these paths also indicate the city's failure to plan for pedestrians. We're left out, excluded. Maybe these lines are attempts at resisting that exclusion. Of course, in Saskatchewan, because of laws against trespassing, there are few footpaths anywhere, except desire paths in cities, so I treasure these lines of bare earth trodden into the grass.

At Tim Hortons the drive-thru is busy. The glass doors are broken and covered in sheets of plywood, but they aren't locked. Inside, I get some coffee, eat a second breakfast, and use the washroom. Then I go outside and wait to cross Prince of Wales Drive. Another mask is lying on the ground. The wind is getting stronger. More desire paths are etched into the lawn beside McDonald's. I ponder the city's decision not to build sidewalks here. Is it just cost-cutting, or is it based on a belief that everyone who matters drives everywhere? I've heard a story about Brasília, the capital of Brazil: the modernist architect who designed the city left out sidewalks because it was to be a city of the future—a future which excluded pedestrians. That story turns out to be inaccurate. Sidewalks do exist in Brasília, but they are twenty-five feet from the curb and built a flight of stairs above street level. "The sidewalk, that traditional ribbon of social exchange, has now been irretrievably severed from the street, broken into discrete lengths, and wrapped around each pavilion as an arcade," James Holston writes.[6] The result: walking anywhere in Brasília is next to impossible. Regina's lack of sidewalks isn't the result of deliberate modernist planning—or is it? The people who designed these streets must have thought nobody would walk on them; perhaps they believed the private automobile would be the only form of transportation in this place. That thinking makes walking here strange, even subversive.

A row of potentilla shrubs is covered with bright yellow flowers. I suddenly realize I've forgotten to bring ibuprofen, the pain reliever of choice for people walking long distances, a cure for swollen feet and sore muscles. The parking lot at the supermarket across the highway is full, so it must be open. Should I retrace my steps to Prince of Wales, cross the road, and buy some? I imagine rules about leaving backpacks at the store's entrance, along with a sign that says the store takes no responsibility for loss or damage, and decide I can do without ibuprofen.

I follow another desire path across a vacant lot and past a thicket of silver buffaloberry shrubs. Plastic bags shredded by the wind are tangled in their branches. I see no birds. Maybe it's been too hot for them during the past couple of weeks, or maybe it's too cold this morning. Still, birds like the soapy-tasting fruit of silver buffaloberry, and I wonder where they might be. A vintage Cadillac is parked behind the Days Inn. A gopher whistles as I cross a lawn. I catch up with Eastgate Drive again. Neither the farm equipment dealer, nor the recreational vehicle dealer, nor the construction equipment dealer is open yet. The only sounds are the traffic and the wind and my boots on the gravel shoulder. I can see the transmission tower at Tower Road standing against the sky; that's the trailhead of my walk, the point where I'll start walking on the Bypass. It's getting closer.

I pass a busy campground. The wind rustles the leaves of the poplar trees along its fence. Large campers are parked beneath them. The business has a new off-season venture: eight-by-twelve-foot storage sheds. I'm reminded of the old song "King of the Road." The singer, Roger Miller, mentions renting rooms that size. And then I'm at Tower Road. I call home to make a progress report, then sip some water. A broken padlock lies on the shoulder of the road. I wait at the corner for the traffic lights to change. After a few minutes, it's clear they aren't going to turn green for me. I see a lull in the traffic and jaywalk across. From this point, I'll be on the Bypass.

///

The highway I'm walking on, and everything else within my field of vision, sits on what was once the bottom of Glacial Lake Regina, which existed about 14,000 years ago.[7] That lake lasted for almost 1,000 years before it drained, quickly and catastrophically, through what are now the Souris River and Qu'Appelle River valleys.[8] Many such lakes formed at the end of the Wisconsin glaciation. "Glacial meltwater typically is full of fine-grained sediments consisting of sand, silt and clay-sized particles often produced by glacial erosion processes," Janis Dale tells us. "When this meltwater reaches a lake basin, it slows and deposits its load of sediment on to the floor of the lake. Former proglacial lake basins are identified by flat, relatively featureless plains composed of fine sediments identified as glaciolacustrine deposits."[9] A flat, featureless plain? That describes perfectly what I'm looking at. Regina, and the land around it, are famous for their flatness. In fact, that flatness has come to define Saskatchewan, even though the southern part of the province has hills, valleys, and badlands, too. The soil of this plain—those fine

sediments—are a blessing and a curse, as Dale notes: "The silts and clays from this former lake support rich agricultural soil but pose considerable engineering difficulties: the clays, dominated by montmorillonite, have a tremendous ability to expand with the addition of water and to contract on its absence."[10] That expansion and contraction, Dale points out, cause sidewalks, roads, foundations, and water pipes—anything built on or under the ground—to heave and crack.[11] I know that from experience: we've had to get the foundation of our house repaired and braced because of that kind of damage. It's a common problem in Regina.

But the idea that this soil is particularly suitable for agriculture is what I want to think about. Most of the grassland that has survived the arrival of settlers is in the province's southwest, on lighter soils more suited to grazing than growing wheat, barley, or canola. The way the heavier soil here retains water is important for farming in a dry place, so little grassland has survived around Regina, where the clay soil was once the bottom of that ancient glacial lake. What was the grassland here like? Was it different than the grasslands I've seen elsewhere in Saskatchewan? Would the grasses and flowers here have been taller because of the soil's ability to hold moisture? If so, would bison have tended to spend more time here during their annual migrations? What would that've meant for the Indigenous people who relied on the bison for everything—food, clothing, tools, shelter, and ceremony? This place, according to Daria Coneghan, "was originally an area where Cree and Métis came to hunt buffalo," and the bones of those animals were piled together here "in a belief that the buffalo would not leave an area that contained the bones of their kind."[12] Those piles of bones are the source of the area's nêhiyawêwin name: *oskana kâ-asastêki*, "where the bones are gathered together." That story leaves me asking about the other histories traced on this land, histories unknown to or ignored by settlers travelling on this highway. Learning those stories could help me turn this highway from non-place into place; it might even help me recognize my relationship with the land that stretches out in all directions from the paved shoulder I'm walking on.

///

South of the old Highway 1, Tower Road disappears into on- and off-ramps for the Bypass. There are a few signs of what was here before the highway: a line of power poles where the road must've been, a back entrance to the retail development where the new movie theatre and Costco are located. Grackles are feeding in the ditch beside the road. A multitude of crickets is singing. A car passes, dragging its muffler on the pavement. Tan bales of hay stand in a green field. Behind Costco, apartments and town houses are arranged in curving lines, receding into the distance.

I climb up onto the overpass that's part of the complex interchange where the two highways meet. I'm walking on the left side of the highway, facing traffic, because it's safer. I never walk with traffic coming up behind me; that's just too dangerous, even here, on this wide shoulder. My left heel is already starting to hurt. To the west, below the highway's opposite lanes, I see the top of an abandoned greenhouse nestled among the trees of a shelterbelt. Some of those trees have died. To the east is a junkyard. Four hawks are circling over the greenhouse, catching the morning light—probably Swainson's hawks, but I can't be sure. A square dugout, surrounded by a fence, sits next to the highway, and I wonder if it's a borrow pit, one of the holes that were dug to provide the earth necessary to build this overpass. Its shape, the fence surrounding it, and its lack of any apparent agricultural purpose makes that likely. There isn't much traffic—less than there is on the old Highway 1—but that could easily change. I sit on a guard rail to rest for a minute, then start walking again. My pack straps rub my shoulders. Across the road, a sign tells me that it's 13.5 kilometres to Highway 6. Can I get that far today? The yard of the deconsecrated church in Rowatt might be a good place to camp. I don't think the archbishop would mind—he's a friend from the long walks on historic trails that my friend Hugh Henry organizes—but I suddenly realize I should've emailed him earlier to ask permission.

There's more traffic now; I'm surprised by the number of vehicles. A piece of Astroturf, shaped like a slice of pie, lies beside the paved shoulder. Overhead, one of the hawks I saw earlier scolds me; its dark-red colour, and its call, confirm that it is in fact a Swainson's. I listen to the crickets, the wind, and the sound of my boots on the paved shoulder, and look at the sun, the blue and cloudless sky, the traffic, and the foxtail barley shining purple in the ditch. I can feel a blister forming on the sole of my left foot. I'm starting to get bored already. That's not surprising: this highway is designed for speeding vehicles, not for pedestrians. Besides, long walks can be tedious. Craig Mod recalls being "luxuriously, all-consumingly bored" during a 620-mile walk in Japan.[13] That boredom gave him "a heightened sense of presence": it became a goal, "the antipode of mindless connectivity, constant stimulation, anger and dissatisfaction."[14] That lack of distraction enabled Mod to perceive things he otherwise would've missed: the hidden Christian messages in small signs along the way, the fact that every small village had at least three barbers or hairdressers, the playgrounds that looked as if no child had touched them in decades. If he'd been listening to podcasts or looking at his phone, Mod wouldn't have noticed those details—or so he believes. I think he's right. We've only got so much attention available, and if we give it to our devices, we'll miss out on what's around us.

Mod is talking about an experience that anyone making a long solo walk probably has had. It's not exactly a meditative experience, or at least it isn't for me: my mind is constantly running with trivia of one sort or another, including how much my feet hurt and when I can stop to rest. The notebook I scribbled in during my walk to Wood Mountain reveals how hard that journey was, although my memories tell me I was having a great time. Maybe both statements are true. I was bored, among other things, and that boredom did lead to an experience that was something like Mod's intense awareness of place. Maybe that awareness is the reason many long-distance walkers describe their experience as somehow spiritual. That's a challenge for this walk: can I find something spiritual—a term I can barely understand—while walking in such a ruderal non-place?

A semi-trailer hauling an oversized load, with a follow vehicle trailing it, approaches, and I step off the shoulder to let it pass. An oversized load of hay follows, without flashing lights or a follow vehicle, and I step off the shoulder again. A dead baby hawk is lying on the highway. The sun is high now, the light harsher than it was earlier. I cross Chuka Creek, which runs under the Bypass in a culvert. I stop for a break and take off my sweater, startling a flock of grey partridges, which fly up from the dry creek bed. Both gantries at the Intermobil terminal to the east are working. Behind them, a windmill spins, generating electricity.

I discover a minor problem: one of my red aluminum water bottles is empty. It had held the electrolyte mixture I drink in an attempt to avoid heat exhaustion, but now there's nothing left. What happened? The top is loose, but is that why it's empty? Has one of its many dents—I've dropped it many times since I carried it across Spain seven years ago—turned into a hole? I don't know. That explains why my sweater is wet. I clip the sweater to my pack, hoping it'll dry in the sun; I'll need it when night comes, since it's always cold when the sun goes down this time of year. Then I start walking again.

Across the highway, a semi coughs to a stop on the on-ramp in a cloud of black exhaust; I wonder if it has broken down. To the west, houses and apartments and a shopping centre fill the space between the Bypass and Arcola Avenue. Not long ago, that neighbourhood was a field of canola. I catch a glimpse of my shadow:

my sweater, a black flag, blows behind me in the wind. I cross the on-ramp and make the gentle climb onto the Arcola Avenue overpass. There's little debris or garbage here; the highway hasn't been open long enough for it to collect. I decide that litter obeys an equation: the number of vehicles that travel a given stretch of road, multiplied by the length of time that road has been open. L=VT. Trash accumulates slowly; it settles, gradually, like the clays that formed this plain.

Crickets are singing all around me. How many could there be? Thousands? Millions? Two racing cyclists ride onto the other side of the highway; I can hear their conversation. Small sunflowers are all over the grass embankment. Now that I'm on top of the overpass, I can see the university, the dome of the Legislature, the office towers downtown, and behind and around them, the sky's blue infinity. If the Earth were the size of an apple, its atmosphere would be as thick as that apple's skin, yet it towers above me, seemingly without limits. I can even see the office building that stands where our street, College Avenue, meets Albert Street. Two ducks fly by. I have a sudden impulse to cross over the median to the westbound lanes and start hitchhiking, to turn the walk into a comfortable ride, but that urge is easy to resist.

Tiny flax plants are growing next to the shoulder. Are they the agronomic version, escapees from a farm, or the native perennial species? I continue down the overpass and cross the off-ramp—the most dangerous part of highway walking, the place where drivers leave the road, not expecting to see pedestrians, where I have to step into traffic to continue on my way. I'm surprised to see the bridge over Wascana Creek so close to Arcola Avenue. There's no sign, but I know it must be Wascana Creek, since no other body of water near Regina is big enough to require a bridge this size. I rest on a guard rail and check the weather forecast. It's supposed to rain tomorrow morning. That would be unpleasant, for so many reasons. I'm not good at getting out of my bivy sack quickly, and

I don't want my sleeping bag getting wet. I don't like eating in the rain, either, and it'll make taking notes difficult. There's nothing I can do about it, though, and in a dry part of the world any precipitation is a gift, so why complain?

Another cyclist approaches, and I step off the shoulder to let him pass. He doesn't nod. A big blue dragonfly catches my attention and then flies away. Wheat is growing on both sides of the highway. A fuzzy caterpillar is trying to cross the shoulder. "Stay out of traffic!" I tell it. It's the first of many I'll see, all apparently on suicide missions, determined to get across two lanes of traffic to the grassy median strip on the other side. Why? What are they looking for? The surprising thing is that I see so many survivors that have made the journey across the highway to the shoulder where I'm walking. It's a good thing for them—for me, too—that the Bypass isn't as busy as its planners anticipated.

The highway arcs southwest. That's its character, to defy the grid of the earlier roads that follow the lines of the Dominion Land Survey. Instead, it swoops from east to west and curves back north, drawing three-fourths of a circle around Regina. I see a row of bins on the horizon: Cargill's chemical depot in Rowatt. A road has been cut in two by the Bypass—Old 16, the road I used to follow when I walked to the Cowessess gas bar and then back into the city, the road Herriot took when he walked to his family's cabin at Cherry Lake as research for *The Road Is How*. I won't be walking that way again. I'm not dashing across the four lanes of the Bypass as part of that journey. Despite my short-lived fantasy about crossing the highway to thumb a ride, I don't want to tempt fate the way the caterpillars do. There isn't much traffic here, but I still don't want to take that risk.

Wild oats and scentless chamomile are flourishing beside the highway here. These introduced weeds imitate a prairie—the wild oats, a grass, in bunches with flowering plants, like scentless chamomile, between them—but the species mix is completely different from native grassland. What would Saskatchewan look like if the highways department—or VINCI, since it's responsible for the maintenance of the Bypass—had to create prairie restorations beside the road? It might not be much different, given the way those restoration projects often end up as wild oats and scentless chamomile. Those weeds inevitably outcompete native plants. Still, scentless chamomile is on the province's noxious weeds list, and it seems unfair that VINCI can let it grow here when I would get in trouble for allowing it to grow in our yard—if a weed inspector came by, that is. On the other hand, the last thing this province needs is more herbicides sprayed around. That's how VINCI would deal with all this scentless chamomile. Given a choice between weeds and 2,4-D, I'll take the weeds.

The wind is coming from the west now, and I'm getting tired. My feet are sore and my pack feels heavier. A trailer's red tail light is lying beside the shoulder, catching the sun. A sign tells me that a pipeline runs beneath the highway; there's a dark repair to the asphalt here, as if that pipeline leaked and needed to be fixed. I can see the landfill on the northeast horizon, and a gas flare at the refinery. The abandoned railway line on the left used to serve the grain elevators at Rowatt before they were torn down. Now it has no purpose. Flea beetles are riding on my sleeve, blown there by the wind. No doubt they've been feeding on someone's canola. Regina is an island in a sea of canola. We can't grow kale or any other brassicas in our garden; those ravenous insects inevitably destroy them.

Rowatt is getting closer now, its chemical bins dark against the sky. Grasshoppers are leaping around on the shoulder. There are no burrowing owls to eat them. The changes we settlers have made to the ecosystem have ended up hurting us: burrowing owls used to eat grasshoppers, which eat crops. Coyotes used to eat gophers and mice, which eat crops. By poisoning the owls and shooting the coyotes, we've left those creatures without predators. Removing vital parts of an ecosystem turns out to have consequences. I'm directly south of the university now. The city's downtown is clearly visible on the horizon. I keep brushing away flea beetles, but more keep landing on me, as if I were a giant cabbage. Two more cyclists pass. One says hello; the other doesn't. Some piece of pipeline infrastructure sits to the left of the highway, on the other side of the railway line. The pipelines and the high-tension lines around me tell me this landscape is now defined by the energy we need to heat our homes, to power our lights and TVs, to run our cars and trucks, even more than agriculture. There are more sunflowers growing beside the highway. I step over slices of roast beef covered in bright orange fuzz lying on the shoulder.

The Bypass bisects Fleet Street, one of the roads I walked along on those journeys to Rowatt and back. There are two exits, though: one carrying westbound traffic north, and another carrying eastbound traffic south. Why here and not at Old 16? What logic was used to plan this highway? I ask myself how much the Bypass has disrupted the lives of the people living near it. Compensation was only offered to those who would lose land to the project; anyone anxious about noise or air pollution or roads being cut by the Bypass was ignored.[15] It's ironic that a project that was supposed to solve traffic problems made travel harder for some rural residents. I guess they didn't count.

///

I think about who counts and who doesn't—whose concerns are heard, and whose are ignored—and that leads to a consideration of what it means to count things, the relationship between being counted and being important, and what it means when things can't be counted, when we just don't know how many there are—or were. Take the bison herds that grazed on the grassland that existed where this highway and these fields of canola are now. We don't know how many bison there were. Estimates range from thirty million to sixty million animals. Those estimates have been made using a variety of methods: direct observation of the great herds during the first half of the nineteenth century, assumptions about how many bison the grassland ecosystem could support, and guesses at the numbers that were killed. That latter method is grisly, but it's not surprising: by the end of that century, only a few hundred bison remained alive. As James H. Shaw concludes, all we know is that tens of millions of bison were still living west of the Mississippi River at the end of the American Civil War in 1865. "Any greater accuracy," he tells us, "seems unlikely."[16]

Those tens of million of bison represented fewer animals than there were before the 1860s. The bison herds on the northern Great Plains, right here where I'm walking, were growing noticeably smaller by the 1850s.[17] By the early 1870s, less than a decade after the end of the Civil War, when the American assaults on Great Plains First Nations and the bison were being pursued with an intense ferocity, the bison here, and the people who lived with them, were in serious trouble. Bill Waiser quotes Winnipeg resident Charles Bell, who reported that the nêhiyaw people who spent the winter of 1874 on the plains had "suffered frightfully" because of the lack of bison; they ate "their horses, dogs, buffalo skins and in some cases their snowshoe laces & moccasins and then died."[18] The precipitous decline in the number of bison returning to what's now southern Saskatchewan every year was one of the primary reasons that First Nations were interested in entering into treaty relationships with Canada in the 1870s. With the bison herds dwindling, First Nations knew they'd have to find a way of living without them, and the federal treaty commissioners' promises to help them become farmers was a powerful argument in favour of treaty making. The hungry winter of 1874 must've been on the minds of the Chiefs who gathered at Fort Qu'Appelle that September to negotiate Treaty 4.

Then, in 1879, the bison suddenly and completely disappeared from the northern grasslands. It happened the way the character in the Hemingway novel describes going bankrupt: gradually and then suddenly.[19] No one could believe it. Edgar Dewdney, then the new Indian Commissioner, claimed in his first annual report that the bison's disappearance had taken everyone by surprise, and during his tour of the territory in the summer of 1879, he kept meeting First Nations people who were worried about surviving the coming winter.[20] In April 1879, Henriette Forget, the wife of Lieutenant Governor David Laird's clerk, Amédée Forget, wrote, "Rumours of starvation, from different parts of the country, the buffalo having disappeared rendered the condition of the Indians most deplorable, what a question to solve."[21] For First Nations people here, who depended on the bison, it must've felt like the end of the world.

Some First Nations responded to the situation by asking for government assistance; others travelled south into the United States in search of the remaining bison.[22] The federal government provided some food aid during the winter of 1880, but it was already regretting the financial commitments it had undertaken when it negotiated the numbered treaties in Western Canada.[23] In fact, James Daschuk tells us that the federal government quickly found that starvation was a powerful weapon against Indigenous Peoples; as the government's point person in the North-West Territories, Dewdney was responsible for implementing this policy of coercion-through-hunger.[24] "Instead of supplying rations to famine-stricken populations 'in a national famine,'" as the treaties had promised, "rations were used as a means of coercing First Nations into submitting to treaty," he explains. "In 1879, a number of bands traded their independence for food."[25] Once they were on reserves, First Nations people were at the government's mercy.[26] A hastily put-together program to reorient the Indigenous economy towards agriculture was doomed, because it lacked details and was too limited to deal with the famine's scope.[27] A cycle of hunger and disease spiralled almost out of control, as outbreaks of smallpox and tuberculosis broke out on reserves.[28] People were starving to death on insufficient rations, and the federal government refused to spend more to address the crisis. Instead, it provided rations at "the absolute minimum to sustain life," even if that meant supplies rotted in its warehouses.[29] Dewdney ordered those rations from I.G. Baker and Company—a Montana-based firm he was financially associated with. He was making money on every single one of those shipments of rancid bacon and rotten flour.[30]

The treaties were supposed to allow First Nations to choose the locations of their reserves, but the weapon of starvation allowed the federal government to tell First Nations where their reserves would be—and then confine them there. In 1882, the government announced that all First Nations would be removed from the territory south of the new Canadian Pacific Railway line. As Daschuk states, "[i]n doing so, the Canadian government accomplished the ethnic cleansing of southwestern Saskatchewan of its Indigenous population."[31] Then, in the aftermath of the 1885 Resistance, the government instituted the pass system, which kept First Nations people confined to the reserves they'd been forced onto. "Essentially, the pass system was a segregationist scheme which, without any legislative basis, required Indians to remain on their reserves unless they had a pass, duly signed by the Indian agent or farm instructor and specifying the purpose and duration of their absence," writes Laurie Barron.[32] The key term in Barron's description is "without any legislative basis": the pass system was never made into law, never debated in Parliament, never discussed openly. It endured in some places until the 1960s.[33] Consider the potential for abuse that was built into the pass system: Indian agents or farm instructors could extort anything they wanted from people who needed their signatures to sell produce at a market in a nearby town or visit relatives on another reserve. Historians have noted that the federal government was aware of cases where Indian agents demanded sex from First Nations women in return for food rations.[34] Why couldn't they have done the same when it came to issuing passes? They had absolute power; they could demand whatever they liked. The potential for corruption was huge.

The highway where I'm walking is south of the Canadian Pacific Railway line, and therefore one of the areas where the ethnic cleansing Daschuk describes took place. This must've been a good place to hunt bison on horseback. There were wetlands here, too, with lots of ducks, geese, and other waterfowl. Those wetlands were drained in the 1960s, and neighbourhoods in the southern part of Regina, like Whitmore Park, were built on top of them. They are notorious for failing basements, broken pipes, and hummocked roads: the marshes that used to be there still exert a powerful force. Still, this place had disadvantages. Wascana Creek was too shallow to be a reliable source of water. There was no wood and little shelter from the constant wind. The Qu'Appelle Valley, some thirty kilometres north of this highway, was a better place to live. Most of the reserves near Regina are in that valley, in a line running east from Piapot First Nation, close to the city, to Ochapowace First Nation 150 kilometres to the east. The people who hunted here would've been forced onto those reserves, or made to move there from other places, like the Cypress Hills that straddle the border between Saskatchewan and Alberta, by the federal government and its policy of starvation. That policy, Daschuk writes, "might have been cruel, but it certainly was effective."[35]

When settlers began arriving here in large numbers in the 1880s, First Nations people would have been visible only through the traces they had left on the land: tipi rings, which would soon be destroyed by the settlers' plows, and bison bones, soon to be shipped east to chemical companies in Illinois and Wisconsin and made into fertilizer.[36] What did those settlers imagine had happened to the people who had lived on this plain? Did they think about the people starving, consider who'd been here before they arrived? Perhaps settlers then, as now, found it easier not to ask too many questions about how they'd come to occupy this land. Who wants to know about the crimes committed in their name?

I stop and take in the land around me, trying to imagine the grass, the massive herds of bison, the unthinkable devastation of the slaughter that led to their near extinction. They were partly killed for commercial profit, for the market in their hides, meat, tongues, and bones, Andrew C. Isenberg explains; the destruction of the bison, he says, was the result of an unsustainable exploitation of a natural resource.[37] They were killed for sport, too, and by diseases introduced to the prairies along with settlers' livestock. Without that invasion—our invasion—the ecological balance between bison and grass and First Nations, a balance that had existed since the glaciers melted, would have continued. Instead, the great slaughter of bison, which began in the eighteenth century in the eastern United States and spread west over the following century, led to a profound ecological devastation, as Wes Olson and Johane Janelle recount. At the end of that slaughter, just 281 plains bison remained alive, out of the tens of millions who had made up the vast herds that had roamed this continent. [38] The effects of the extirpation of the bison are difficult to imagine, Olson and Janelle tell us: "Countless millions of insects lost their food supplies, and so countless millions of birds, reptiles, amphibians, and small mammals lost theirs. All were forced to find an alternate food source or perish trying."[39] Never mind the effects on the people who also depended on the bison; they were left without homes and starving.

Describing the bison as a natural resource rather than relations is part of the thinking that drove them to the brink of extinction. Here, where I'm standing, bison were hunted by employees of the Hudson's Bay Company (HBC); pemmican, that mix of berries and bison meat and fat, was the fuel of the fur trade. In the 1820s, the HBC, fearing the economic power of the Métis buffalo hunters who lived at Red River, now Winnipeg, asserted a monopoly control of pemmican production, driving prices down so that in 1827 it was worth a quarter of what it had been worth five years earlier. Those lower prices meant that hunters had to kill more bison to pay their debts to the HBC.[40] As the pemmican trade grew, the hunt expanded deeper into the interior of the plains. By the 1850s, there was increasing tension between First Nations and Métis peoples over access to the diminishing bison herds, tension which continued for decades.[41] Along with the demand for pemmican came the trade in bison robes: in the 1840s, the American Fur Company (AFC), which operated south of the forty-ninth parallel, was sending 100,000 bison robes east every year.[42] The HBC and the AFC were bitter rivals, but both considered the bison to be an unlimited natural resource, the way settler hunters thought the passenger pigeon and the northern curlew were infinite, the way our provincial government and forestry companies now imagine the boreal forest to be an endless supply of oriented strand board and toilet paper.[43]

The robe and pemmican trades were not the only way that settlers destroyed the bison. The occupation of bison habitat by settlers, and our conversion of grassland to cropland, was also a factor.[44] In addition, as industries expanded in the east, the demand for bison leather belts also grew, since eastern mills needed heavy leather belts to drive their machinery.[45] Bison hide was cheaper and more durable than cowhide; the expansion of the railway network in the United States facilitated the shipment of hides to the east; and bison hunters adopted powerful new rifles, such as the Sharp "big fifty," which allowed them to kill bison in safety, from several hundred yards away.[46] Millions of bison were killed by hide hunters, beginning in the 1860s, and estimates of the number of hides they shipped east don't include the hides wasted by the hunters, who often wounded animals without killing them, or the hides they damaged as they flayed them, or the ones they failed to stretch and dry properly.[47]

By the end of the 1870s, few bison remained anywhere on the Great Plains, although the slaughter continued until 1883, when the hide hunt collapsed because there were no animals left to kill. Then the bone trade began. Starving First Nations people scavenged the prairie for bison bones, which were sold to chemical companies that turned them into fertilizer that was shipped back west for the use of settler farmers [48] The bison bones that gave Regina its nêhiyawêwin name met the same fate.

Killing the bison was also a military strategy. The US federal government, which was at war with First Nations on the plains, believed that destroying the bison would help to defeat their enemies and force them onto reservations.[49] "This might seem like cruelty and wasteful extravagance but the buffalo, like the Indian, stood in the way of progress," wrote General Nelson A. Miles, a Civil War hero who led campaigns against the Lakota and the Nez Perce in the 1870s, in his memoir.[50] General Philip Sheridan, another veteran of the Civil War who led soldiers during the Sioux War and the Red River War, believed that the hide hunters had done more "to settle the vexed Indian question, than the regular army has done in the last thirty years":

> They are destroying the Indian's commissary, and it is a well-known fact that an army losing its base of supplies is placed at a great disadvantage. Send them powder and lead, if you will; for the sake of a lasting peace, let them kill, skin, and sell until the buffaloes are exterminated.[51]

Exterminating the bison was, for Sheridan, an essential element in the genocide that was being carried out against First Nations. Kill one, kill the other.

Even in the 1870s, though, not everyone agreed with the slaughter of the bison. The American Society for the Prevention of Cruelty to Animals, founded in 1866, declared the hide hunt to be cruel, which led to a public-policy debate in the United States about the fate of the remaining animals.[52] That attempt to curb the slaughter merely kept a handful of the animals alive, in places like Yellowstone National Park, established in 1872,[53] and Buffalo National Park near Wainwright, Alberta.[54] The rest perished. All plains bison alive today are descendants of that remnant. As Candace Savage explains, bison have become nearly "ecologically extinct."[55] The massive wild herds of bison that roamed these plains for tens of thousands of years no longer exist. True, during the winter of 2016, some thirty-five bison escaped from a ranch near Tisdale, Saskatchewan, and spent the winter roaming free;[56] they weren't returned to their owners until the following summer.[57] I wonder how they hid from their pursuers, where they found space for themselves. They must've been enjoying themselves, living the way their ancestors had.

During those decades of slaughter in the nineteenth century, both the bison and the First Nations people became "brutes that needed to be erased," and settlers did all they could to make that erasure happen, as nêhiyaw writer and filmmaker Tasha Hubbard tells us.[58] Indeed, Hubbard contends that the destruction of the bison was an act of genocide: not only against First Nations, for whom the animals provided everything, but against the bison themselves, since according to Indigenous ways of knowing "humans do not hold exclusive title to personhood, and therefore neither to genocide."[59] Indigenous Peoples saw the "buffalo genocide as a war on buffalo," an animal that was their protector and which "took a position on the front line in the genocidal war against Indigenous peoples."[60] The bison and Indigenous Peoples shared the same fate: "Through a complex and interrelated policy of buffalo genocide, enacted by the state, military, and hide hunters, the buffalo disappeared from the land, forcing the disappearance of Indigenous people at the same time."[61] Nevertheless, Hubbard concludes, while the bodies of the bison were destroyed, their spirits were not: "Our stories, still told and still understood, tell us the buffalo will return one day."[62]

One sign of that return is the Buffalo Treaty between Indigenous Peoples and the bison. A series of dialogues began in 2009 between First Nations on both sides of the Canada-US border about the possibility of bringing back the bison. Those conversations were rooted in the idea that Indigenous philosophies are, as Leroy Little Bear has written, "holistic and cyclical or repetitive, generalist, process-oriented, and firmly grounded in a particular place," and that Indigenous societies are made up of interconnected circles of kinship that constitute a "spider web" of relations.[63] Little Bear argues that colonization fractured this way of thinking and being, creating "a heritage of jagged worldviews" among Indigenous Peoples.[64] The discussions that led to the Buffalo Treaty, and the Buffalo Treaty itself, set out to heal those fractures by focusing on relationships between humans, and between humans and bison.

For Little Bear, bison are a keystone species—a term that, in his usage, goes beyond its usual ecological implications. Instead, he sees the bison as a keystone in Indigenous cultural, economic, and political paradigms.[65] The bison are part of what Little Bear calls "buffalo consciousness," something experienced not just through the natural world, culture, governance, and learning, but also as a form of economic strength that supports Indigenous self-determination.[66] Buffalo consciousness sees the bison as teachers and research partners as well. According to the authors of "Awakening Buffalo Consciousness: Lessons, Theory, and Practice from the Buffalo Treaty," buffalo consciousness is a political and ethical imperative created by ongoing interactions with bison. Those animals, they argue, "build a self-perpetuating and recursive consciousness in plains societies, evoking with a glance or thought a web of memories, stories, lessons, and strength in the minds of Indigenous people—all of which is situated within an appreciation for how the buffalo hold together a world for humans and other relations on the plains."[67] Métis writer and educator Chelsea Vowel suggests that this way of thinking is a rejection of the notion that Indigenous Peoples need to accept and adapt to a post-contact reality in which traditional ways of living are gone; instead, it asserts that Indigenous "kinscapes" can be restored, which will in turn lead to a restoration of the reciprocal obligations that exist between humans and their more-than-human relations. "Instead of accepting that the buffalo and our ancestral ways will never come back, what if we simply ensure that they do?" Vowel asks.[68]

The Buffalo Treaty,[69] a 2014 agreement, answers Vowel's question. The Buffalo Treaty is about building relationships that exist beyond and outside of colonial systems of governance.[70] It is a renewal of Indigenous treaty-making practices, which existed long before settlers arrived here.[71] It's an example of Indigenous internationalism.[72] It's Indigenous resurgence in action, too, because it creates a different future by making a different present, one that centres Indigeneity and allows that centring to change those who participate in it.[73] By 2019, some thirty First Nations had signed on to the treaty; conservation organizations have also been allowed to participate.[74] The bison are taken seriously as treaty partners, taking the project "beyond conservationist orientations and toward a more capacious understanding of human-buffalo relationality."[75] By coming together out of a concern for the buffalo and their relationship with them, the treaty parties "build an inter-Indigenous governance framework," a framework of relationality that's facilitated by the bison themselves.[76]

The return of bison to the plains, in parks and conservation areas and on Indigenous lands on both sides of the Canada-US border, is a tangible sign of the effect of the Buffalo Treaty. Bison have been reintroduced to Alberta at Banff National Park and to Saskatchewan at Grasslands National Park, Wanuskewin Heritage Park in Saskatoon, Old Man on His Back Prairie and Heritage Conservation Area, Batoche National Historic Site, and many other places. Such reintroduction efforts are often led by First Nations. In fact, Indigenous people played a central role in saving the bison from extinction. In *Buffalo Nation: American Indian Efforts to Restore the Bison*, Ken Zontek describes how James McKay, a Métis hunter, captured a small group of bison somewhere between what are now Moose Jaw and Regina in 1874. As that herd grew, it became the nucleus of other remnant herds on both sides of the Canada-US border.[77] Zontek's research shows that First Nations and Métis people are leaders in the return of bison in both countries. "Native people have demonstrated through their actions that they always sought a home for the buffalo to roam, a landscape capable of again nurturing the prolific herds," he concludes. "Indians have demonstrated phenomenal cultural perseverance—spanning more than 125 years—in reinstating the bison once again as part of a sacred symbiosis."[78]

The presence of bison on the grasslands they evolved with helps keep that ecosystem healthy: their pointy hooves aerate the soil and disperse seeds, and when they wallow, or roll on the ground to shed their winter coats or find relief from biting insects, they create depressions in the ground that fill with rainwater and snowmelt, encouraging plants to grow and providing habitat for microorganisms, amphibians, and insects.[79] But, as Jordan Daniels, a member of the Mistawasis Nêhiyawak (Cree) Nation, told *National Geographic*'s Karen Gardiner, "nothing outweighs the cultural factor of having bison back here."[80] Violet Meguinis, consultation director for the rewilding project being carried out by the Tsuut'ina Nation on the southwest edge of Calgary, agrees. "It's fulfilling because our spirituality is so dependent on our connection with the land, the animals," she told CBC Radio's Mouhamad Rachini. "It makes us whole again."[81] That sense of connection, of relationship, is precisely what the Buffalo Treaty is all about.

These reintroductions, also known as "rewilding," are different from ranching. When bison are rewilded, they interact with predators, including wolves, and shape the ecosystem as they did for tens of thousands of years.[82]

Gigantic herds of migrating bison, numbering tens of thousands of animals or more, are unlikely to return to the plains: there are too many highways and cities in the way, too many fields of wheat and canola, too many pipelines and fences, cities and towns. The rewilded bison in parks and on First Nations land often live in paddocks or on smallish pastures, since large areas of open grassland are now so rare. Much of what little grassland still exists is occupied by cattle, and because bison are thought to carry diseases like brucellosis, beef ranchers want to keep them far away from their herds. Nevertheless, rewilding bison creates tremendous benefits for the people and for the land. It's important work worth celebrating.

I think about my tendency to negativity, to ignore the good side of things and preclude future possibilities, and once again consider Rebecca Solnit's suggestion that hope is located in "the spaciousness of uncertainty" which allows us room for action.[83] Rewilding bison is hopeful, because it's based in the possibility that the future can be different from the present. It's an attempt to do something that'll change the relationship between people and the land. This walk, too, is hopeful, I realize. I don't know if I'm going to be able to recognize my relationship with the land by walking beside this highway, but it's a possibility—one I'm taking seriously, one step at a time. After all, if I really didn't think it could happen, I would've stayed home.

///

My pack straps—nylon, not leather of any kind, and so the product of a different kind of destructive resource extraction, the petroleum industry—are creaking with every step I take. I look at the sun and at Fleet Street, which curves to meet the highway at a perpendicular angle, and decide I'm still walking southwest, rather than west. The direction of my travel doesn't matter, of course—if I stay on the highway, I won't get lost—but I'm trying to orient myself in relation to the four cardinal directions. As I'm puzzling this out, without much success, another cyclist passes. "How's it goin'?" he asks, smiling. "Good, how about you?" I answer, but he's already behind me. I've walked twenty kilometres already, and I'm beginning to stumble on my blistered feet. To carry on much further risks making this journey about my body, its aches and pains. I want to keep both my body and the land itself in view, to maintain some kind of balance between them, but that gets harder the farther I go. A rock shaped like a stone hammer lies beside the paved shoulder. A motorcycle with two guitars strapped to the back zips past. I think I hear a voice speaking to me but decide it's only the water sloshing in my pack.

I stop to rest beside the old railway tracks, on the edge of the embankment they're built on. I admire the striped patterns of swathed canola to the south, beyond the tracks, before I sit down. Across the highway stands a stark pile of dirt—perhaps left over from the construction of one of the overpasses. I've picked an unusual spot to rest: I'm lying beside a clump of Canada wild rye, one of the few native grasses I'm likely to see on this walk. It's a big surprise to find it in this place. I greet it politely: "Hello, grass. Thanks for being here." Then I eat a cereal bar and a handful of dried blueberries and drink some water. I take off my boots and my socks. My feet are covered in heat rash and pruney with sweat—their normal state after walking this far. A raven croaks. A combine rolls slowly down the highway, heading west. I doze in the warm sun. Grasshoppers start taking me for granted, finding me a warm place to rest. A pickup stops on the shoulder, and a young man gets out to pee. He doesn't notice me. After an hour or so, I decide to push on. I gather my things, put my socks and boots back on, apply sunscreen. Then I stand, stretch my stiff legs, and start walking again.

The blister on the sole of my left foot seems to have grown while I rested. The wind is stronger now. My pack straps groan with each step, sounding even more tired than I am. I pass beneath more high-tension lines. A truck's mudflap lies in the ditch. An array of cameras has been installed over the highway. What are they for? Photo radar? Licence plates? A way to collect tolls in the future? Now I can see the overpass at Highway 6 on the horizon. I pass more pipeline infrastructure on the edge of a field of barley. On the shoulder, cannibal grasshoppers feed on the bodies of their dead comrades. A creek passes beneath the Bypass, and I wonder what it's called. I reach the on-ramp from Highway 6. The fields to the south have already been combined; to the north, golden wheat waits for the machines. A grid road runs alongside the Bypass, parallel to the highway, and I briefly consider crossing the ditch to walk on it instead of on the highway. It would be a change, but it would also violate the spirit of this walk, which demands that I remain on the highway. I decide to stay where I am.

The wind is from the south now, a blast of hot air. I walk down Highway 6 to Rowatt. The wind is shirring through the poplar trees there. A sign warning about the presence of the pipeline bangs against its post in the wind. An angry dog is barking. I decide to rest in the shade of a shed belonging to the Regina South Pipeline Public Utility Board instead of pressing on to the church—partly because of the dog, partly because I'm too tired to talk to the dog's owner about what I'm doing. There's a slough next to the shed, and a single frog gives one last chirp before going silent. Ladybugs hover around me, and large black flies bite my legs, leaving bleeding wounds behind. They look like houseflies, but they can't be, since houseflies don't bite. Or do they? On the other side of the shed, traffic is rushing along Highway 6. The grass whispers in the wind. That dog is still barking; it's clearly agitated, almost hysterical. The church might not be a safe place to camp after all. Besides, if that dog barks all night, nobody's going to get any sleep.

There are five hours until sunset, when I'll feel comfortable making camp. What am I going to do for five hours? The dog and the flies make this a bad place to rest and a worse place to camp, but I'm too tired to find a different spot. Both of my heels are sore now. I think about the weather forecast. A cold and rainy night, an angry dog, and these voracious flies: I decide that Rowatt isn't a good place to sleep after all. I'm only twelve kilometres from my own bed. Why don't I go home and come back tomorrow morning? That way I could eat something decent and get some rest. I call my partner for a ride.

I swat flies and wait, glumly comparing myself to Robert Macfarlane. He wouldn't go home in this situation. He always sleeps outside, even when it's cold and rainy, even when other accommodations are available. I remember a story he tells in his book *The Wild Places*, about waking up in one of the few old-growth forests left in Scotland, sheltered only by the base of a fallen birch tree, his sleeping bag covered in snow.[84] Macfarlane likes to swim in the ocean in the Hebrides, too, despite the freezing water temperatures. I guess I'm just not as tough as he is. I like sleeping in a bed. Maybe, faced with these big, biting flies, Macfarlane might go home, too. Or maybe he wouldn't. I can't imagine him striding down the shoulder of a paved highway, either. Such ruderal places don't appeal to him.

I stand and stretch. Fine, then, Robert, I mutter. Be a hero. I take my phone out of my pocket. I'm going to sleep in my own bed tonight and drink a cup of coffee in the morning before coming back here to start walking again. You stay here with the flies and the dog. I'll see you tomorrow.

SEVEN

FUTURES TRADING

AUGUST 30, 2020

The next morning, my partner drops me off back at Rowatt. The forecasted rain didn't amount to much, but the ground is wet, and there's a smell of wet poplar, or maybe wet canola—I can't tell which—in the air. I'm tired this morning, and I'm glad I decided not to camp here last night. The dog is silent; maybe it sleeps inside and wouldn't have bothered me. Maybe the flies would've gone away, too. I'll never know.

I head up Highway 6 to the interchange. It's cold and damp. I'm not used to walking two days in a row, and my muscles are stiff. The thick line of cloud suggests a front is passing through from the northwest. It's supposed to drop to three degrees tonight. I've added a down coat and a wool hat to my pack; I'm going to need them. I'll have to wear all the clothes I'm carrying tonight inside my sleeping bag. I can hear the trucks rumbling along the Bypass. The wind is cold enough that I consider zipping the legs onto my shorts, but I don't want to stop walking and fumble with them. Two motorcycles on the Bypass sound like helicopters, and

I briefly recall the movie *Apocalypse Now*. As I'm walking down the on-ramp, a truck pulls over on the other side of the highway; I hear its air brakes hissing. A seemingly infinite line of power poles runs along the side of the road.

A massive field of lentils waits to be combined on the south side of the highway. The scale of agriculture here is hard to comprehend. This is a landscape for driving, not for walking, and it's been that way since rural Saskatchewan started losing its settler population in the 1930s. Before the introduction of horses, though, Indigenous people here walked everywhere. Maybe part of the difference lies in the change from grassland to cropland; walking for miles on prairie must feel different from walking down a highway beside fields of canola and barley. A flock of birds flies out of the

ditch beside me into the path of a passing semi; they've decided that I'm more of a threat to them than the traffic. I figure they were grey partridges and write that in my notebook. The new pavement on the Bypass is clean and unblemished, unlike other highways in this province; the colour is a uniform black, and it shines with rainwater, especially the rumble strip, where puddles have collected. I hear crickets, although not as many as yesterday—or else I'm not yet attuned to them this morning. I seem to be hearing individual insects, rather than hearing them together, as a chorus, the way I did yesterday. Maybe they're cold.

The sky to the southeast is grey, almost black. It must be raining hard there—the weather I wanted to avoid. A dead field mouse, wet from the rain, lies on the shoulder; it's the same dark colour as the pavement. A light-grey band of cloud stretches across the western sky. I suddenly wonder if this landscape—the lentils, the highway, the sky—can evoke love. Isn't that the point of this walk? Leanne Betasamosake Simpson told Naomi Klein that the relationship she has with the land is one of love, the kind a child has for her mother.[1] I always find a sense of wholeness in grassland, an interconnected web of grasses and flowers, of birds and animals, that makes it easy to love. But this highway, a non-place that people pass through instead of spending time in—can it be loved? I watch the passing semis. Do truckers love the highway? It's possible. Non-places could become places for people who spend time in them. Someone who works at an airport, for instance, will come to know that non-place as a place: this door that sticks, that shortcut to the coffee shop, the one washroom that always gets dirtier than the others. Stories will accumulate there, and those stories, the knowledge they contain, suggest the possibility of place. But does that change from non-place to place necessarily suggest love? I wave at the truckers speeding past; most of them wave back. That's the extent of our relationship. Is their connection to the space they're driving through just as shallow? I'm convinced that as I walk I'm turning this non-place into place, at least temporarily, but by not sleeping at Rowatt last night, I missed a chance to engage with it more deeply. Maybe that was a mistake. I think about the dog, the flies, Macfarlane. I'll sleep outside tonight, see if that makes any difference to how I feel about the spot where I end up camping. Ahead, the grey band of cloud has developed curved peaks on the top, like a child's drawing of an ocean.

///

I'm still wondering what the farmland this highway crosses looked like before settlers arrived, and if the explorers who travelled through southern Saskatchewan—Captain John Palliser and Henry Youle Hind in the late 1850s, and botanist John Macoun in the last decades of the nineteenth century—left any hints. The purpose of Palliser's expedition was to fill in a blank space on the map: the northern plains were largely unknown to outsiders. "Without first-hand, dependable information, the public and politicians alike had only rumour, conjecture, and controversy as a basis for decisions as to policy," Irene Spry writes.[2] Nobody in eastern Canada knew whether there were forests here, what the soil and climate were like, whether the land was fertile or a desert, or if any rivers flowed into the South Saskatchewan River's right bank.[3] With its focus on answering these questions, Palliser's expedition obviously served the colonization of the western grasslands. It was funded and organized by the British government's Colonial Office, which sent a botanist, an observer of the earth's magnetic fields, a combination geologist/naturalist/medical doctor, and an astronomer, who was also the expedition's secretary, along with Palliser. In 1857, the party travelled by steamboat and canoe to the starting point of their expedition: Fort William, a fur-trading post on the north shore of Lake Superior, now part of Thunder Bay.

Palliser and his companions journeyed from Fort William to Fort Garry, now Winnipeg, and then headed west, using horses and Red River carts. On their way to the so-called "Elbow" of the South Saskatchewan River, the party passed very near what is now Regina—in other words, close to where I am walking. Palliser's account of his travels near here reads:

> September 15th. Off at 4:30 a.m. and halted for breakfast at 10 o'clock beside a small lake; from this we had an extensive view of the Prairie Coteau, extending away to the north-west. Our Indian guide, the peace-maker, to whom we had given the name of Nichiwa, or friend, counselled us to cut wood and bring it along in our carts, as he said it was the last we should see to-day; there is now no more wood except in the valleys of the rivers. Our course was due west, and as far as the eye can reach nothing but desolate plains meet the view; at noon reached a small creek called "The Creek before where the bones lie;" here we found water and a little grass, also a few willows and cherry bushes, but no wood fit for fuel. This creek rises from a small lake about 8 miles to the south of the Qu'appelle Lakes, into which it ultimately flows. Two Indian lodges are here, containing an old man with some women and children; the young men are away in all directions in strong parties hunting buffalo. In the evening reached the Creek where the Bones lie, where we found water and very little grass; a few willows also grew here but no wood fit for fuel.[4]

I'm not sure what the first creek Palliser mentions might be, but the second is definitely Wascana Creek, which meanders through Regina before emptying into the Qu'Appelle River to the north.[5] Palliser's description of the grassland here as "desolate plains" contradicts my hunch that the grassland here would've been particularly lush because of the heavy, moisture-retaining clay soil. Maybe my hunch is incorrect, or maybe people used to the eastern forests didn't understand grasslands, or maybe before Palliser arrived here bison had eaten the grass or fires had burned it. However, his suggestion that the young men from the group of people he met were hunting bison supports my guess; the plant life here might've indeed been tall and rich, if bison came here in large numbers.

The following year, Hind's exploratory expedition (organized by the Legislative Assembly of Canada[6]) passed near here, and his description of the area is very similar to Palliser's. Hind describes the area south of what he termed the Fertile Belt as a northern extension of "the Great American Desert":

> The northern limit of the Great American Desert is an imaginary line drawn from the Touchwood Hills to the Moose Woods on the South Branch, then south of the Battle River as far as long. 112°, when turning south it sweeps along the flanks of the Rocky Mountains at 115°.[7]

Regina, this highway, and everything I can see lies within the territory Hind describes here. He has nothing else to say about this place; instead, he focuses on the "Fertile Belt" to the north, which, he states, possesses a "singularly favourable disposition as to soil and climate," along with a wealth of natural resources.[8] Only the "Fertile Belt" would lend itself to agricultural exploitation and settlement; the desert to the south was, Hind suggests, uninhabitable—at least for settlers, since Indigenous Peoples had been living there for thousands of years.

How are we to understand Palliser's and Hind's conclusions about this place? It's not a desert; the fields of barley and canola surrounding me make that clear. Did they misunderstand the productivity of what geographers refer to as the moist mixed grassland ecoregion?[9] Of course, the prairies experience frequent droughts, including the catastrophic drought that occurred in the decade after 1929, but does that make them "desolate plains"? Palliser's expedition crossed the plains during a period of drought, which explains his reports of little rain, dry rivers, and arid country. [10] In addition, S.A. Wolfe, C.H. Hugenholtz, and Olav B. Lian explain, "with limited technical knowledge of the day, the Expedition tended to judge the quality of the soil mainly by the vegetation type, and their impression of aridity was further reinforced by plagues of grasshoppers and plains eaten bare by buffalo."[11] Palliser's conclusions about these "desolate plains" may have been influenced by his encounter with active dune fields in what's now southeastern Alberta.[12] That may have been a factor in Palliser's overall impression of what came to be known as "Palliser's Triangle," but it doesn't explain why Palliser would have described the place where I'm walking as "desolate," unless the droughts were particularly bad in the 1850s.

David J. Sauchyn and Alwynne B. Beaudoin examined tree rings in logs used to build structures in the late nineteenth century to learn about historical droughts. The driest twelve-month record they found was the period between August 1773 to July 1774, when just 242 millimetres of rain fell in the Cypress Hills. Precipitation for the period between August 1857 and July 1858—the period when Palliser and Hind were crossing the northern plains—was, at 313 millimetres, well below the average for the 313-year tree-ring record, 373 millimetres.[13] Perhaps that drought explains the explorers' descriptions of the land they travelled through. However, W.F. Rannie relies on the accounts of the weather in the reports published by those expeditions to argue that while what is now southern Alberta was indeed experiencing dry conditions in 1857 and 1858, the situation elsewhere on the prairies was very different: Palliser reported rain frequency that was below normal in 1857, but not so low as to be considered a drought, and Hind's account suggests that his expedition "encountered abundant and frequent rainfall everywhere he went east of the South Saskatchewan River."[14] The lack of grass in the region, Rannie argues, was due to fire, grasshoppers, and the effects of buffalo grazing, so the notion that Palliser's impressions of this place were affected by a drought is only partially correct.[15]

Why did Palliser and Hind both consider the place where I'm walking to have been a desert? Could it be that they equated a land without trees—which a grassland would be even in a wet year—to a desert? Did they think trees equalled agricultural fertility, that a land without trees was not fit for farming? Bill Waiser thinks so. "The failure to recognize the treeless prairie as a distinctive North American physical environment had accounted, in part, for Palliser's and Hind's pessimistic conclusions," he writes.[16] They had no conception of grasslands; they saw any territory without trees as a desert. Roger L. Welch argues that in the nineteenth century the word "desert" meant something different from what it means now: rather than referring to sand dunes or cacti, it merely denoted any land without trees.[17] Maybe the key to Palliser's and Hind's description of this land is linguistic, not meteorological.

Other outsiders visited the northern plains before the arrival of settlers and plows, too, leaving written descriptions of what they saw. George Dawson, who was appointed geologist and botanist to Her Majesty's North American Boundary Commission in 1872, published a report detailing his observations of what is now southern Saskatchewan. Dawson passed to the south of this highway, but his report reminds us what this place might have looked like while bison—a few, anyway—still roamed here. Despite the character of his appointment, Dawson's report is the work of a geologist, rather than a botanist, and his descriptions of the flora of the northern prairies are secondary to his interest in the area's geology. Nevertheless, he does remark that "[f]rom the second crossing of the Souris to the foot of the Missouri Coteau"—in other words, the country about a hundred miles south of this highway—"the prairie still shows a gently undulating surface, and in most places a short, thick growth of grass."[18] Another visitor to the area was Macoun, who had been part of Dawson's expedition. In 1880, he described “a broken, clay plain” west of the Souris River and east of the Missouri Coteau—perhaps the very plain I am looking at—with few animals and little water, but with tall, green grass. Macoun was surprised by its height.[19] In a letter addressed to his wife, noting his location as “somewhere in the ‘Great Lone Land,’” Macoun wrote: “On Friday morning we entered on this plain and only saw water once at sundown after we had made 27 miles.... The surface of the ground was so rough that we thought our carts would have been shaken to pieces. Some of the cracks were 2 feet deep and the whole surface was constantly uneven.”[20] That uneven ground must’ve been the result of clays containing montmorillonite, which expand and contract dramatically in the presence or absence of water, like the soil on which Regina has been built,[21] so “somewhere in the ‘Great Lone Land’” might’ve been close to where I’m standing—perhaps the badlands near Avonlea, Saskatchewan, southwest of Regina.[22] Dawson’s and Macoun’s words suggest that the prairie here was richer and more productive, as agronomists would say, than the grassland I’ve seen in southwestern Saskatchewan. If so, this place would’ve provided food for large herds of bison, along with other animals and birds. That means it would’ve been important for First Nations people, too. That’s what I suspected, but it’s good to have my hunch confirmed.

Even after the bison had been extirpated and the people confined to reserves, the grassland songbirds remained. In 2005, ornithologist Stuart Houston told Trevor Herriot that the prairies of his youth, where he was surrounded by “the music of longspurs, lark buntings, grassland sparrows and pipits pouring down from the sky,” were like “standing beneath a ‘canopy of song.’”[23] Today, walking alongside this highway, I can’t hear any birds at all, just traffic and crickets and my own footsteps. No wonder: as far as I can see, all the way to the horizons on every side, the grassland habitat those birds depended upon has been destroyed and the land silenced.

///

I pass a field of wheat that's been combined and inhale the wet straw smell of the stubble. I haven't seen any shoes yet, but a bag that once held a folding camp chair lies in the ditch. There isn't much traffic, but it's early on a Sunday morning, so that's probably normal. I'm walking past a lot of discarded water bottles now. Most of the cars heading east have Manitoba plates; those folks are hurrying home. The wave-like shapes in the grey band of cloud ahead of me have subsided. I can see where the Bypass curves northwest now, but I have several kilometres to go before I get there. Behind me, the sun is trying to break through the clouds. A forest of light poles to the west marks what must be the Courtney Street exit. I pass a sign that tells me another oil pipeline runs under the Bypass. Somewhere in the distance I hear a train horn sounding at a level crossing; it's almost inaudible. On the horizon, to the northwest, I can see the overpasses where this highway meets the Ring Road, and I realize that what I took to be a train horn must've been a truck at that interchange. Two semis with the word *Bison* painted on their trailers move west in tandem.

The pavement is drying, and behind me the clouds are becoming a magnificent swirl. I'm walking past a large, square pit filled with water and surrounded by a chain-link fence festooned with DANGER signs. It looks like another borrow pit, but there's no overpass nearby. I try to take a picture, but I'd need to be someone like Canadian photographer Edward Burtynsky, with a large-format camera and a helicopter, to get a decent image in this strange light. Then the sun breaks through the clouds behind me, and I take photographs of the sky instead. The cold air feels like the first day of fall. I pass a spiky rubber ball at the side of the road, a model of the novel coronavirus, and another water bottle filled with what looks like pee. I used to think pee-bottles were an urban legend, but I guess they're real. I can't imagine being too pressed for time to stop and take a leak at the side of the road, instead fumbling with my zipper while trying to keep my vehicle in its lane, but then I'm not a trucker, locked into a schedule that pays only for kilometres travelled. Across the highway is a huge farm with dozens of grain bins. Does the farmer own land on both sides of the road? How would that farmer get equipment from one side of the highway to the other? It's not long before I get an answer: there's an exit, marked by at least a kilometre of lights, at Courtney Street, the at-grade kind that expects drivers to make turns into oncoming traffic that's moving at 110 kilometres per hour or more. Those interchanges have been replaced at Balgonie and Pilot Butte and Emerald Park by overpasses, and I thought the new highway would do the same. I was wrong. It's a question of money. Why build an overpass for a handful of farmers? As the highway banks into its northwest curve, it gets harder to walk on a slanting surface. A sign reads IMPORTANT INTERSECTION.

Walking demands patience, as Craig Mod suggests, because it's slow. It's going to take me fifteen or twenty minutes to get past Courtney Street, its exit, its line of lights, and it's going to take another hour or more to get to the overpasses that are creeping closer. I'm not a patient person; maybe walking will eventually help me develop that virtue, though it hasn't yet. The crops on both sides of the Bypass have been harvested; I'm walking between fields of stubble, except for a small field of barley between the Bypass and Courtney Street that still waits for the combines. Not one of the trucks passing me is hauling a container, which suggests they aren't coming from or heading to the Global Transportation Hub. Instead, they're passing through. Sunflowers and flax are growing in the ditch, beside unripe wheat that must've been blown there on the wind. An equipment dealer's truck turns onto Courtney Street and heads towards a farm; someone's combine must need emergency service. A second truck follows the first. A third vehicle uses the exit to turn around and head back west;

I catch sight of the driver as she passes. She looks lost. Maybe this exit gets more traffic than I thought.

A phalanx of trucks approaches, and I step off the shoulder onto the grass to be safe. Swathed canola paints a field in tan and pale green stripes. The sky behind me is dark but the sun is fully out now. A truck honks its horn—at me, perhaps—and I put on some sunscreen. I can see the airport on the northern horizon, and the city's downtown east of that. I pass another truck's mudflap in the ditch. How often do they come loose? A sign tells me that the big interchange is now just one kilometre away, although it looks farther. My nose is running in the cold wind. I'm walking directly north now; the highway's long, gentle arc has straightened out. I can see the Loblaws warehouse at the Global Transportation Hub. I'm starting to feel anxious about getting through the interchange ahead, because I'll have to cross multiple on- and off-ramps where motorists won't expect to encounter a pedestrian. I pass beneath more high-tension lines. To the left, a meadowlark sings—a sound I haven't heard since June. I can smell the swathed canola on my left. The sun is warm now, but the northwest wind is still cold. Another pipeline crosses beneath the Bypass. The blister on the sole of my left foot is stinging again.

Then, suddenly, I'm at the interchange. The earthen embankments supporting the overpasses will probably be here until the next ice age. So much dirt was moved for this project; settlers walk heavily on the land. It's true that some Indigenous Peoples built lasting monuments: I've seen the pyramids and stone buildings at Chichen Itza, for instance, and I've read about the Cahokia mounds near St. Louis, where Indigenous people built earthen pyramids that were part of a large city. But the people who lived here, where I'm walking now, left lighter traces on the land: tipi rings, medicine wheels. So few have survived. Most were destroyed along with the prairie when the land was broken. I startle a rabbit, which runs across the silent highway and hides in the median strip.

To the east I can just make out the white shell of Mosaic Stadium, empty this year because of the pandemic.

I walk beneath the first overpass and listen to the hollow bangs of traffic passing above and the cooing of pigeons roosting underneath it. A cyclist approaches, heading south. I can see the Canadian Pacific intermodal terminal now. Ahead, the highway gently arcs west, towards Rotary Avenue and the Global Transportation Hub. Once I'm away from the overpasses, I decide to take a break. I rest my pack against a light pole, then lean against it and watch the sparse traffic pass. The wind is still cold. I take a photograph of a light pole against the sky's thin blue. Google Maps tells me it's still a long way to Rotary Avenue. I wonder how far I'll get today, and what I'll find when I'm too tired to go any farther.

///

Everything I can see from the shoulder of this highway—all the land, stretching far beyond the horizon in every direction—was the exclusive territory of Indigenous Peoples before settlers arrived and claimed ownership. What gives me—or any other settler—the right to be here? Is there any ethical basis for my presence here on Treaty 4 land? Or am I here only because of colonialist arguments like *terra nullius*, the doctrine of occupation, and the doctrine of discovery?

Terra nullius, the doctrine of occupation, and the doctrine of discovery are three arguments that try to defend the Crown's (and therefore settlers') title to the land. *Terra nullius*, the notion that land not being used for agricultural purposes has been abandoned by its owners, is the basis of the doctrine of occupation, which, as Anishinaabe legal scholar John Borrows points out, holds that "[o]ccupation by a political grouping on a territorial basis is one reason for recognizing broad legal rights over a territory."[24] According to Borrows, the doctrine of occupation should be rejected because it is factually incorrect: "if the doctrine of occupation were applied without bias," he contends, "most people would likely conclude that at Canada's formation the Crown had not effectively *occupied* Indigenous lands in this manner such as to justify displacing their laws."[25] In addition, "[e]thnocentric standards concerning occupation"—such as the claim (derived from seventeenth-century philosopher John Locke) that Indigenous Peoples had not worked the soil and were therefore not owners of the land, or the claim (derived from eighteenth-century jurist William Blackstone) that Indigenous Peoples were not organized in such a way as to claim group occupation—"should be discarded as a basis for diminishing Indigenous law," including Indigenous title to territory.[26] Finally, the doctrine of discovery is the claim that the arrival in (or "discovery" of) North America gave the title of that territory to the Crown. That argument, according to Sylvia McAdam (Saysewahum), "no longer has legal standing in international discourse," even though Canada continues to apply it in court. The doctrine of discovery "was unacceptable at the time of treaty and is unacceptable now," she states.[27] Although Supreme Court of Canada rulings have upheld the doctrine of discovery, "it is factually apparent that at Canada's formation there was no first *discovery* on the part of the Crown that would justify displacing Indigenous law," Borrows argues. "Indigenous peoples had already discovered most land within their territories and exercised jurisdiction over it prior to the arrival of Europeans."[28] Even if the doctrine of discovery gave "the Crown the ability to claim exclusive or pre-eminent legal authority in areas that were *terra nullius*, literally 'barren and deserted,'" the territories of Indigenous Peoples when the Crown arrived in North America were neither barren nor deserted.[29]

The doctrine of discovery, the doctrine of occupation, and *terra nullius* are all connected, Borrows suggests, and not only because they are wrong. For nêhiyaw lawyer and writer Harold Johnson, they are simply racist. There is no coherent theory that explains the sovereignty of the Crown in this territory, Johnson argues, unless one relies on "the outmoded doctrine that you have a right to this territory because you are superior to my family"—by "family," he's referring to the nêhiyawak—but this is a doctrine that, he contends, properly belongs to the KKK or the Aryan Nations.[30] "Discovery cannot be justification for your family's occupation of this territory," he continues. "Your family did not discover this place. It was never lost."[31]

And yet, those doctrines are still used to explain the presence of settlers on this land. If they are wrong, and they obviously are, then what justifies settlers living here, building highways or arguing about who owns the land and how much money it's worth? These are difficult questions, the kind we settlers rarely ask ourselves.

But Indigenous people who write about decolonization demand answers to them. For instance, Unangax̂ education professor Eve Tuck and K. Wayne Yang contend that the goal of decolonization for Indigenous Peoples is "the repatriation of land and life": "all of the land, and not just symbolically."[32] For settlers, such a process of repatriation will, Eva Mackey writes, "require engagement with the difficult yet necessary task of unsettling attitudes and practices based on settled expectations."[33] The notion of becoming unsettled does not sound comfortable; nor does the prospect of responding to the demand that land be repatriated. However, the argument that land must be returned in order for decolonization to happen is common in writing about settler colonialism. Echoing Tuck and Yang, Mackey suggests that "settler colonialism is a complex and singular social formation concerned with the appropriation of Indigenous land," and for that reason "decolonization must also be a material process"; that is, it must involve returning land to Indigenous Peoples.[34] For Emma Battel Lowman and Adam J. Barker, decolonization describes "an intensely transformative process with the goal of regenerating Indigenous nationhood and place-relationships while dismantling structures of settler colonialism that oppose or seek to eliminate Indigenous peoples from the land."[35] Land is the word that links these three different examples of settler-colonial theory: for decolonization, land—who owns it, and who belongs on it—is the central concern.

This emphasis on land separates decolonization from ideas of reconciliation. When the authors of the summary volume of the multivolume report of the Truth and Reconciliation Commission of Canada state that we must "return what must be returned,"[36] they're talking about land, since the report's authors consider matters beyond the history and legacy of Indian residential schools in Canada. "What is clear to this Commission is that Aboriginal peoples and the Crown have very different and conflicting views on what reconciliation is and how it is best achieved," the report states. On one hand, "the Government of Canada appears to believe that reconciliation entails Aboriginal peoples' acceptance of the reality and validity of Crown sovereignty and parliamentary supremacy, in order to allow the government to get on with business." Indigenous Peoples, on the other hand, "see reconciliation as an opportunity to affirm their own sovereignty and return to the 'partnership' ambitions they held after Confederation."[37] However, the word "decolonize" appears only once in the summary of the TRC report: it is used by Shirley Flowers, a survivor of the residential school system, who recognizes that the purpose of the residential schools was "part of a bigger scheme of colonization." She concludes, "We have to learn to decolonize."[38] Because decolonization requires the repatriation of all the land, according to Tuck and Yang's definition, it is a more radical solution to settler colonialism than reconciliation. It would also be more unsettling for settlers, more uncomfortable, more anxiety-producing.

The question of what decolonization will look like, or how it will end, is an open one. For Lowman and Barker, decolonization is "a call to fundamentally change how we generate political power and conceive of land."[39] "Decolonization is open ended and multiple, creating more and more different possibilities as it is pursued," they argue, and it is "embodied in the creation of social movements and communities that sustain themselves on the land, revitalize traditional trade and treaty networks, promote Indigenous cultural expression, and challenge narrow identity binaries, all of which can combine to make the structures of settler colonialism irrelevant and impotent."[40] Tuck and Yang make some suggestions about how decolonization might be shaped. They write that decolonization will mean the enacting of an ethic of incommensurability, which would mean "relinquishing settler futurity, abandoning the hope that settlers may one day be commensurable to Native peoples," they write. "The Native futures, the lives to be lived once the settler nation is gone—these are the unwritten possibilities made possible by an ethic of incommensurability."[41] The term "settler futurity" isn't defined by Tuck and Yang, but in a later essay, Tuck and Rubén A. Gaztambide-Fernández cite Andrew Baldwin's suggestion that "futurity" refers to our attitudes towards the future.[42] Baldwin's examples are fear and hope: "Both are simultaneously embodied experiences and atmospheric qualities animated by imagined futures: one fears the yet-to-come and the other hopes for better things to come. In both, the here-and-now of the psyche or of [the] collective mood is shaped by the yet-to-come."[43] For Tuck and Gaztambide-Fernández, as well as Tuck and Yang, settler futurity seems to be a synonym for the ongoing replacement of Indigenous Peoples by settlers—the logic of elimination Patrick Wolfe describes. No wonder Tuck and Yang, and Tuck and Gaztambide-Fernández, call for the abandonment of settler futurity. For them, that term describes an ongoing genocide.

What about the idea that settlers are incommensurable with Indigenous Peoples? According to the *Oxford English Dictionary*, "commensurable" means "measurable by the same standard or scale of values," or "[p]roportionable in measure, size, amount, etc.; having a suitable proportion, proportionate *to*."[44] For Tuck and Yang, settlers cannot be measured by the same standard or scale of values, because their futurity is based on a genocidal ambition to replace Indigenous Peoples through Wolfe's logic of elimination, whereas the futurity of Indigenous Peoples is based on a resistance to that logic. We also see this notion of incommensurability when Tuck and Yang discuss James Fenimore Cooper's Leatherstocking Tales, and their protagonist, Natty Bumppo, as examples of one of the ways settlers imagine themselves: settler adoption fantasies. Such fantasies "can mean the adoption of Indigenous practices and knowledge, but more, refer to those narratives in the settler-colonial imagination in which the Native (understanding that he is becoming extinct) hands over his land, his claim to the land, his very Indian-ness to the settler for safe-keeping," they write. "This is a fantasy that is invested in a settler futurity and dependent on the foreclosure of an Indigenous futurity."[45] Cooper's Leatherstocking Tales are an example of this fantasy. My desire to come into relationship with the land might be one, too, although I hope that's not the case. "In the unwritten decolonial version of Cooper's story, Hawkeye would lose his land back to the Mohawk," Tuck and Yang write. "Hawkeye would shoot his last arrow, or his last long-rifle shot, return his eagle feather, and would be renamed Natty Bumppo, settler on Native land. The story would end at the moment of this recognition."[46] That imagined ending, though, would still leave a number of questions open: "Would a conversation follow after that between Native and the last settler? Would the settler leave or just vanish? Would he ask to stay, and if he did, who would say yes? These are questions that will be addressed at decolonization, and not a priori in order to appease anxieties for a settler future."[47]

And yet, while the claims of settlers to legitimacy here might be based in racism and genocide, we're unlikely to simply vanish. If we can't find some ethical basis on which we can justify living here, then our presence is just a case of might making right. Neither the doctrine of discovery, nor the doctrine of occupation, nor *terra nullius* will provide that legitimacy. Settlers need to find some just way to live together with Indigenous Peoples and share the land. In addition, given the demographic reality of the number of settlers living here, it would seem apparent that building alliances and relationships with those settlers will be necessary if decolonization is to happen. All of that seems to be a tall order, given the ongoing history of genocide perpetrated upon Indigenous Peoples by settlers. Luckily, a potential model, both for a sharing of the land and for establishing an ethical relationship between settlers and Indigenous Peoples, exists: the historical and modern treaties between Indigenous Peoples and the Crown.

Unfortunately, that model is fraught with problems. Everything I can see from where I'm walking was once Indigenous land, it's true, but it's also Treaty 4 land. Over a few days in mid-September 1874, nêhiyaw, Anihšināpē, and Nakoda Chiefs, and Alexander Morris, David Laird, and William Christie, the treaty commissioners representing the Crown, came together to negotiate Treaty 4 near Fort Qu'Appelle, then a Hudson's Bay post, located east of here in the Qu'Appelle Valley. Treaty 4 is an agreement which enables settlers, at least in theory, to share the land with First Nations. Two stories are told about that treaty, and about all the nineteenth-century numbered treaties: one by Indigenous Treaty Elders, and the other by Canada's federal government. Comparing those stories can help us understand what those treaties might mean.

The federal government claims that the numbered treaties—including Treaty 4—were real-estate transactions, in which First Nations Chiefs surrendered their lands in return for, among other things, assistance with the transition to an agricultural economy and small reserves. That story relies on the so-called "surrender clauses" in the written treaty texts by which First Nations allegedly extinguished their title to their land. In Treaty Commissioner Alexander Morris's account of the negotiation of the first seven numbered treaties on the southern prairies, it is clear that from the outset extinguishing Indigenous title was the federal government's goal, because Indigenous title to the land was a barrier to white settlement. In his book's dedication to Lord Dufferin, for example, Morris writes of "obtaining the relinquishment of the natural title of the Indians to the lands of the Fertile Belt on fair and just terms,"[48] a statement that is both a recognition of underlying Indigenous title and an admission of the Crown's desire to extinguish it.[49] Similar language is used in Morris's accounts of the treaty negotiations from the Robinson Treaties in Ontario ("the Government of the late Province of Canada, deemed it desirable, to extinguish the Indian title"[50]) through to Treaty 5 ("it was essential that the Indian title to all the territory in the vicinity of the lake should be extinguished so that the settlers and traders might have undisturbed access to its waters, shores, islands, inlets and tributary streams"[51]). The language of the written version of Treaty 4 is consistent with the first five numbered treaties:

> The Cree and Saulteaux tribes of Indians, and all other the [*sic*] Indians inhabiting the district hereinafter described and defined, do hereby cede, release, surrender and yield up to the Government of the Dominion of Canada for Her Majesty the Queen and her successors forever, all their rights, titles, and privileges whatsoever to the lands included within the following limits...[52]

However, that kind of language doesn't appear in Morris's discussions of Treaty 6 or Treaty 7, perhaps because by then it was unnecessary to explain that the government wanted to extinguish Indigenous title: that point had already been made.

The differences between the way the Crown negotiators seem to have understood Treaty 4, and the way the First Nations negotiators understood that agreement, are complicated by the fact that, as Sheldon Krasowski points out, there is no evidence the Crown negotiators ever mentioned the "surrender clauses" in the written treaty texts during the negotiations that led to Treaty 4,[53] or in the negotiations of any of the other numbered treaties. Those acts of lying by omission call the validity of the treaties into question for Krasowski, and if the treaties are not valid, then settlers have no right to be here. Nor have governments over the past 146 years lived up to the commitments made in the written text of Treaty 4 (or any of the other numbered treaties),[54] never mind the oral understandings of the agreement kept by Treaty Elders. Given this history, if all we have to rely on to justify the presence of settlers in Western Canada are the written treaty texts, then it's true, as Simpson argues, that treaties are simply a vehicle for settler colonialism, and that their intention was simply to clear the land of Indigenous bodies prior to settlement.[55] nêhiyaw lawyer Harold Cardinal is just as blunt. Even though he describes the treaties as "an Indian Magna Carta,"[56] he concludes that everything that's happened since the treaties were negotiated shows that First Nations' settler treaty partners were "slick-talking, fork-tongued cheats."[57] This view of the treaties concludes that they are worthless, and that settlers therefore have no ethical basis for their presence here.

Another view of the treaties comes from Treaty Elders, who tell a story that is very different from the government's version. As Julie Jai suggests, Treaty Elders hold that the treaties were sacred agreements, made according to First Nations protocols and ceremonies, that were meant to establish mutual and ongoing arrangements of sharing and caring between First Nations people and settlers, including a sharing of the land.[58] The principles of the treaties, according to Treaty Elders, included mutual respect between peoples; a relationship of peace; an understanding that the treaty was a sacred covenant with the other government and the Creator in which all parties recognize divine sovereignty; a recognition of First Nations' rights to maintain their relationship with the Creator, including the laws given by the Creator, which include the right to self-government, the right to use the lands and resources, harvesting rights, and the right to maintain their way of life; an ongoing familial relationship, since according to Indigenous traditions, entering into a treaty means entering into a relationship with your treaty partner and bringing them into kinship; a mutual sharing of resources; a continued right to livelihood and way of life; and a sharing—not surrender—of land.[59] Those principles are the reason the Chiefs agreed to the historical treaties, and that Treaty Elders remain proud of them today.[60]

The idea of a familial relationship between treaty partners is essential to understanding Indigenous views of the treaties. Johnson argues that the treaties were ceremonies in which First Nations adopted settlers as family. Johnson uses the word *kiciwâminawak*, "our cousins," to refer to settlers, and assures us that, because the treaties were negotiated according to Indigenous ceremony and protocol, they remain valid, despite the Crown's chicanery at the time and ever since, and that settlers therefore "have a treaty right" to share the land.[61] Borrows agrees; he argues that "[t]he laws surrounding Canada's formation in many treaty territories are profound because they are meant to encourage the spiritual, moral and legal capacities of all the people who would come to live here." Because the treaties are sacred in nature, "many First Nations would not consider abandoning them despite generations of government neglect. It would be a violation of the Creator's law, sacred law, to turn away from their promises to him and others in maintaining peace and order throughout the lands on which they lived."[62] If Borrows, Jai, Johnson, and the Treaty Elders interviewed by Cardinal and Walter Hildebrandt are correct, the treaties could provide an ethical justification for the presence of settlers on this land, as they were intended, although we would have to do a much better job of honouring our treaty obligations and relationships. Today, for instance, First Nations reserves constitute only 1 percent of the land in Saskatchewan, despite the millions of dollars in Treaty Land Entitlement money that have been spent by First Nations on buying land back from settlers, a situation that can hardly be described as a fair and equitable sharing of the land. That must change. A more equitable sharing of land might be what "repatriation of Indigenous land and life" means—what decolonization might mean.

Decolonization might also mean that settlers would have to reconsider the importance of the historical numbered treaties. Anishinaabe scholar Aaron Mills/Waabishki Ma'iingan argues that treaties are, or ought to be considered, first-order constitutional matters.[63] However, because they are seen as second-order matters of distributive justice, Canada is founded on domination over Indigenous Peoples and Indigenous lands,[64] since Canada continues to claim "radical title to all of Turtle Island, knowing full well that Indigenous peoples were already living on it as persons, peoples, and confederacies of distinct constitutional orders before settlers arrived"—a claim supported by the Supreme Court of Canada in the *Tsilhqot'in Nation v British Columbia* case.[65] Canadian courts are simply incapable of building a doctrine around treaties that would reflect a translation of Indigenous understandings, Mills continues, and instead the Supreme Court of Canada "consistently chooses to account for the unique political status of Indigenous peoples *within* the contract-confederation story," rather than "situating treaties as the very things which empower settler legitimacy," something which is assumed without justification.[66] "From an Anishinaabe constitutional standpoint," he writes, "this is outrageous," because treaties are the way "we constitute ourselves as communities of communities, across our difference."[67] For Mills, the change that needs to happen in the relationship between settlers and Indigenous Peoples must be structural: "We have to transform that very structure to allow Indigenous legal traditions to stand within their own constitutional worlds, not contain and re-express them post-fact within the existing terms of the settler contract."[68] Mills sees the eighteenth-century Treaty of Niagara as a model of the intercultural achievement of a commitment to a relationship based on practices of mutual aid, represented in the Covenant Chain wampum belt.[69] The Treaty of Niagara, he continues, articulates a vision of a shared political community, of a living relationship between settlers and Indigenous Peoples that creates a foundation for settler citizenship.[70] That vision is what Canada needs to return to, and Canada's construction on the basis of domination needs to be abandoned. In this argument, Mills is applying Borrows's contention that Canadian law needs to recognize and develop Indigenous legal traditions to Canadian constitutional law.[71]

If Canada, and Canadians, were to do this work of recognizing and developing Indigenous legal traditions and resituating the treaties as first-order statements of the relationship between settlers and Indigenous Peoples, then perhaps the work of decolonization in this country would be able to begin. In other words, if we believe the story about the historical numbered treaties that is told by Treaty Elders, Jai, Borrows, Johnson, and Mills, it's possible that an acknowledgement of the Indigenous perspectives on the treaties and commitments to share the land fairly and to honour and develop our treaty relationship might constitute the beginnings of a form of decolonization. At the moment, though, there is little recognition among settlers of the need to rethink the treaties as partnerships and agreements based upon relationships and an equitable sharing of the land. How can the range of acceptable political ideas in Canada be shifted to include the possibility of decolonization—even a version of decolonization which is far from the call to return *all* the land to Indigenous Peoples?

I don't have an answer to that question. And, according to nêhiyaw/Anihšināpē political scientist Gina Starblanket and nêhiyaw writer Dallas Hunt, a renewed understanding of the treaties isn't necessarily a solution to the problems caused by colonization. Starblanket and Hunt "are not implying that people in the prairies can simply turn to treaty to remedy the myriad issues surrounding the Indigenous-settler relationship"—in fact, they contend that "there is no *easy* or *straightforward* solution to issues that are now several centuries in the making and have become well-sedimented in these spaces."[72] In order to implement the treaties as they were intended by Indigenous Peoples, "the current settler colonial structure" would have to be dismantled.[73] That's a tall order. Where would that process begin? Can nothing be done without such radical change? Or would recognizing the treaties as first-order constitutional matters be the beginning of the end of settler colonialism?

Starblanket and Hunt suggest that the treaties "provide important sources of inspiration for alternate ways of interpreting, understanding, and responding to the many inter-societal and political tensions that remain alive in the prairies."[74] The most important aspect of the treaties, they argue, is the way they provide a framework for relationship and dialogue:

> Treaties, at a basic level, are mechanisms for talking to strangers and bringing them into relationship with us. It is no small feat to be able to dialogue and negotiate forms of relationship across linguistic, cultural, political, juridical, economic and spiritual differences. It's even harder to do this when the other party poses (or is perceived to pose) a threat to the other. In negotiating treaty relations, Indigenous leaders already saw the damage that was being caused by newcomer presence; they saw the impact on their traditional way of life and to their animal and human kin, who were succumbing to illness and death. Nevertheless, they sought to enter into negotiations in good faith in the interest of cultivating a better relationship for future generations to inhabit. These negotiations required humility, trust, risk and sacrifice. They required parties, to employ the words of Treaty 6 Elder Peter Waskahat, to undertake a willingness to "meet each other halfway." No part of this is easy. And neither is the process of activating treaty in our relationships today.[75]

"Treaty is work; it takes labour to be in relation with other people, and to hold them accountable to a community or communities," Starblanket and Hunt continue. And we cannot predict where those relationships enabled by treaty will take us: "treaty, in all its messiness and complexity, allows for a relationship that is not pre-determined or fixed."[76] Instead, that relationship "is active, something that must be restored and worked on at different times and in different spaces."[77]

This description suggests that treaties are by nature meant to be renegotiated and renewed as time passes and events cause ruptures in the relationships they establish. Mending those broken relationships is complicated and difficult, just as keeping relationships whole can be hard work.[78] Starblanket and Hunt argue that

> [i]f the modes of relationship that we currently have at our disposal are ill-equipped to allow us to affirm these entangled relations, then perhaps we need to reimagine them, which in turn requires us to contend with the possibility that this might not be possible in the world as it is currently constructed.[79]

Reimagining treaty relationships would mean dismantling settler colonialism, a task that would involve tackling a settler-colonial version of what Robin DiAngelo calls "white fragility." White people are socialized to believe they are superior to others, something we don't realize or can't admit to ourselves, and as a result, we tend to become upset by conversations about race and consider discussions of racism to be challenges to our image of ourselves as good, moral people, DiAngelo explains. For that reason, we resist attempts at connecting us as individuals to larger systems of racism. Even the suggestion that being white means something generates defensive reactions like anger, fear, and guilt, all of which lead to arguing, silence, and withdrawal.[80] Because those responses refuse the challenge of thinking about systemic racism, they end up short-circuiting any possibility of change. For that reason, white fragility, DiAngelo argues, is not a form of weakness; it's a way to protect the advantages that come along with having white skin in North America.[81]

In white fragility's settler-colonial manifestation, settler Canadians refuse to think about the way we have benefited from the displacement and dispossession of Indigenous Peoples. Lee Maracle describes that refusal when she notes that Canadians never ask how authority over the land shifted from Indigenous Peoples to us.[82] I understand that reaction. We all want to see ourselves as good people, as deserving people who have earned what they have. When we're asked to think about the ways we're enmeshed in a brutally unfair, genocidal system, when we're asked to consider the fact that we don't deserve the benefits we have received, we might feel afraid and ashamed—and anger and defensiveness are easier to handle than shame and fear. Becoming unsettled, as writers on settler colonialism demand, is hard. There's no way around that. "Settler people wanting to confront the colonialism pervasive in our lives and societies must accept that this process will be uncomfortable and unsettling," Lowman and Barker contend. But staying with that discomfort, "going further into situations and conversations that are unsettling," can help us "identify points of contention in our lives where settler colonialism exerts pressure on us through our particular, personal vulnerabilities." If you're a settler, and you feel uncomfortable, they continue, "you are probably in the right place."[83] Nobody wants to feel uncomfortable, I know that, but then again, that kind of discomfort is a lot easier to take than ongoing experiences of colonial oppression and racism. Those experiences must be intensely uncomfortable. More than uncomfortable—harrowing, heart-wrenching, deeply painful. Settlers need to remember that.

Is the uncertainty that is part of treaty relationships and decolonization, that is part of becoming unsettled, related to the uncertainty Solnit sees in hope, in the possibility that things can be different? I stop walking, look at the highway, the fields around it, the sky. Could hope as uncertainty be a way to reframe settler discomfort with decolonization? Unlike optimism or pessimism, which are settled and definite, which are certain about the future, Solnit argues that hope embraces what we don't know, even what is unknowable. Doing something, even if we don't know if it will work, even if we never learn what its effects might be—that's what hope looks like, Solnit tells us. Maybe being unsettled isn't all that different.[84] Surprised by what feels like insight, I start walking again.

Doing something is what hope requires, though—that's essential. Starblanket and Hunt decry "superficial engagements with treaty that too easily declare that 'we are all treaty people.'"[85] Instead, they argue that we need "to recognize the messy, interpersonal work we need to do in order to live together in a good way on these lands." Living together would mean rethinking how Indigenous people and settlers relate to each other. For instance, they ask, what would happen if we placed "a higher importance on the type of hard work involved in talking to strangers and providing them with assistance, even if you perceive them to represent a threat?"[86] I hear the echoes of the killing of Colten Boushie behind those words. Thinking of treaty as a way of assisting and relating to strangers would lead to profound changes. For instance, "if the provision of justice in Saskatchewan was carried out in accordance with a treaty frame, Indigenous people would have a more significant role in the structure and implementation of justice systems," since each of the numbered treaties "contains an iteration of a commitment from Indigenous peoples to maintain 'peace and order' between themselves and between Indigenous and settler people," a clause which affirms the jurisdiction of treaty Chiefs while limiting the Crown's authority.[87] "Indigenous jurisdiction in areas of law and governance represent[s] a vital, even if largely unrecognized dimension of treaty implementation," Starblanket and Hunt state. Recognizing Indigenous legal jurisdiction over law and governance would even make Canadian law more just. Indigenous legal traditions "could inform a far broader conception of justice than the measures of justice available under Canadian law," because "they are fundamentally relational" and account for the harms committed against a person's many relations as well as the victim of the offence.[88] Limiting the authority of the Crown, and fundamentally rethinking Canadian law, would move us all towards dismantling settler colonialism, and therefore towards decolonization.

The call Starblanket and Hunt make for dismantling the structures of settler colonialism feels overwhelming. After all, individual settlers can't overcome those structures, in which we are all entangled, by ourselves; that kind of political action, which would require completely reworking our social and political and legal structures, would have to be collective, and it would no doubt meet with intense resistance from settlers and our governments. And a self-reflexive investigation by settlers of their complicity in colonialism might be, as the French-Tunisian writer Albert Memmi tells us, next to impossible. Memmi argues that the colonizer who wants to refuse to be a colonizer is bound to fail: "everything confirms his solitude, bewilderment and ineffectiveness. He will slowly realize that the only thing to do is to remain silent."[89]

I think about Memmi's pessimism and Solnit's words about the open-endedness and uncertain possibilities of hope. Maybe dismantling settler colonialism is possible, despite the difficulty Memmi identifies. It would have to be done in solidarity with Indigenous Peoples—that much is certain.[90] In *Decolonizing Solidarity: Dilemmas and Directions for Supporters of Indigenous Struggles*, Clare Land discusses the complexity involved in settlers working together with Indigenous Peoples in struggles against settler colonialism. Her focus is on southeastern Australia, but those complexities exist elsewhere, too, including in Western Canada. In her introduction, Land notes that white people who begin that work often meet with obstacles and problems which lead them to either "look in the mirror, adopt a questioning attitude and reaffirm their determination to stay involved" or else "walk away thinking 'It's too hard'" or that "Aboriginal people are ungrateful or unreliable."[91] Land's intention is to provide "an urgently needed new framework for action by non-Indigenous people in support of Indigenous struggles,"[92] one that focuses on the complexity of relationships between settlers and Indigenous Peoples.

Apologies and processes of reconciliation will not, Land argues, lead to decolonization. What is required instead is both a commitment by settlers to engage in political work with Indigenous Peoples, along with a self-reflexive attention, by settlers, to behaviour that reproduces white privilege,[93] although Land also wonders if it's possible to be a white critic of whiteness, since that requires the difficult understanding that one is part of the problem one is trying to articulate.[94] Settlers need to examine our complicity in colonialism, thinking about our identities, cultures, and histories, as well as how we have benefited from the way things are.[95] That critical self-reflection, she continues, "is a non-Indigenous effort in parallel with the Indigenous project of *indigenizing*."[96] Settlers also need to internalize "an Indigenous view of whiteness, a recognition of the historical and political specificities of the moment in which it is salient...and the struggle to overcome the self-hate that can flow from that."[97] I hear DiAngelo's argument echoing in Land's words.

In collaborative political struggles, non-Indigenous supporters need to think about issues like initiation, participation, and control, which means, in part, that projects or collaborations need to be initiated by Indigenous people.[98] "The principle of Aboriginal people initiating and being in control of their own struggle is politically, concretely important," Land states; it is a way for them to solve their own problems, to add to pride and self-confidence in a context of denigration and oppression.[99] In addition, since conditions are not always right for dialogue, coalition, or collaboration, working separately might be more appropriate than those things.[100] So walking alone on the land might be politically useful after all. Because the ongoing history of colonialism will inevitably affect attempts at dialogue or collaboration, making trust, co-operation, and equality difficult, settlers "must strive to be trustworthy" without expecting to be trusted in return; in that way, we can acknowledge "our colonizing past and present, as well as the riskiness of trust across colonizing power differences."[101]

Some non-Indigenous activists, because they don't trust themselves to identify their own racism, may end up withdrawing from work with Indigenous communities.[102] That might be an example of "the ultimate privilege," in which "members of dominant groups" don't engage in social justice work because they're afraid of making mistakes, although it can also reflect anxiety about hurting people.[103] Land insists that the focus in social justice struggles ought to be on the work itself, rather than potential ancillary benefits, such as friendship.[104] For that reason, non-Indigenous people need to be honest about their motives: do they find pleasure in the work itself, or are they hoping for friendship, redemption, or some other "assumed dividend"?[105] Are our motives merely extractive, in other words?

Land presents a list of questions that can help settlers understand Indigenous struggles, including "What happened to Aboriginal people where you now live?" and "Why are you interested in being supportive of Aboriginal people?"[106] These questions can lead to the critical self-reflection non-Indigenous people need to engage in if they are serious about being involved in the struggle for justice for Indigenous people.[107] However, Tuck and Yang argue that a focus on "decolonizing the mind" is merely a first step, not the only or final one, and that focusing on cultivating a critical consciousness can end up being a "move to innocence" that stands in "for the more uncomfortable task of relinquishing stolen land."[108] Indeed, they argue that "the front-loading of critical consciousness building can waylay decolonization, even though the experience of teaching and learning to be critical of settler colonialism can be so powerful that it can feel like it is indeed making change."[109] Tuck and Yang would likely condemn my walk around the Regina Bypass, and the book you're reading, as mere conscientization; while they might help begin to decolonize my mind, and possibly the minds of readers, my efforts won't do anything to return land to Indigenous Peoples.

The "Land Back" movement, which calls for the transfer of land back to Indigenous Peoples, constitutes a different way of thinking about decolonization. Since 90 percent of Canada is Crown land, ceding that territory to Indigenous Peoples would go a long way towards returning land to Indigenous Peoples.[110] "Despite fear-mongering that often accompanies discussions of Indigenous land rights, First Nations leaders aren't interested in displacing settlers—they simply want to make decisions about what happens to their lands," writes Justin Brake in his discussion of "Land Back."[111] Indeed, as Anishinaabe sociologist Hayden King and geographer Shiri Pasternak argue, "Land Back" is about ceding legal jurisdiction over the land to First Nations, Inuit, and Métis Peoples.[112] Saskatchewan could return provincial Crown land to First Nations and Métis political entities, for instance; that seems like a straightforward way to start undoing the ongoing historical wrongs committed against Indigenous Peoples here. Instead, the Saskatchewan Party government is auctioning off Crown land to the highest bidder as fast as it can, something it's been doing for years.[113] In response, Carry the Kettle Nakoda Nation is taking the provincial Ministry of Agriculture to court, arguing that it has failed to consult with First Nations over selling Crown land in southern Saskatchewan, thereby violating the terms of Treaty 4.[114] Decolonization would require the court to find in Carry the Kettle's favour. Whether it will rule that way, though, is anybody's guess. Meanwhile, the sale of provincial Crown land in Saskatchewan continues. Our government needs the money: we have to pay for this highway somehow.

My walking obviously isn't going to return land to anybody, and to be honest, I'm not suited, temperamentally or by experience, to collaborative political work. If I were, I might not be the kind of person who's comfortable going on long walks by myself. A walk like this one might be a form of political engagement if it were an embodied territorial acknowledgement, a form of walking with the land rather than just talking about it, a way of putting some flesh on the bones of verbal land acknowledgements, which are often maligned as incorrect, rote, and thoughtless.[115] Maybe this kind of walking could be a way of having a nonextractive encounter with the land or building a relationship with it. Perhaps the self-reflection such walking might occasion could play a role in processes of decolonization. After all, decolonization needs to begin somewhere. Or maybe I'm kidding myself: maybe I ought to quit walking and start marching, together with others, or get over my dislike of meetings and organizational politics and work towards more tangible forms of justice. Maybe this solo walking practice, this desire to find a relationship with the land, is a dead end.

Not to mention self-indulgent—a way to write a book on a trendy topic and not much more. That's what some people would argue: these walks and this book have nothing to do with decolonization. They might be the expression of a need, a hunger, to connect with the land, yes, but little more than that. Perhaps, by walking on the land, even on the side of a highway, I'm just another colonizer inspecting the property. Perhaps the treaty which I imagine might give me an ethical basis on which to live here is an instrument of settler colonialism, and the ongoing legacies of colonialism make it impossible to make tangible the relationships represented (at least potentially) by the treaties. All these doubts nag at me; they are shadows trailing behind me as I walk.

I think about the words of Michael Asch, who contends that the treaties are the only thing that could possibly give settlers like me an ethical way to be on this land—one beyond the racism of the doctrines of discovery and occupation or *terra nullius*. "Treaties offer us the means to reconcile the fact that we are 'here to stay' with the fact that there were people already here when we first arrived," he states.[116] What settlers need to do, he continues, is renew our commitment to the principles he finds in the treaty-making process, even if the federal government's behaviour during those negotiations, and afterwards, ignores every single one of those principles: gaining consent from those who were here first, keeping our commitments to them, and rectifying the harm our actions have caused.[117] Perhaps, in a context where treaties exist, and where they are recognized as foundational, that is what decolonization could look like. That alternative is a situation where the only justification for the presence of settlers here, including me, is the racism of *terra nullius* and the doctrines of discovery and occupation, along with the belief that might makes right.

I open my pack, find my food bag, and eat two tasteless cereal bars. I drink some electrolyte mix. I'm shivering in the cold wind. A ladybug tries to catch a ride in my pack, and I gently shoo it away before I pull the drawstring that closes the pack and fasten its lid in place. Then I stand up, haul my pack onto my shoulders, and start walking north again.

EIGHT

TREATY, KINSHIP, CEREMONY

AUGUST 30, 2020

As I plod north in the wind, I seem to be making no headway. It's as if I'm walking on a treadmill: my body is moving but I'm going nowhere. I've had this experience before, walking in rural Saskatchewan and seeing some landmark in the distance—a grain elevator or an inland terminal, usually, since they're the tallest things on the horizon—which never seems to come any closer as I make my way towards it. Then, always suddenly, I arrive. One minute I seem to be immobile; the next I realize that immobility was an illusion, that I was getting somewhere, slowly, all the time. As I've said, I've never been a patient person, but walking is trying to teach me that virtue, slowly. Sometimes I wish it would hurry up.

A cyclist approaches and I step off the shoulder to let him by. He seems to be wearing a GoPro camera on his helmet. The videos he makes must be like the notes I'm taking. The difference is in the duration: I wouldn't be able to relive this walk in real time, nor would I want to, but those videos would have to be watched that way, wouldn't they? Unless he's planning to watch them sped up, a time-lapse experience of his ride around the city. I remember doing that once. I drove across Ontario with a Super 8 camera shooting one frame of film through the windshield every sixty seconds. That entire journey ended up condensed into three minutes. If that's the cyclist's plan, then my appearance will be brief, almost unnoticeable, like the trace of my footsteps on the land. Given its immense age, given all the changes it's seen since the glaciers melted, the land might not even notice I was here. In that case, how could I form a relationship with it? A friend who is Algonquin assures me, though, that the land remembers those who walk upon it. Maybe I ought to have more faith in its powers of attention and observation.

The land's more short-lived creatures are definitely aware of me. A flea beetle lands on my glasses. Grasshoppers are active now, perhaps because the sun is warm despite the cold wind, and one of them, taking flight in the gale, hits me in the mouth. There are so many fuzzy caterpillars now that I stop noting them in my book. The instruments of settler colonialism are in motion, too. On the northern horizon, a train of hopper cars is moving east. Sheep are feeding in a pasture on the other side of a grid road that runs parallel to the Bypass. Alpacas or llamas—I'm not sure which—dot the green grass of an adjacent pasture. On the eastern horizon, a gas flare rises from the oil refinery. There are layers of settler occupation here, old roads and new ones, farms and pastures, industrial sites. It's all visible on the surface of the land, recent scars compared to the signs of prior Indigenous occupation, which have been mostly erased by the plows that tore up the grassland and then the heavy equipment that built this highway.

A sign confirms another suspicion: this new road *is* called Highway 11. I wonder what the old Highway 11, or at least the part that runs from the interchange with the Bypass to the city, is called now. Perhaps it has no name, or there are two Highway 11s now. That would be confusing to first responders, wouldn't it? A gopher squeaks; I can hardly hear it over the wind. I step over the dry shell of a dead bird; it's been lying here for quite a while. As the highway bends northwest, I'm walking right into the gale. Another cyclist is heading south. We exchange waves. The overpass at Centre Road is a wind tunnel. Beyond it, a huge field of wheat spreads to the west. I can see Dewdney Avenue on the horizon. I climb up a gentle slope onto the overpass that carries the Bypass over the Canadian Pacific Railway tracks. My blister hurts; I'm limping. A hawk courses over the highway, and a mask lies next to the shoulder.

The highway begins to curve back towards the north. The wind gusts shove me towards passing traffic. I'm holding onto my hat, and my camera is swinging on its strap. The wind wouldn't bother passing motorists, though. They wouldn't feel it, comfortable inside their vehicles, insulated from the weather. Yes, they're inconvenienced by rain or snow, but not like pedestrians, who are open to the elements. If it were raining, I'd be wet, while people inside their vehicles would be dry. That's part of Tim Ingold's take on walking: when we walk, we experience "the contours of the landscape" with our bodies, through the "muscular entailments" that climbing and descending require, and as a result, kinaesthetically, walking is "directly incorporated into our bodily experience."[1] That kinesthetic experience might be impossible to separate from our experiences of place. As Yi-Fu Tuan suggests, "[t]he feel of a place is registered in one's muscles and bones."[2] Our experience of place, the land through which we walk, is a sensory one: along with the heat of the sun or the chill of the rain or wind, we are more likely to hear birdsong or smell flowers or petrichor than are travellers sealed inside vehicles. This level of sensory engagement is a characteristic of walking; it might be what makes walking so different from other modes of transportation, what makes it unique. Our cars are like shells we wear, providing us with a sense of safety—one that might be illusory, but that feels real.

I step over what looks like a dead mole on the bridge—how it got up here is a mystery. I look down at the train tracks. The wind is even stronger on top of the overpass. When I first started going on long walks, I didn't carry a phone, and I would have dizzying feelings of freedom and anxiety, finding myself miles from shelter without the apparent safety of a vehicle. Perhaps, for most of human history, that's how people felt when they were alone and far from home. Maybe they were used to it. Or maybe they felt at home wherever they were.

I tire of holding on to my hat and stow it in my backpack. I put sunscreen on my face and the top of my head, hoping it will keep my scalp from burning—a hazard of walking while balding. I'm growing tired and stop to rest again. I look at the sky, the Global Transportation Hub, the train tracks. Crickets run past me. There are so many of them singing now, so loudly, over the sound of the wind, their music like tinnitus. Foxtail barley, alfalfa, sweet clover, quack grass, smartweed, and sow thistle are everywhere. I wonder what VINCI plants on these embankments, and at how quickly the weeds take over. The huge empty fields at the Global Transportation Hub might be the source of all these weeds. Mowing all those square kilometres of empty space must be a huge job. The wind is howling now. I'm not convinced the sunscreen will protect me—after my youngest sister died of melanoma, I started being more careful about the sun—and I pull my merino wool Buff up over my head, like a hood. I close my eyes. I could almost fall asleep, but I still have eight or ten kilometres left to walk today, and I have no idea how I'm going to do it. Reluctantly, I get to my feet, slowly, grab my pack, and set off.

///

The question of land was very much on the minds of everyone at the Treaty 4 negotiations. The Crown negotiators were seeking the extinguishment of Indigenous title over a large territory, but the nêhiyaw and Anihšināpē Chiefs were angry about the sale of Rupert's Land to the Dominion of Canada by the Hudson's Bay Company six years before. The HBC had been granted an exclusive charter to trade in Rupert's Land, all the territory that drains into Hudson Bay, by King Charles II in 1670. Indigenous Peoples were not consulted when that sale took place.[3] Meeting at an HBC post made the Chiefs even angrier, which didn't encourage them to agree to begin the negotiations.[4] The negotiations were also delayed because not all the Chiefs had arrived. When talks finally began on the third day, Alexander Morris explained what the Queen planned to do for them—the same offer as had been made to the Anishinaabe at the Lake of the Woods the previous year: an annuity of five dollars "as long as the sun shines and water flows," a promise to buy powder and shot and twine for fishing nets, reserves for farming (a square mile of land for every family of five), agricultural equipment, school and schoolmasters, and other items.[5] Morris made it clear that these terms were not negotiable, since they were the same as those accepted the previous year during the Treaty 3 negotiations. He told the Chiefs,

> [R]ecollect this, the Queen's High Councillor here from Ottawa, and I, her Governor, are not traders; we do not come here in the spirit of traders; we come here to tell you openly, without hiding anything, just what the Queen will do for you, just what she thinks is good for you, and I want you to look me in the face, eye to eye, and open your hearts to me as children would to a father, as children ought to do to a father, and as you ought to the servants of the great mother of us all.[6]

In this speech, we see not only Morris's refusal to dicker, but also his professions to openness and fair dealing. We see his use of kinship metaphors, too, although the suggestion that their relationship is one of father to son might've been inappropriate, even offensive. Elsewhere Morris speaks in terms of brotherhood,[7] and tells the assembled Chiefs that "we have done all that men who love their red brothers can do."[8] Brotherhood is a more appropriate metaphor than fatherhood, since the latter connotes superiority, and it fits better with the metaphor of the Queen as "the great mother of us all," but Morris uses both. That's no surprise: Morris's impulse is connected to the twin imperatives of Christianizing and colonizing Indigenous Peoples. To Christianize them, settlers had to recognize that they shared a common humanity with the people they were proselytizing, otherwise God wouldn't be interested in their souls; but to colonize them, settlers had to claim that Indigenous Peoples were inferior, that they were children who required guidance and management from the more civilized settlers. The nineteenth-century belief in social Darwinism required that Indigenous Peoples be seen as less developed than settlers, who were alleged to be further along on the ladder of civilization. The brotherhood analogy enables the first idea; the parent-child analogy the second.

The Chiefs were blunt about the reasons they were angry. The Gambler, an Anihšināpē Chief, told Morris,

> The Company have stolen our land. I heard that at first. I hear it is true. The Queen's messengers never came here, and now I see the soldiers and the settlers and the policemen. I know it is not the Queen's work, only the Company has come and they are the head, they are foremost; I do not hold it back. Let this be put to rights; when this is righted I will answer the other.[9]

When Morris asked The Gambler what the Company had stolen, he replied, "The earth, trees, grass, stones, all that I see with my eyes."[10] Not only had the Hudson's Bay Company sold the land, which the Chiefs felt it had no right to do, but it had also been surveying lots for settlers around the fort where the negotiations were taking place. "The Company have no right to this earth," The Gambler continued, "but when they are spoken to they do not desist, but do it in spite of you."[11] Chief Pasqua ("Pis-qua" in Morris's text) pointed at the HBC factor and stated, bluntly, "You told me you had sold your land for so much money, £300,000. We want that money."[12] Morris's response to The Gambler, according to the official record, was that the Great Spirit made the land "for all his children to use, and it is not stealing to use the gifts of the Great Spirit."[13] Journalist F.L. Hunt, who was covering the negotiations for *The Manitoban* and was married to a Nakoda woman, recorded the response of Pahtahkaywenin, one of the Chief's speakers: "True, even I, a child, know that God gives us land in different places and when we meet together as friends, we ask from each other and do not quarrel as we do so."[14] For Sheldon Krasowski, that response "represented the essence of the treaty relationship: the Cree and Saulteaux had their lands, and the Europeans had their lands, and the negotiations should be based on sharing and mutual respect."[15] Hunt seems to have understood this: he described Pahtahkaywenin's response as "a grand act simply and perfectly well done."[16]

Morris tried to mollify the Chiefs' anger, telling them that the Company had only sold its trading monopoly—not the land. The Queen, he stated, "took all the lands into her own hands and gave the Company a sum of money in place of the rights which she had taken from them. She is ready to deal with you justly."[17] However, the following day, the discussion returned to the Hudson's Bay Company. The frustration on both sides of the negotiations is palpable in the shorthand transcription published in Morris's book. There was little mutual understanding. Finally, on the morning of the sixth day, the nêhiyaw Chief Loud Voice told Morris and the other commissioners, "Let us join together and make the Treaty; when both join together it is very good."[18] Those words, however, seem to be more about forming a relationship—about joining together—than they are a response to any of the specifics in Morris's offer to the Chiefs.

As I walk, I try to imagine what those negotiations were like: the warm late-summer days, the cold nights, the way that the Crown negotiators sat on chairs while the Chiefs sat on blankets spread out on the ground. The symbolism of those chairs is not encouraging: the Crown negotiators were putting themselves above the Chiefs and separating themselves from the land they were talking about. The chairs were a power play, an assertion that the Crown negotiators were better than their counterparts. And yet, there would have been a practical reason for them: the môniyâwak negotiators would have found it difficult to sit on the ground, unlike the Chiefs, whose muscles were used to sitting down and standing up again, gracefully. I think about the clumsy way I drop to the ground beside this highway when I stop to take a break, my body's awkwardness when I scramble to my feet. The Chiefs must have laughed to themselves at these môniyâwak whose bodies were too enfeebled by chairs to share a blanket with them. They must have pitied these men who were unable to sit upon the earth.

As Krasowski points out, despite the importance of extinguishing Indigenous title to the Crown negotiators, and despite the attachment of the Chiefs to their land, as shown by their anger at the thought that the Hudson's Bay Company had sold it behind their backs, there is little evidence that the meaning of extinguishment or surrender or cession of title was explained to the nêhiyaw and Anihšināpē Chiefs gathered at Fort Qu'Appelle in 1874. Arthur J. Ray, Jim Miller, and Frank Tough note that Morris's language on this point is vague, compared to the detailed and precise wording of the treaty document.[19] For instance, in his account of the negotiations, Morris tried to compare the arrival of settlers to the recent arrival of the Anihšināpēk (or, in Morris's account, "Ojibbeways") in what had been nêhiyaw territory:

> We have two nations here. We have the Crees, who were here first, and we have the Ojibbeways, who came from our country not many suns ago. We find them here; we won't say they stole the land and the stones and the trees; no, but we will say this, that we believe their brothers, the Crees, said to them when they came in here: "The land is wide, it is wide, it is big enough for us both; let us live here like brothers;" and that is what you say, as you told us on Saturday, as to the Half-breeds that I see

> around. You say that you are one with them; now we want all to be one.[20]

These words can be understood as a statement about forming a relationship, rather than surrendering land, but the analogy Morris is drawing is imperfect at best. As Ray, Miller, and Tough point out,[21] the Treaty 4 document is much more specific about how settlers will live together with the nêhiyawak and Anihšināpēk (and Métis) "like brothers"; that togetherness would be accomplished by extinguishing Indigenous title to the land. There is a vast difference between pretending that the arrival of settlers will be like the arrival of the Anihšināpēk, suggesting that the land will be shared between settlers and Indigenous Peoples the way it was shared between the nêhiyawak and Anihšināpēk (among others), and the words *cede*, *release*, *surrender*, and *yield up*. Could the negotiating parties have understood each other, given their different cultural and legal frameworks? It seems unlikely.

Another example of that lack of mutual understanding lies in the claim that the nêhiyaw and Anihšināpē Chiefs surrendered their land by entering into Treaty 4. The Treaty Elders interviewed by Harold Cardinal and Walter Hildebrandt, for instance, rejected the notion of extinguishment of title wholeheartedly: "The Elders maintained that such extinguishment was never agreed to by First Nations during treaty negotiations." In their discussions with Treaty Elders, when the "extinguishment clauses" of the written treaty texts were read, translated, and explained, those Elders reacted with "incredulity and disbelief." "They found it hard to believe that anyone, much less the Crown, could seriously believe that First Nations would ever have agreed to 'extinguish' their God-given rights," Cardinal and Hildebrandt report.[22] Moreover, according to Sylvia McAdam (Saysewahum), the male Chiefs could not have made such a decision without consulting first with their nations' women, particularly the *okihcitâwiskwêwak*, a word that means "clan mothers" or "warrior women." "During and prior to treaty making, it would have been the okihcitâwiskwêwak who would have been consulted regarding the land, because authority and jurisdiction to speak about land resides with the women," she writes.[23] Besides, as Harold Johnson tells us, "I do not say that I own this land; rather, the land owns me."[24] If you do not own the land, if rather you are in a relationship with it, as the nêhiyawak believed, then how could you extinguish or surrender your title?

"The most controversial difference between the Treaty 4 oral and written accounts is the surrender clause," Krasowski writes.[25] The oral histories say there was no surrender, only an agreement to share the land to the depth of a plow—about six inches.[26] Mineral rights thus remained with First Nations. That part of the agreement was violated when the federal government transferred the right to control the development of natural resources to the prairie provinces in 1930.[27] The written sources, on the other hand, "show that Morris and the treaty commissioners utilized two main strategies when dealing with the cession of land."[28] The first was to discuss only the benefits of the treaty and ignore the drawbacks. There is no evidence, for example, that the surrender clause was mentioned, or that the written text of the treaty indicated that hunting and fishing rights could be regulated by the government.[29] The second strategy had to do with the reading of the written treaty text at the end of the negotiations. At the end of Treaty Four, Morris asked interpreter Charles Pratt to interpret the written text of the treaty into nêhiyawêwin and Anihšināpēmowin. Pratt's surprised response, recorded by eyewitnesses, suggests that he was not prepared to do that. "Pratt was known as an exemplary interpreter," Krasowski writes, but the surrender clause, and much of the text of the written treaty, "would have been difficult to translate because of the legalistic language."[30] According to Treaty Elders, in fact, translating the surrender clause would've been impossible.[31] As an interpreter for missionaries, Pratt often "changed elements of the Christian teachings to soften their Eurocentric edges and avoid critiques of Indigenous traditions," Krasowski contends, and he might've done something similar with the treaty text, explaining the surrender clause in terms that were more appealing to his audience.[32] Besides, since Pratt wanted the treaty negotiations to be successful—he was concerned about what would happen if the bison disappeared from the prairies—he might've thought it politic to skip over that part of the text.[33] The negotiations were difficult, after all, and it's possible that the surrender clause would've scuttled them entirely. Of course, this argument is conjecture; nobody knows exactly what Pratt said, because his nêhiyawêwin and Anihšināpēmowin translations weren't recorded by eyewitnesses. Nevertheless, given the surprised response of Treaty Elders to the surrender clause, Krasowski's interpretation rings true.

Even if Krasowski is wrong, and the extinguishment clause was explained to the First Nations negotiators, that clause would not have meant, as the *Indian Act* and other federal laws and policies suggest, that the First Nations represented at Fort Qu'Appelle in September 1874 became subordinate to the federal government through Treaty 4. Michael Asch's reading of the shorthand transcription and other documents leads him to conclude that nothing "supports an interpretation of the extinguishment clause as resulting in the political subordination of the Indigenous parties to the government of Canada." Instead, he contends, "it is more consistent with the evidence to conclude that the shared understanding of Treaty 4 resulted in a direct political allegiance with the queen."[34] Asch is supported in this conclusion by the words of Treaty Elders. For instance, Treaty 4 Elder Danny Musqua echoes Johnson's argument that the treaty was an adoption, although for Musqua it was an adoption of First Nations people by the Queen, instead of the other way around, as Johnson argues. Musqua tells us, "The Queen has adopted [First Nations] as children...a joint relationship will come out of that. And so we have a joint relationship with the Crown because the Queen is now our mother."[35] Regardless of who adopted whom—perhaps the adoption was mutual—other commentators from outside Treaty 4 agree that the result was the establishment of a kinship relation. Treaty 6 Elder Jimmy Myo states: "They said, we came here as your relatives. They said, the Queen sent us here, the Queen wants to adopt you Indians . . . as her own children."[36] According to Anishinaabe legal historian Aimée Craft, when the Treaty 1 negotiations became a kinship ceremony, the Anishinaabe "pledged to the Creator to share the land with the Queen's other children, in accordance with principles of kinship, equality, and reciprocity."[37] Nehetho Elder D'Arcy Linklater from Treaty 5 agrees. "We also should talk about the Treaty and how the Queen became our relation," he states. "Relationship is sacred. She said that she would like to take care of her children. If that were true we would be well off just like her children who live in big houses and are wealthy. . . . We adapted to change. We need to talk about this."[38] That call for a continuing conversation is characteristic of Indigenous perspectives on treaties as living agreements that are the basis for further discussion and negotiation, in contrast to the settler belief that treaties are finished and closed after an agreement has been reached and a paper signed.

According to oral histories, part of the delay in beginning the negotiations was the fact that the nêhiyawak and Anihšināpēk needed time to prepare themselves. Those preparations included Sacred Pipe Ceremonies, which protected the foundation of the treaty relationship: peace and harmony.[39] Unlike the other numbered treaties, though, there was no Sacred Pipe Ceremony between the Indigenous negotiators and the treaty commissioners during the Treaty 4 negotiations, and for that reason, some Elders believe that Treaty 4 is incomplete, since "the bond of the treaty was not formed until the ceremony took place."[40] The lack of ceremony in the Treaty 4 negotiations could complicate the claim that they resulted in an adoption. Ceremonies, especially the Sacred Pipe Ceremony, were vital parts of the other treaties.[41] As Johnson states regarding Treaty 6, "[i]t was in accordance with the law of adoption that my family took your ancestors as relatives. We solemnized the adoption with a sacred pipe." For Johnson, the promises made by his ancestors "are forever, because they were made under the Creator's law. This adoption ceremony is what we refer to when we talk about the treaty."[42] But the Sacred Pipe Ceremony was not just a part of this adoption. According to Cardinal and Hildebrandt, the use of the pipe and sweetgrass signified the oneness of the negotiating parties "in the undertaking that nations represented in the treaty would place their new relationship created by treaty in the hands of the Creator," and that this relationship "would be governed and conducted according to the principles symbolized by the sweetgrass and the pipe."[43] Those principles include *manâtisiwin* (respect), *yôspâtisiwin* (gentleness), *kisêwâtisiwin* (kindness), *kwayaskâtisiwin* (honesty and fairness), and *kanâtisiwin* (cleanliness), among others, and they were to guide the evolving relationship between the treaty parties—"an undertaking at the fundamental level that the relations between the parties would be non-coercive, non-adversarial, and non-antagonistic."[44] The Crown negotiators might not have recognized the significance of the Sacred Pipe Ceremony, although Morris did notice its absence and complained to The Gambler that when he arrived at the Treaty 3 negotiations the previous year, he was given "the pipe of peace" and "paid... every honour."[45] That statement seems more like wounded vanity than an acknowledgement that an adoption didn't happen. However, even if the treaty commissioners didn't understand what it meant, the Chiefs they were talking to did.

In fact, the Chiefs may have considered the 1874 negotiations to be merely preliminary—without a Sacred Pipe Ceremony, they could not have been finalized, according to nêhiyaw and Anihšināpē spiritual and legal traditions—and the following year they attempted to increase the annuities and gifts the treaty provided and get additional tools and training to make the transition to farming. "Most of these demands were reasonable and showed a willingness to farm," Krasowski writes, "but the Canadian government chose not to grant the requests even though many of the farming implements were included in Treaty Six two years later."[46] The Chiefs were given additional ammunition and twine for fishing nets only. When their demands were not met, many Chiefs abandoned their reserves and returned to the Cypress Hills to hunt; they were not going to take up farming unless forced to do so by the disappearance of the bison.[47]

The Chiefs who met with Morris, Laird, and Christie that September clearly saw the negotiations as creating a relationship: one of kinship, given the frequency with which both sides used kinship metaphors in the shorthand transcription, which suggests that the Chiefs did see the result as an adoption. Remember Chief Loud Voice's words: "Let us join together and make the Treaty; when both join together it is very good."[48] This statement refers to creating a relationship rather than surrendering land or extinguishing title. Morris, on the other hand, despite his use of kinship metaphors, seemed focused on getting the Chiefs to sign the written text. On the last afternoon of the negotiations, he tells the Chiefs,

> Since we went away we have had the treaty written out, and we are ready to have it signed, and we will leave a copy with any Chief you may select and after we leave we will have a copy written out on skin that cannot be rubbed out and put up in a tin box, so that it cannot be wet, so that you can keep it among yourselves so that when we are dead our children will know what was written.[49]

Morris refuses to describe himself as a trader, but his focus on getting signatures on the treaty reminds me of the credo of salesmen everywhere: Always Be Closing. Indeed, the proceedings ended once the Chiefs signed the paper, and annuities and provisions for the trip home were distributed immediately afterwards.[50] Morris's goal had been achieved, and he and the other commissioners soon returned to Winnipeg. No wonder the nêhiyawêwin word for treaty is *kihci-ostêsimâwasinahikan*: "the elder brother's paper." That's what the government negotiators cared about—all they cared about.

Asch argues that Treaty 4 was the product of good-faith negotiations, and that this makes it a remarkable achievement, a shared understanding arrived at despite cultural differences, and that it represents a path forward that goes beyond colonial relations.[51] That interpretation is only possible, however, because Asch rejects the validity of the written text. He believes that "the interpretation of the terms of Treaty 4 offered by our Indigenous partners today more accurately reflects the agreement we reached than does the version transmitted to us through the written text." In other words, "to gain their permission to settle on lands we recognized as belonging to them, we asked only to share the land with them (not take it over by purchasing it)," and in return, "we promised to do our utmost to ensure that our presence on these lands would result in benefits to them, and certainly would cause them no harm." The evidence also shows that "we treated our partners as independent political actors with their own leaders and a right to make the final decision on our request," and nothing in the treaty terms changed that relationship. "Put succinctly, but perhaps too mechanically, the agreement was this: they would share the land, and we would treat them like our own brothers and sisters," Asch concludes.[52]

If the treaty commissioners lied, however, then the treaties become worthless pieces of paper, no longer worthy of being described, in Cardinal's words, as "an Indian Magna Carta."[53] But, according to Asch, Morris was neither a liar nor a fraudster.

As lieutenant governor of Manitoba, he advocated for the faithful implementation of the spirit of the treaties, which put him at odds with his superiors in Ottawa. In 1876, the Department of Indian Affairs reduced his involvement in treaty implementation because it felt he had been too generous in the negotiations leading to Treaty 6, and the following year his authority in that area was removed. In 1878, when Sir John A. Macdonald returned to power, Morris was pushed out as lieutenant governor, and Dewdney became commissioner of Indian Affairs for the North-West Territory, where he introduced those infamous policies of deliberate starvation and residential schools.[54] Morris's honesty is, for Asch, a sign that the Indigenous interpretation of the treaties is the correct one.

Morris did advocate for the proper implementation of treaty promises; he writes,

> [T]he provisions of these treaties must be carried out with the utmost good faith and the nicest exactness. The Indians of Canada have…an abiding confidence in the Government of the Queen, or the Great Mother, as they style her. This must not, at all hazards, be shaken. It can be easily and fully maintained.[55]

One senses here an anxiety about what might take place if Indigenous confidence in the government were to be lost, and just five years later, the North-West Resistance showed what could happen—even though for the most part First Nations did not participate.[56] Nevertheless, Morris's understanding of the treaties is not, as Asch would like to believe, based on oral history and verbal promises. Rather, Morris immediately lists the characteristics of the southern numbered treaties, beginning with the extinguishment clause.[57] In addition, he includes the text of the treaties in an appendix to his book. Clearly the written documents were important to his conception of what he had accomplished as a treaty commissioner. Those documents were what the Crown negotiators understood—what they cared about.

There is also the question of whether the negotiations were conducted under duress. James Daschuk suggests that hunger played a role in the completion of the Treaty 4 negotiations.[58] Can hungry people freely negotiate their future? And Morris's take-it-or-leave-it stance during the negotiations was likely to produce a result that was less than fair to the nêhiyaw and Anihšināpē negotiators. On the fifth day of the difficult negotiations, he said,

> Must we go back and say we have had you here so many days, and that you had not the minds of men—that you were not able to understand each other? Must we go back and tell the Queen that we held out our hands for her, and her red children put them back again? If that be the message that your conduct to-day is going to make us carry back, I am sorry for you, and fear it will be a long day before you again see the Queen's Councillors here to try to do you good.[59]

That threat was followed by a second: "The Queen and her Councillors may think that you do not want to be friends."[60] No doubt both of those threats were empty, since the federal government desperately wanted a treaty with the nêhiyawak and Anihšināpēk—it wanted the Indigenous title to the land extinguished in order to facilitate the arrival of the railway and settlers. The government also wanted the negotiations to come to an end; every day of the negotiations was costing it money, since it had to feed the 3,000 people who were camped at Fort Qu'Appelle while they continued. Still, a threat is a threat, and given everything that took place at the Treaty 4 negotiations, it seems clear that if Morris was not a liar nor a fraud, he was no saint, either. Moreover, if he failed to ensure that the meaning of the extinguishment clause was understood, as Krasowski argues, then he lied by omission.

If the treaty commissioners were silent about the surrender clause, if they were lying by omission, what does that mean about the treaty they negotiated? "At least," Krasowski writes, "the absence of the surrender clause during the discussions casts doubt on the validity of the complete surrender of Indigenous Lands."[61] He concludes that the treaty relationship between settlers and Indigenous Peoples was based on sharing the land so that settlers could earn a living by farming, and that it established peaceful relations with First Nations. In partnership with Indigenous Peoples, settlers would also be called on to act as stewards of the land.[62] The treaty relationship and the model of governance it established were supposed to be an equal partnership between settlers and First Nations, one that recognized the shared rights and responsibilities of the treaty partners.[63] Of course, neither the federal government, nor our provincial governments, understand the numbered treaties in this way. If, for example, the treaties are an agreement to share the land for agricultural purposes only, then mineral rights remain with Indigenous Peoples. If there was no surrender of land, the government had no right to survey and sell all the land outside of the reserves, and there's no such thing as Crown land at all: what we call "Crown land" would actually belong to First Nations, not the Crown. Krasowski's argument has profound implications for our understanding of the relationship between settlers and First Nations people. I hope settlers like me have it in us to accept what seems to be the truth: there was no surrender of land.

Contemporary legal scholars and historians, Indigenous and settler alike, may have identified a way to bring the mutually incompatible visions of Treaty 4 together, using earlier treaties as a model. First, as Craft argues, during the Treaty 1 negotiations two distinct systems of law were in operation. However, she continues, by adopting both the procedural and substantive forms of

Anishinaabe *inaakonigewin*, or law, to secure the treaty, the Crown representatives ended up adopting and operating in Anishinaabe law, even if they did not realize that was what they were doing.[64] For that reason, it is not acceptable to consider the interpretation and implementation of the treaty only in terms of Canadian common law.[65] Craft argues that "the true spirit and intent of the treaty can be explored and perhaps ultimately resolved by understanding the systems of law that informed the treaty negotiations."[66] That would mean focusing on relationships, rather than the written text, and recognizing that in Anishinaabe inaakonigewin, relationships never end, but are instead fostered, redefined, re-examined, renegotiated, tended, fuelled, and nurtured.[67]

Second, as Michael Coyle points out, we need to bring together the written and oral versions of the historical treaties. He writes, "Some way must be found to reconcile the fact that while the treaties themselves were clearly intended to endure indefinitely amidst inevitable changes on the ground, the written texts of the land treaties were framed in very narrow and precise terms," outlining articles of agricultural assistance, for instance, that would only have been relevant to the period immediately following the treaty negotiations.[68] Coyle believes that the only way to accept this contradiction is to realize that the treaties were designed to be renegotiated, in good faith, over time, to address the evolving needs and interests of both treaty parties.[69] For Coyle, as for John Borrows, Julie Jai, and Aaron Mills, a model for this kind of relationship already exists, in the metaphors of the Two Row Wampum and the Covenant Chain, which were accepted by both the Crown and over 2,000 Indigenous Chiefs from across North America, including nêhiyaw and Lakota Chiefs, at the Treaty of Niagara in 1764.[70] The Two Row Wampum, which depicts a canoe and a sailing ship moving in parallel down a river, represents an understanding of a mutual relationship of peace and non-interference in each other's ways of life by both Indigenous people and the Crown, and it was reaffirmed and accepted by the Crown at the Treaty of Niagara negotiations.[71] The Covenant Chain, a wampum belt that depicts settlers and Indigenous people linked together by a silver chain, is, according to Mills, a representation of the need for mutual aid between the Crown and Indigenous Peoples. The Treaty of Niagara, he suggests, represents the intercultural achievement of an understanding of mutual aid and a commitment to a relationship based on practices of mutual aid, oriented towards harmony, which are represented in the Covenant Chain wampum belt.[72] The Treaty of Niagara, he argues, created a shared political community, a living relationship between settlers and Indigenous Peoples, and a foundation for settler citizenship.[73] The best way to under stand the historical numbered treaties, then, may be through the lens of these earlier agreements. That would mean rethinking the importance of the written text of those treaties, and focusing more on the way that they founded relationships between Indigenous Peoples and the Crown. Even if that mutual understanding has never existed, it could be created now, by reinvigorating the model of the Covenant Chain and Two Row Wampum. If that means turning away from the written texts of the treaties, so be it.

However, as Jai points out, the Treaty of Niagara was negotiated at a time when First Nations people and settlers were relatively equal in demographic and political power, while the later numbered treaties were not; although First Nations have recovered in numbers and influence from their nineteenth-century nadir, they are still less powerful than the federal government and fewer in number than the settlers who live in their territories.[74] For that reason, returning to the relationship models provided by the Covenant Chain and the Two Row Wampum would require tremendous political courage, imagination, and commitment by the federal government and/or the Supreme Court of Canada. As Mark D. Walters suggests, "the fate of the Covenant Chain...was sealed by the general phenomenon of *colonialism*,"[75] and so as long as Canada behaves as a colonizer, the models represented by the Covenant Chain and the Two Row Wampum will remain beyond our reach. We may find that the Covenant Chain, rather than merely being rusted and tarnished, is broken beyond repair, and that any attempt at polishing it by developing stronger and more mutually affirming relationships will be doomed to fail. Nevertheless, the attempt is worth making, because, as Asch suggests, if the historical numbered treaties resulted in mere mutual incomprehension, the right settlers have to live here disappears.[76] Rather than resigning ourselves to that fate, to accepting that we are here only because of practices of colonial domination, including the doctrines of *terra nullius*, occupation, and discovery, we could try to reinvigorate our treaty relationships. We have much to gain by making the attempt, and much to lose by refusing. Reinvigorating those treaty relationships would help decolonize the relationships between settlers and First Nations. Renewing those relationships wouldn't be enough to undo a century and a half of settler colonialism, as Hunt and Starblanket remind us,[77] but it seems like a place to start.

///

The sky is changing: clouds are forming to the west, although I'm not sure what they mean, since there's no rain in the forecast. A black-and-white spotted moth is sitting in the weeds next to the shoulder. A train pulling a long line of containers on flatcars slowly crawls towards the horizon. I have blisters on the bottom of both feet now, a matching pair, and my right heel hurts as much as my left. A pickup passes and I smell a skunk. Sunscreen is running into my eyes—it stings. A dead seagull lies in the weeds. I pass Rotary Avenue. A truck exits, heading to the Global Transportation Hub. A large billboard is advertising land for sale at the GTH without mentioning its name—avoiding the controversy attached to the development, I suppose. I walk beneath the overpass that carries

Dewdney Avenue over the highway. Out of the wind, it's suddenly silent, except for the passing traffic, which is immediately louder. On the other side of Dewdney, I'm back in the wind.

An old-fashioned galvanized steel windmill is spinning on the west side of the highway. The steel mill is visible now. I can't quite see the Regina Indian Industrial School cemetery yet, but I can see the buildings next to it. I keep walking. Soon I can make out the new white fence around the cemetery, which was completed and painted this past week. In the distance, I can see the streetlights that mark the exit at 9th Avenue North on the horizon. I walk across the overpass at the Canadian National tracks. A dead gopher lies in the road—at least, that's what I think it is. The corpse has a long tail; maybe it's a muskrat, although there's no water nearby, and the presence of an aquatic mammal here would make little sense. I don't brave the traffic, sparse as it is, to investigate. Gulls wheel above, white against the blue sky. Bales of hay lie golden in a field of the same colour—a Saskatchewan harvest cliché. Swathed canola in shades of tan and green makes another cliché. Photographs of such landscapes end up on calendars; they're beautiful, it's true, but they're also artifacts of settlement, like this highway. Of course, everything I can see from here reflects the massive changes settlers have wrought since we started arriving in the 1880s. It's all ruderal.

Another flying grasshopper hits me in the mouth. In the distance, a pair of bridges takes the Bypass over Wascana Creek again. I hadn't realized I'd cross the creek twice on this journey. It twists across the landscape, serpentine. I sit down to rest. I'm stopping more frequently now, fighting my exhaustion, looking for places where I might camp. This spot is okay, but I need to walk farther so that tomorrow's journey is shorter. It's a good place to sit for a minute, though. I slide off my boots and my feet relax. I'm hungry, but I'm too tired to bother opening my pack to find something to eat. I doze for an hour. When the sun goes behind a cloud—puffy white clouds dot the immense sky now—the sudden cold shakes me awake. I eat another cereal bar. I try some trail mix, but it's stale and inedible. I consider dumping it out, but don't want to litter, or attract animals to the highway, where they'll be in danger of being killed by traffic. I drink some water, zip my pant legs onto my shorts, and repack my knapsack. All that takes a half hour. Finally I'm ready to go, my muscles complaining about being asked to move after my long rest.

As I pass through the underpass at 9th Avenue North, I smell freshly cut grass. On the other side, a bearded, grinning man is mowing the steep embankment with a tracked robot. He holds the remote control in his hands. A jet is climbing through the air from the airport to the south. A black car pulls onto the shoulder, flashing its hazard lights. It's my friends Glenn and Kathleen. I knew they were coming back from Saskatoon this afternoon, and I know that Glenn likes to take this route; I wondered if I might see them. They invite me to sit in the car for a minute, but I'm afraid that I won't be able to force myself up off the padded upholstery, so I decline the offer. They ask how I'm doing and whether I need anything. Oh, everything's fine, I say. I consider lightening my pack by giving them the stale trail mix I'm carrying, but I don't want to go through the ritual of unfastening my pack so soon after hauling it up onto my shoulders. Kathleen takes my picture. She emails it to me later. I look ridiculous with the orange Buff pulled up over my head. We say goodbye and I continue walking past fields of swathed canola. Houses stand beyond them. I'm walking the interface between the country and the city: a shallow space, with fields butting up against houses, industry and agriculture commingled. The stubble is a rusty colour. Crispy blue J Cloth towels, scraps of sky, are caught in the roadside weeds.

I get to Armour Road. Like Courtney Street, it's a level intersection, without an overpass. I could stop to camp here, but the streetlights along the highway here would keep me awake, so I keep walking. A combine is working a field to the west, raising a cloud of dust. Ahead the highway begins climbing to cross the low hills marking the boundary between the Wascana Creek and Boggy Creek watersheds. Another grasshopper hits me on the head. North of Armour Road, the highway swings northeast, towards old Highway 11.

I need to find a place to camp, even though it's several hours until sunset, when I'll feel more comfortable rolling out my bivy sack. I don't want to attract the attention of a passing Mountie; wild camping, especially on private property, is illegal. I imagine the scenario: being nudged awake by a polished black boot, a light shining down in my eyes, a police officer asking, "What do you think you're doing?" That would be the end of my walk: the handcuffs; the ride in the backseat of a cruiser to the detachment; the call to my partner, asking to be picked up. It's not the possibility of a ticket that bothers me. It's having to abandon my journey, along with the humiliation of trying to explain myself to someone who would think I'm out of my mind. That's never happened: this is a big province, with lots of roads and not many cops to patrol them, so I shouldn't worry. And I'm aware that my fears are mild, a sign of white privilege, compared to what could happen to someone not white, male, middle class, and cisgendered in that situation. I do sometimes fret about the possibility of a pickup truck full of good old boys coming home from the bar deciding to have a little fun with me—an echo of the bullying I experienced as a boy—but that's never happened, either; my bivy sack is a dark colour, well camouflaged, resembling a garbage bag or the shadow of a dead deer instead of a camp site. But even if these scenarios are unlikely, I still fret about them.

Up ahead, a grain bin sits on the edge of a field beside the highway. That might be a place to rest for a minute; I could sit on the leeward side, out of the wind. I wonder if it might make a decent camping spot. I circle the bin. At first, I'm not optimistic. It's on the edge of a field of peas that's been combined, leaving stubble behind. On the leeward side there are thistles. Out of the wind it's quiet, but the shade of the bin is cold, so I find a spot on the other side, where chaff covers the ground, and sit. It's surprisingly comfortable. I'm mostly out of sight of passing cars and trucks. After walking twenty kilometres, I'm tired and ready to stop. I put on the light down jacket I packed this morning and shiver in the wind. The noise the traffic makes is blocked, a little, by the bin. A murder of silent crows flies past. The straw is dusty and makes me sneeze. Peas are sprayed with a desiccant like glyphosate before they're harvested, so that the plants don't clog the combines, and I'm sitting in the residue. Maybe that's why I'm sneezing. I can see the refinery's gas flare from here, along with the landfill, the steel

mill, the towers downtown. There are cirrus clouds high overhead. A dog barks in the distance, but it likely isn't allowed to roam free because of the highway and won't cause me any trouble.

I decide to unpack my bivy sack and sleeping bag and crawl inside them. I listen to the crickets and the traffic. The dog barks occasionally. The moon rises, and I try to get a photograph. I want to sleep, but I can't quite get there. It's getting colder. I hear strange noises and poke my head out of the bivy sack to discover that I'm surrounded by grey partridges, gleaning the stubble for peas the combine missed. They take to the air when they realize I'm looking at them. As the sky darkens, I hear coyotes singing. I prefer them to the dog; they're less likely to bother me. I listen to the sounds of traffic and coyotes until I finally drift off to sleep.

NINE

FLYING-UP MOON

AUGUST 31, 2020

All night long the cold keeps me awake. I finally get up at six o'clock, as the sun is rising. It's still freezing, and I wish I'd remembered to bring a pair of gloves. I break camp quickly, shove a couple of cereal bars in my pocket, and start walking. I eat with numb fingers. The road curves over a hill—such a rarity in this flat plain—and into the shallow Boggy Creek valley. I'm walking quickly, trying to get warm, wondering if sleeping on the land made any difference to my connection with it. Nan Shepherd would tell me that it did. "No one knows the mountain completely who has not slept on it," she argues, and by sleeping on the mountain, one "dwells in pure intimacy with the tangible world."[1] Such outdoor sleeping, she suggests, empties or uncouples the mind. "I do not ascribe sentience to the mountain; yet at no other moment am I sunk quite so deep into its life," she writes. "I have let go my self. The experience is peculiarly precious because it is impossible to coerce."[2] If that was true of the mountains where Shepherd walked and slept, might it be true of these flat plains as well? Did I manage to sink deeply into the land's life by sleeping in the chaff of that field of peas? No doubt it's an experience that I'd have to repeat many more times before I could figure out whether it was even close to Shepherd's. She spent decades hiking in the Cairngorms; I'm spending just a few days on this highway. To be honest, last night wasn't very pleasant: between the cold and the hard ground, I kept waking up and rolling over, shivering. Shepherd doesn't complain about such things. No doubt, like Robert Macfarlane, she was tougher than I am.

Maybe what makes sleeping on the ground important is the way it eliminates some of the barriers between ourselves and the earth itself. When I'm walking along this highway, my feet are encased in socks and boots, and there are layers of asphalt and gravel between those feet and the earth. But last night, much less separated me from the land: clothes, a sleeping bag and a light pad, and the bottom of my bivy. Maybe the fewer barriers there are between us and the earth, the greater the possibility of some kind of intimate relationship. That's Jeffrey Lockwood's argument in favour of walking barefoot, and the reason Trevor Herriot encourages his readers to lie down in the grass. But I'd have to travel many kilometres to find a piece of unbroken grassland to lie on or walk across. The best I can do is the field I slept in last night, land that's been broken. It's worth thinking about the connotations of that word. The settlers who arrived and began breaking the prairie might have understood, at some level, the violence of that process, suggested by their use of the word *breaking* to describe what they were doing. I've heard stories about roots snapping against the plow blade with sounds like gunshots and screams. I have to believe that something of the land remains—in the sky, the wind, or the earth itself—but much has been lost with the conversion of grassland to cereal agriculture. I'm not accusing or blaming anyone; I'm just as dependent on the food grown in these fields as anyone else is, and I know that without agriculture this province couldn't feed its population, let alone export food to the rest of the world. But I still wonder if it's possible to develop any kind of intimacy with what is, essentially, an industrial site. It might take years of walking here to answer that question.

///

When settlers arrived on the plains, they eradicated the buffalo, tore up the grass, and made the prairie into something new: the miles of wheat and canola and barley I've been walking through. We think of agriculture as a natural process, since it involves growing things, but contemporary agriculture is an industrial, extractive use of the land, one upon which people depend, but that has terrible effects on more-than-human creatures. Writing in 1945, Aldo Leopold, who studied the tall-grass prairie of southern Wisconsin, suggested that agricultural progress brought with it "three fundamental weaknesses":

1. Wildlife habitat in fertile regions is being destroyed faster than it is being rebuilt.
2. Many imported and also native species exhibit pest behavior. A general disorganization of the wildlife community seems to be taking place.
3. Private initiative in wildlife management has grown very slowly.[3]

Even then woodlots were being cut down, marshes drained, and creeks channelized, processes intended to increase agricultural yields but which eliminated wildlife habitat.[4] Modern chemical pest controls—Leopold's example is DDT, almost twenty years before Rachel Carson's famous book, *Silent Spring*, which woke people up to the dangers of that pesticide—were also supposed to improve yields, but they might turn out to be "as dangerous as the pests themselves."[5] The farm, Leopold continued, was becoming "a food-factory," a monoculture where anything other than crops had no place.[6] "It was inevitable and no doubt desirable that the tremendous momentum of industrialization should have spread to farm life," Leopold concluded. "It is clear to me, however, that it has overshot the mark, in the sense that it is generating new insecurities, economic and ecological, in place of those it was meant to abolish."[7] Industrial agriculture was turning out to be bad for both the natural world and farmers.

Contemporary agriculture continues to be hard on farmers and the ecosystem. Faced with rising costs and increasingly tiny profit margins, farmers put every square metre of land into production, leaving nothing—no crop margins, wetlands, or windbreaks—where wildlife can live. The reliance on herbicides and pesticides is another problem. I think about the pea field where I slept, the potentially cancer-causing glyphosate residue that's all over my pack and bivy sack and boots, and the story Herriot tells about the chemical carbofuran, a poison used against grasshoppers in the 1980s.[8] Carbofuran is a deadly neurotoxin. "A quarter teaspoon of the liquid form is enough to kill a human being; a single grain of the granular form will kill a songbird," Herriot notes, "but in the 1980s our farmers were told to use it on cropland, grassland, easements, ditches, and rights-of-way all over the northern Great Plains."[9] As many as one million birds each year were killed by the granular form of carbofuran alone before it was phased out in the 1990s.[10] In addition, with insects like grasshoppers eliminated, birds that eat them were left to starve. Carbofuran's replacement, terbufos, is nearly as toxic to birds.[11] Birds also die after eating canola seed treated with lindane, "a persistent toxin that has made its way around the globe by travelling in the atmosphere," ending up in water in the remote Arctic, polar bear fat, and breast milk.[12] Lindane is linked to breast cancer.[13] It took decades for these dangerous chemicals to be partially deregistered by governments under pressure from environmental organizations. According to

Herriot, government regulatory agencies are "rolling the dice" on our behalf, "justifying the risk of cancer and the killing of birds and other creatures to ensure that high-yield agriculture continues on its inexorable path."[14]

Meanwhile, bird populations are crashing across North America—survey data show that there are three billion fewer birds on this continent now than there were in 1970[15]—and new chemicals, like neonicotinoids, are killing insects and birds.[16] Add the indiscriminate use of biocides to the continuing loss of habitat, the presence of microplastics in the water and soil, and the ravages of climate change, and it's not a surprise that the world has lost two-thirds of its wild creatures in the past fifty years.[17] All of us bear some responsibility for this planetary catastrophe, including the farmers whose fields I have been walking past and everyone who buys and eats the crops they grow. Including, of course, me. And yet, perhaps because all of us are to blame, it seems impossible for us to take action to stop the destruction. We watch ourselves collectively speeding towards the edge of an ecological cliff, apparently powerless to take our feet off the gas pedal. If I look carefully, I can see all this clearly from my vantage point on the shoulder of this highway, and it terrifies me.

///

I pass under buzzing, spitting high-tension lines. A train's horn sounds at a level crossing somewhere nearby. Now I can see the old Highway 11. The Bypass is about to end. A dead bird lies on the road, probably a grey partridge. The highway designers have left space to expand this interchange. Will there ever be enough traffic to make that worthwhile? A field of canola next to the highway is half-swathed. I realize this is a bad time of year to sleep in a field; if farmers are anxious about getting their crop into the bin, they'll combine all night, and I doubt my dark-coloured bivy sack would be visible from the cab of a combine harvester. My hands are warm now. I take off my down coat, then cross old Highway 11 on the overpass and start down the on-ramp. Not for the first time, I wish I'd been able to share this experience with someone else. It would've been less lonely, more fun.

I head south towards the city. This highway, the road between Regina and Saskatoon, is busy, as it always is. The traffic is loud. There are too many vehicles speeding by for this to be a safe place to walk. The animal feed processing operation across the road is emitting a loud whine that I can hear between vehicles. It's giving off a terrible smell, too, one that takes me back to my hometown, where a mill that made chicken feed produced a similar stench. Between the stink and the traffic, this is a dispiriting place to walk. I sing to keep my energy up. I pass beneath the same spitting high-tension line I walked under an hour ago. My blisters are growing painful again. Three sheep are feeding in a large pasture. I'm limping again. The steel mill is just ahead; it'll take me at least an hour to get past it. Dump trucks roar by, leaving behind the smell of asphalt. I can see the downtown now. Birds are feeding in a stubble field. So many wild sunflowers are growing beside the shoulder. I pass a lost tarp and plod on, passing the exit to Pasqua Street. There is so much more garbage on the side of the road here than there was on the Bypass; my theory about traffic, time, and trash seems to be accurate. I walk past a slough where geese are swimming; when they see me, they take wing, arcing into the sky, reminding me that this is the last day of the Flying-Up Moon, *ohpahowi-pîsim*, the month when the birds born in the spring learn to fly.

///

If the invasion of Indigenous lands by settlers is a structure rather than an event, as Patrick Wolfe argues,[18] if it's an ongoing process, what might it look like to those who are being invaded? I have no direct knowledge of that experience, the frustration and anger it must occasion, or what it's like to still be fighting for survival centuries after that invasion began. I consider the long list of our failures to live up to the terms of the treaties we made with First Nations here. Rather than a nation-to-nation relationship, which was implied by the process of treaty making, Canada has imposed—and continues to impose—the *Indian Act* on First Nations, distorting every aspect of their systems of government[19]; instead of local schools in each community, the horrors of residential schools; instead of the promised assistance with the transition to an agricultural economy, the social Darwinist peasant-farming policy, which prevented Indigenous farmers from competing with their settler neighbours by reneging on treaty promises to supply them with modern agricultural implements.[20] Add to those cruelties the pass system—illegal because it was not enabled through legislation—which confined First Nations to reserves for decades after 1885;[21] a century and a half of starvation and disease—from epidemics of tuberculosis on reserves and in residential schools in the nineteenth and twentieth centuries, to epidemics of diabetes, substance-abuse disorder, and suicide in the twenty-first; a refusal to share land and resources equitably, leading to unacceptable rates of poverty on and off reserves; the slow motion genocide of murdered and missing Indigenous women, girls, and two-spirit people;[22] and staggering rates of incarceration caused by a legal system defined by systemic racism rather than justice.[23] All of this—and so much else—constitutes the dry facts of the case; the emotional reality must be very different, something beyond my grasp, except perhaps through novels and poems and plays and films about the experience of being Indigenous in Canada. They must convey some small part of that emotional reality, the way that my attempts to convey the reality of these walks to readers passes on only a fraction of what they were really like. All those past injustices need to be recognized, and the present injustices need to end. That's something settlers could do. Our governments, though, are unwilling to make the necessary changes: to negotiate an abolition of the *Indian Act* with First Nations, or to do something concrete about the suicide epidemic in northern Saskatchewan, to give two examples.[24] Instead, we make symbolic gestures that do nothing to repatriate Indigenous land and life, as Eve Tuck and K. Wayne Yang demand.[25] We are unwilling, collectively, to begin behaving as if we were family, to start considering the treaties to be living relationships that require attention and care—to approach the treaties the way that Treaty Elders do. And I don't know what I might do, as one person, to push for those changes; settler colonialism is a systemic problem, which makes it hard to grasp in its entirety, let alone begin to change. Trying to develop a relationship with the land by walking is one thing I thought I could accomplish, even if that walking has taken place on roads; it's been, if nothing else, a way to witness the land, turn it from non-place into place, think about what a relationship with it might entail. It's not enough—I know it's not nearly enough—but it's something.

///

I smell another skunk. The refinery is clearly visible on the horizon now, all of its stacks, not just the one flaring gas. I'd hoped that I'd get to a fast-food restaurant on the edge of the city to use the washroom, but my bowels have other ideas, and I realize that since I'm still at least an hour from the city, I'm not going to make it. What to do? There's an empty field next to the highway, with a tall, rusty steel power pole on its far edge. Maybe I can squat behind that. I cut across the field. At the pole, I drop my pack and fish out my toilet paper and orange plastic pack trowel. As usual, my pack trowel is useless for digging a hole in the hard ground. This is humiliating, I tell myself. I drop my pants, squat against the pole, and let go. It's an ignominious necessity, but nothing that people all over the world don't do every day. When I'm finished, I fumble my roll of toilet paper and drop it. It's caught by the wind, unfurling in a grand white flag of surrender. On the highway behind me, a car horn honks.

Afterwards, I limp across the ditch to the shoulder of the highway on my sore feet. A switching engine in the yard of the steel mill hoots. I see rose hips and wormwood in the grass. I step past an abandoned windbreaker and someone's discarded mask. The wind is getting stronger after the early morning calm. Barley fields wait for the combine on both sides of the highway. To the south the city begins: houses, apartments, car dealerships. A torn mattress lies in the ditch, along with a floor mat thrown from a passing car. I'm running out of time to see a lost shoe. I pass yet another dead bird. I make my way over the bridge that carries this road across Highway 6. There's a lot of nameless debris here, but still no shoes. A gopher squeaks. A dog in the new neighbourhood that's been built east of the highway barks. Passing trucks throw grit in my face and a hot wind sucks at my hat. I step over a strand of barbed wire. Paving work is underway where Highway 6 becomes Albert Street, and the shoulder hasn't been finished; I can feel the rough surface through the soles of my boots, and it hurts my blisters. Traffic is slow here, though, because of the construction—a blessing. I sit on the guard rail for a minute. I've walked three hours without resting, and I'm getting tired. Then I cross the overpass at Ring Road—there are no sidewalks on this side of the street—and stop at a fast-food place to eat something and drink some coffee. The hard plastic seat is more comfortable than the ground, and I think about the treaty commissioners and the chairs they brought to the Treaty 4 negotiations 146 years ago.

Outside, I keep going south on Albert Street. Annual flowers planted beside the busy traffic artery fill the air with a beautiful scent above the stink of exhaust. I see yet another discarded mask. My feet complain with every step; they're becoming the focus of my consciousness. I pass the Saskatchewan Indian Institute of Technologies campus. A lunch truck is parked outside; it's break time. I wait to cross 1st Avenue North. The wind blows dust at me. To the east, a train is approaching the CNR's level crossing. A winter's worth of sand has been left on the sidewalk, and I add my footprints to the ones already there. A man shouts instructions to someone through a sewer hatch. The receiver in a phone booth is broken. I cross 4th Avenue, then 5th Avenue. Two tough-looking young men pass me, recounting last night's exploits. I cross Dewdney Avenue. A young woman carrying a bigger backpack than mine passes me; she waits to cross Albert Street. I'd like to ask where she's going, but I'm too tired to speak. Finally, I spot an abandoned shoe—a child's Croc—and take a photograph. On the other side of the street, a Riders fan dressed in green and white is walking north. I walk through the underpass beneath the CPR tracks. There are no pigeons here today. I wait to cross Saskatchewan Drive. A broken chair lies on the sidewalk. I'm limping and stumbling now. I cross Victoria Avenue. I'm tired of the traffic noise and turn west onto 13th Avenue, where it's a little quieter.

This is my neighbourhood, Cathedral. After three days and seventy kilometres of walking, I'm almost home. I walk by the remains of a heritage building that's been demolished to make way for a private liquor store. There's a powder blue bathtub in the basement, visible through the broken floor. All of this wood and brick is going to end up in the landfill. That bathtub, too. I cross 13th Avenue, cut across the Safeway's parking lot, as I always do, and trudge down Robinson Street. I turn on 14th Avenue, then Cameron Street. This is the path I take home from the supermarket or the pub; I've walked here so many times. Will I relate to these half-dozen blocks differently now? I seem to be looking at them in a new way, but that could be an illusion caused by exhaustion and sore feet. I can't tell. I cross 15th Avenue and turn onto College Avenue, the street I've lived on for more than twenty years. Finally, after three days of walking, I limp into our front garden. I put down some tobacco and step over it, the way that Lifespeaker Noel Starblanket suggested I do when I finished. It's a gesture of respect, a silent prayer of gratitude to the land I've been walking on. When an Elder invites me to participate in a ritual like this one, I feel as if I've been welcomed into a circle; as if, despite my settler origins, I've been allowed to become, however tentatively, part of something else, something better. I think about Willie Ermine's ethical space of engagement, a place where Indigenous people and settlers can meet to share ideas, and wonder if such invitations bring me into that space. I hope they do.

As I take off my boots and drop my pack on the floor, I think about the walk I've just completed. Was I able to turn non-place into place over those three days of walking? Yes, I decide, even if only temporarily, if only in a ring around my body, one limited by the reach of my senses. And my larger goal of coming into a kinship relation with the land? That's harder for a settler like me to accomplish, I think. To experience that relationship, to feel it in my body, would require more walking, more time with the land. But, after this walk, I'm certain it's possible—difficult, perhaps, but possible. I think about the sky, the birds, the patch of Canada wild rye I napped beside two days ago: despite the massive changes that settlers have wrought, the land is still there, still with us. It endures; it waits for us to recognize that we're its kin, that we're all related. It's good to realize that truth.

Then, yawning, I lie down on the couch in our sunporch and fall asleep.

EPILOGUE

LOOKING BACK

A long, dreary pandemic winter finally ends. Spring arrives. I still wonder sometimes what all my walks accomplished—whether I managed to achieve the goals I set for myself. In some ways, yes. I can see my relationship with the land in a way I couldn't have before. I sense that I'm at the beginning of some new kind of connection, but it feels tentative, evanescent. I'm sure it'll take more work, more time, more walking, to develop it. Like colonialism, building a relationship is a process, I realize—a structure rather than an event. It unfolds over time; it doesn't happen all at once. But does discovering that sense of relationship count as decolonization? It's a start, I decide. A way to begin.

Another year passes, and then another. I finish my PhD, winning the President's Distinguished Graduate Student Award. I publish a few poems and essays about walking, history, and ecology, which makes me feel like I'm becoming the writer I dreamed about when I was a boy.[1] I'm back to teaching a full load of courses every semester now, and my weeks are too full with prepping lectures and grading papers, with reading and writing, to go on long walks around the Bypass or to plod up Pinkie Road's drifts of thick gravel to visit the RIIS cemetery, but I find time every day to walk to the university and back across Wascana Centre. I never liked Wascana Centre that much; its paved footpaths, its lawns and trees, always struck me as too manicured while, at the same time, given the invasive weeds that flourish there, it seemed abandoned, too, unloved, as if nobody cared for it. But after all those daily walks through the park, I'm surprised and happy at how much I've grown to appreciate it. The secret, as I suspected, is repetition: walking again and again in the same place does create a sense of connection and belonging—of relationship, in other words. So does seeing how it changes over the seasons. Appreciation, affection, intimacy, knowledge: these seem to be the building blocks of connection. If I had spent as much time in the places where I walked in the summer of 2020, I'm certain I would've come to know them better, too. I would've begun to see our connections, our kinship. The sense of wâhkôhtowin I was hoping to find would've become clearer.

Other things have been happening, too. For instance, after just thirty minutes of debate, Regina's city council recently refused to rename Dewdney Avenue. One suggestion for a new name was the Lakota word *tatanka*, which means "bison."[2] The two councillors who made the motion to change the name, Andrew Stevens from Ward 3 and Dan LeBlanc from Ward 6, argued that not celebrating Dewdney by putting his name on a major thoroughfare in Regina would be a concrete commitment by the city to the spirit of truth and reconciliation. Only three councillors voted in favour of the motion, however; the other seven voted against. Just one, Ward 9 councillor Jason Mancinelli, apparently speaking for the majority, explained his opposition: renaming Dewdney Avenue would cost residents and businesses too much, he said.[3] Mayor Sandra Masters also said cost was a factor in her decision to vote no. Those arguments contradicted city manager Niki Anderson, who pointed out that the city's research indicated that the change would cost residents, and the city itself, next to nothing.[4]

After the meeting, LeBlanc said that the decision went against the city's past and present statements and decisions about Indigenous issues: its public commitment to the Truth and Reconciliation Commission of Canada's 94 Calls to Action; the Indigenous framework it's developing, which would bring Indigenous ways of thinking into its policies and procedures; and the fact that every city council meeting begins with a land acknowledgement.[5] "[W]e're not even at the truth stage of truth and reconciliation," LeBlanc told reporters.[6] Stevens suggested that the decision would harm the city's reputation among Indigenous residents. "I think any member of the [Indigenous] community would be right to question whether or not we're listening and whether or not it means anything to engage," he said.[7]

According to Mayor Masters, it would make more sense to invest whatever changing the street's name would cost in other projects, "whether that's programming or artwork, [or] other kinds of signage," such as educational banners along the road. That kind of spending, she said, wouldn't be as "divisive" as removing Dewdney's name from street signs.[8] But the history of colonialism here, especially Dewdney's role in that history, is itself divisive; that's a kind word for the policies of deliberate starvation and residential schools that he facilitated. First Nations people, from the Federation of Sovereign Indigenous Nations to activists like BigEagle-Kequahtooway, have been telling us how they feel about having Dewdney celebrated by having a major street in this city named after him. They didn't ask for artwork or signage or programming; they asked our city council to listen to their concerns—something it has refused to do.[9]

Meanwhile, Saskatchewan's provincial government is planning to build an eight- to ten-lane highway, called the Saskatoon

Freeway, through that city's Northeast Swale and Small Swale—areas of grassland and wetland near the South Saskatchewan River. The swales are islands of biodiversity in an ecologically impoverished landscape, providing habitat for deer, badgers, waterfowl, and rare indigenous plants. They are important recreational and educational assets for city residents, too. One man I met during a recent visit to the Northeast Swale, a newcomer to the city named Pratik, described that place as "the best part of Saskatoon." If the province builds that freeway, "the best part of Saskatoon" will be buried under concrete and asphalt. It's hard to imagine that a ten-lane freeway—that's about the size of Highway 401 in Toronto, a city twenty times the size of Saskatoon—will ever be necessary there, and I find myself wondering if the province will once again spend billions of dollars on an expensive, empty road. At least the Regina Bypass only paved over fields of wheat and canola. As activists Candace Savage and Meghan Mickelson, co-chairs of Swale Watchers, a community organization in Saskatoon that's trying to protect the swales, argue, the provincial highways department is "offering 1950s answers to 21st century challenges."[10] What's more important: protecting ecologically sensitive places or building massive highways to nowhere? Our government's answer to that question is pretty clear. Do the rest of us agree?

The provincial government is also moving ahead with the Westside Irrigation Rehabilitation Project, its $1.15 billion plan to expand irrigation around Lake Diefenbaker. Construction of the first phase is supposed to begin in 2025; if the rest of the project is completed, the total cost is projected to be $4 billion.[11] That's a lot of money, but the project's initial economic analysis, which was prepared by the accounting firm KPMG and released in late September 2024, just prior to the provincial election, predicts that over the next fifty years it could increase the province's gross domestic product by as much as $5.9 billion while creating 43,000 jobs.[12] The thirty-one-page report, which took more than three years to finish, calls the project a "generational opportunity for Saskatchewan."[13] Sounds great, doesn't it?

Economists who looked at the analysis, though, said that the government's big investment is unlikely to pay off. The estimated tax revenue the project will return to taxpayers is just $410 million,[14] which means that it'll end up being a $600 million subsidy to the farmers who use it to irrigate their crops.[15] The government argues that those farmers will end up paying something towards the project's costs, but nobody seems to know how much.[16] Nobody's even sure what crops farmers will grow on their newly irrigated land. Potatoes, apparently: while an acre of wheat adds $400 per acre to the provincial gross domestic product, an acre of irrigated potatoes adds $5,500 to the provincial GDP.[17] However, only 4,800 of the 112,000 acres that are currently irrigated using water from Lake Diefenbaker—just 4.3 percent of that land—were used to grow potatoes in 2023. Other specialty crops, including vegetables and hemp, were grown on another 2 percent of that area. The rest was used to grow grain, oilseeds, forage crops, and pulses. Dave Marzolf, who farms near Lake Diefenbaker, told the CBC's Geoff Leo that he keeps asking the Water Security Agency how many acres of irrigated land would need to be used to grow specialty crops before the province's billion-dollar investment would make sense. "Nobody answers that question," he said.[18] Maybe they don't know.

The possibility of cost overruns is another issue. Peter Phillips, a professor emeritus of economics at the University of Saskatchewan's Johnson-Shoyama School of Public Policy, pointed out to Leo that governments planning megaprojects "tend to underestimate costs and time to completion, and overestimate benefits." That's especially true of water projects, which typically cost 20 percent more than anticipated.[19] In addition, the initial economic analysis assumes that more irrigation will lead to more food processing, an idea that Phillips compared to the movie *Field of*

Dreams: "If you build it, they will come." "Might work in movies," Phillips told Leo, "but not in real life."[20] If most of the newly irrigated land is just used for growing grain, like the land near Lake Diefenbaker that's already being irrigated, the dream of more food processing isn't going to happen. It sounds like a lot of risk for a project that's probably going to directly benefit only fifty farmers.[21]

The fact that the initial economic analysis lacks crucial information is another red flag, according to Phillips: the authors' names are absent, there are no tables of data showing how they arrived at their conclusions, and it's missing a clear statement of whether the benefits of the project will outweigh the costs. Those omissions, Phillips stated, are unusual.[22] I find it surprising that the government plans to spend more than a billion dollars on a project supported by an economic analysis that's only thirty-one pages long—not much longer than a graduate student's term paper. Isn't that a little skimpy? Is an initial economic analysis enough to justify this project? Where's the feasibility study? Don't we need a little more information before we commit to a megaproject this big and expensive?

Another question: how will this project affect Lake Diefenbaker and the Saskatchewan River system? Peter Leavitt, a professor of biology and Canada Research Chair in environmental change and society at the University of Regina, noted that the lake is experiencing blooms of cyanobacteria, something that hasn't happened before and which indicates that its water quality is getting worse.[23] When people drink or wash with water containing cyanobacteria, they can end up with rashes, diarrhea, fevers, and respiratory problems; cities drawing water from lakes and rivers containing cyanobacteria need to invest in new water-treatment facilities to keep their citizens from getting sick.[24] And, because the irrigation canals will cross creeks that run into the lake, the project is likely to end up dumping fertilizers and other agricultural chemicals into the water, damaging the ecology river system even more.[25]

Given these possibilities, why hasn't the project been through an environmental assessment?

First Nations in Saskatchewan are troubled by the government's lack of consultation with them. Chief Bobby Cameron of the Federation of Sovereign Indigenous Nations called on the province to respect First Nations' inherent and treaty rights and include First Nations in decisions about infrastructure projects that "impact our traditional lands that we have been stewards of since time immemorial."[26] First Nations are also concerned about the project's effect on the Saskatchewan River delta, where water levels have declined by 20 percent in the past century, mostly because irrigation projects and growing cities, including Regina and Saskatoon, have been taking more and more water from the river.[27] Leavitt predicted that the concerns of First Nations will be ignored unless they take the government to court over the project.[28] It's a familiar story, isn't it? môniyâwak and our governments doing whatever they like, paying no attention to the people who were here before us. What will it take for us to behave differently?

The provincial government isn't thinking about what climate change will mean for the Westside Irrigation Rehabilitation Project, either. Water levels in the South Saskatchewan River, of which Lake Diefenbaker is a part, are currently at historic lows after years of drought.[29] That drought is almost certainly caused by anthropogenic climate change, which is central to the idea of the Anthropocene; there's a clear consensus among scientists about what's happening to our climate, and many people, including artists and writers, are engaged with the issue.[30] It's not clear to me, though, that Premier Moe understands what climate change is or what it could mean for this province. After all, he's bitterly opposed to the federal carbon tax, deciding early in 2024 to refuse to remit carbon-tax revenues to Ottawa, and in 2022, he told an audience at an event held by the Prince Albert and District Chamber of Commerce that he didn't care that Saskatchewan has the highest carbon emissions per capita in Canada.[31] He seems to hold the same beliefs as the delegates at the 2024 meeting of the Saskatchewan Association of Rural Municipalities, who passed a resolution on carbon dioxide and climate change that described "policies that vilify CO_2" as "illogical and unpredictable" measures that damage "our existing crop production systems and economy."[32] The resolution's denial of the reality of climate change and its causes was shocking to anyone who grasps the urgency of the issue. The people who voted for it are part of the Saskatchewan Party's rural political base. It seems that, like them, Moe considers economic growth to be more important than a stable climate—as if we can have the first without the second. I'm not sure there's any other explanation for the things he says and does, including doubling down on the provincial economy's reliance on fossil fuels and investing in an irrigation project that could run out of water. Neither am I certain that huge infrastructure megaprojects are the best way to make use of our limited resources. The Regina Bypass, the Saskatoon Freeway, the Lake Diefenbaker irrigation project: what if we spent those billions of dollars on health care and education? What kind of economic impact might that kind of investment have on this province?

Refusing to rename Dewdney Avenue and building new megaprojects haven't been the only recent news items worth thinking about. On September 15, 2024, the sesquicentennial of Treaty 4 was celebrated at the powwow grounds in Fort Qu'Appelle. I wanted to be there, but I was recovering from a bout of COVID-19—the first time I'd fallen ill with the virus since the pandemic began—and had to stay home, reading media reports about the event. Most of the journalists who wrote about the anniversary focused on the written treaty text and the federal government's continuing failures to live up to that document. In a lengthy feature article, for instance, filled with interviews with First Nations Chiefs and journalists as well as settler historians, the *Regina Leader-Post*'s

Murray Mandryk focused on the creation of residential schools instead of the local on-reserve schools promised in the treaty text; the lack of support for the shift by First Nations to an agricultural economy, another promise in the document; and the pass system.[33] Part of the motivation for these decisions was that the federal government simply refused to spend the money required to fulfill the promises it had made in the written treaty document; another part was simply racism against Indigenous Peoples. nêhiyaw journalist Doug Cuthand echoed Mandryk's argument. "The treaties were never properly executed and after 150 years there is still unfinished treaty business," he wrote. "While the Prairie provinces grew and prospered, the First Nations languished in poverty with no prospects for a viable future."[34]

Mandryk, Cuthand, and anyone else who points out the government's multiple and catastrophic failures to live up to the promises made in the treaty document are absolutely correct, and yet the focus of those arguments on the written treaty document is incomplete, partly because they lead us back to the core of the treaty text: the fraught notion that First Nations extinguished their title to the land by entering into treaty, the idea that the treaty was essentially a real-estate transaction. There's more to Treaty 4, and the other numbered treaties, than that piece of paper. That truth does manage to sneak in around the edges of the discussion. Cuthand points out, for instance, that while the treaty commissioners promised they would get together with First Nations annually to discuss the progress of the treaty, that only happened once, and the event was never repeated. "The result was that treaties became fossilized in the 19th century," he notes.[35] Had those ongoing meetings taken place, the relationship the treaties heralded might have become a reality. And relationship is at the core of the treaties, as Zagimē Anishinabēk First Nation Chief Lynn Acoose told CBC News at the Treaty 4 gathering. Knowing more about the treaty, she said, might encourage settlers "to learn more and develop deeper relationships with First Nations people."[36] The future of the treaty itself, she continued, must involve First Nations coming together with their settler treaty partners "to form a more equitable relationship."[37] Chief Acoose's words remind me of the ones spoken by Chief Loud Voice 150 years ago: "Let us join together and make the Treaty; when both join together it is very good."[38] Had settler governments understood the treaties as relationships, rather than real-estate deals, then the cruelties Mandryk and others rightly criticize might never have been committed.

And what about the Global Transportation Hub? It's slowly acquiring new tenants. In August 2021, the agribusiness giant Cargill announced that it would build a canola-crushing facility in the GTH. In a statement, the company indicated that it had chosen that location because of the GTH's "excellent existing highway and rail infrastructure."[39] That $350 million project is supposed to open in 2025.[40] Morguard has constructed a warehouse in the GTH, as has the Saskatchewan Liquor and Gaming Authority; SaskPower is building an operations centre on its land in the GTH as well, which will open in 2026.[41] Smaller businesses have also set up shop there.[42] The GTH is still in debt, and almost 500 acres of its land is still vacant,[43] but who knows? Maybe the naysayers and nitpickers—me included—will be proven wrong; maybe in twenty years the Global Transportation Hub will be an important part of the region's economy, instead of an expanse of empty, weedy lots. I think back to those vacant lots, the silence of the streets there, the dead-looking Canada goose that raised its head and stared defiantly at me, the sound of the wind and, in the distance, the crashing of shipping containers being stacked at the intermodal terminal and the beeping of the tractors jockeying them around. Even if the GTH becomes a success, though, even if the Regina Bypass turns out to have been a wise investment, the larger questions about the land and the treaty that allows settlers to be here, about the relationships to land that are ignored or violated by settlers, will remain unanswered—or, perhaps more accurately, unasked, except by those of us who keenly feel their illegitimacy on this land and who want to find an ethical way to live here, one centred on relationships, on connection.

I stand up and stretch my back, sore and stiff after months of sitting, writing, revising. I look through the kitchen window. There's a strong breeze—the elm trees are dancing, shaking their branches, their yellow autumn colours looking glorious in the bright sunlight—and a few clouds scud across the clear prairie sky. It's a perfect day to go for a walk. I lace up my boots, put my sun-bleached ball cap on my head, and open the front door.

ACKNOWLEDGEMENTS

So many people have contributed to *Walking the Bypass*, and I want to thank everyone who helped make this book happen. As I've noted in the first chapter, this book came out of my PhD research in the Faculty of Media, Art, and Performance at the University of Regina. I am grateful to my co-supervisors, Sherry Farrell Racette and James Daschuk, for their guidance and helpful feedback, and to the members of my committee, Jesse Rae Archibald-Barber, Kathryn Bracht, Kathleen Irwin, and Michael Trussler, for their support and engagement. I am also thankful to my external examiner, Dwayne Donald of the University of Alberta, for his thoughtful questions. My research was funded, in part, through scholarships and awards from the Faculty of Media, Art, and Performance and from the University of Regina; I'm grateful for the support. I'm also indebted to the members of the committee who chose me to receive the President's Distinguished Graduate Student Award in 2023—an honour I never expected to receive.

The first drafts of what became this book were written in the 2020 creative nonfiction workshop at the Sage Hill Writing Experience. I owe so much to Sage Hill for including me in that workshop, and to that organization's amazing staff, Tara Dawn Solheim and Caitlin Terfloth, for making that emergency pandemic remote-meeting version of its summer programming work so well; to the workshop facilitator, Tanis MacDonald; and to my workshop colleagues: Erika Batdorf, Kim Fahner, Adrienne Gruber, Roberta Laurie, and Lisa Richter. Your responses to those preliminary drafts made them better and suggested to me that this project was worth pursuing. Since those ten days in July, we have continued to meet as a group over Zoom to discuss our work with the addition of two more writers, Ariel Gordon and Elizabeth Ross, and I am beyond grateful to be included in that community. Maybe someday we'll all get to meet together in person! I also want to thank the Access Copyright Foundation for a grant that covered part of my Sage Hill tuition.

Other writer friends have read parts of this book, and their careful feedback made it better. Matthew Anderson, my friend, walking companion, and sometimes co-author, kept me from wandering into Old Testament territory beyond my level of competence, and Danica Klewchuk's notes were always helpful and honest.

Tanis has not been my only inspiring creative-writing teacher. I'm thankful to Jenna Butler, Yvonne Blomer, Lorri Neilsen Glenn, Ariel Gordon, Rachel Laverdiere, and Michael Trussler for helping me to develop as a writer. "The lyf so short, the craft so longe to lerne," Chaucer wrote in the first line of *The Parliament of Fowls* (words I have never forgotten from a poem on which I wrote a terrible undergraduate essay nearly forty years ago—thanks for making me read Chaucer, Dr. Wurtele!), and while like every other writer I will never stop learning my craft, my teachers have taught me more about writing than I could have learned in several lifetimes by myself.

The manuscript of *Walking the Bypass* won the 2022 City of Regina Writing Award. I am thankful to the City of Regina for funding that award and to the Saskatchewan Writers' Guild for administering it, as well as to the judges who selected my manuscript—Jane Munro and Eddy Boudel Tan—and the staff of the Guild, particularly Yolanda Hansen, whose email informing me that I had won the award astonished me. That award confirmed my sense that what I was writing might find readers—a tremendous encouragement.

My nêhiyawêwin teachers, Solomon Ratt, Bill Cook, Arok Wolvengrey, and Darren Okemaysim *kâki-itêt*, helped me to glimpse a way of thinking about the world I would not have considered without their assistance, and I'm incredibly grateful for their knowledge—and their patience. I'll never be a fluent speaker of nêhiyawêwin, but I learned so much from them, and from my classmates, in the language courses I took at the First Nations University of Canada. Thanks also go to Darian Agecoutay, one of my classmates, who translated my PhD dissertation abstract into nêhiyawêwin—a task I could not have accomplished. I am particularly indebted to Solomon Ratt, who repeatedly answered my vocabulary and spelling questions as I worked on this book. Getting the nêhiyawêwin right, he says, is a way to show respect to that language, and if I were to make mistakes that conveyed a sense of disrespect, I would be violating the spirit of this book. Of course, the responsibility for any errors that may have crept into these pages is entirely mine.

Thank you to Marilyn Dumont, who graciously permitted me to quote from her poem "Letter to Sir John A. Macdonald."

I'm grateful to Sky Dancer Louise Bernice Halfe and to Lifespeaker Noel Starblanket *kâki-itêt* for their wisdom, guidance, and open hearts. Louise, I hope we get to walk together again soon!

Hugh Henry answered my questions about farming, explaining things I didn't understand about how that industry works, and I will always be grateful for his hard work in planning the walks he organized in rural Saskatchewan during the past ten years, which helped to shape this project in ways I'm just beginning to understand. If you'd like to learn more about those walks, Matthew Anderson's book, *The Good Walk: Creating New Paths on Traditional Prairie Trails*, published by the University of Regina Press in 2024, provides a thoughtful and thorough account of three of them. It's a lovely book, well worth reading. I'm thankful for the friendships I made on those walks, too; among others, I want to recognize the late Richard Kotowich, who gave me advice about my PhD research while we walked along a grid road on a hot August afternoon; Pat Erhardt; Fred Ludolph; Connie Sykes; Harold Stepphun, for teaching me about prairie geology and for walking so much faster than me; Sharon Pasula; Kristin Enns-Kavanagh; Kristin Catherwood; Simone Hengen; Sister ReAnne Letourneau; Madonna Hamel; Peter Butt; Laurent (Larry) Dudragne; Dave Cyca; Barbara Anderson; and Donald Bolen. I hope we all get together someday to cross another pasture, or at least trudge up another grid road.

Other friends suggested I read things that became essential parts of this book. Geoff Travers, whom I met on the Camino de Santiago more than a decade ago, suggested Craig Mod's article to me, and Lindsey french, a former colleague in the Faculty of Media, Art, and Performance at the University of Regina, introduced me to Bettina Stoetzer's notion of the "ruderal." I am thankful to you both, and Geoff, I look forward to more walks together.

First Nations University of Canada, Luther College, the Department of Film, and the Department of English and Creative Writing, all at the University of Regina, provided me with teaching opportunities while I wrote and revised this book. After the pandemic began to recede, and people were allowed to teach face-to-face at the university again, most of that writing and revising was done in the office that the Department of English and Creative Writing and the Faculty of Arts allocated to me. That office, which gives me an excuse to walk across Wascana Centre almost every day, has been a godsend. The Department of English and Creative Writing also provided financial support for this project, for which I am grateful.

I also want to recognize Regina's Spafford Books and the much-lamented Penny University Bookstore, as well as the staff at the John Archer Library at the University of Regina and the First Nations University of Canada Regina Campus Library, for their assistance in finding research materials.

Everyone at University of Regina Press has been wonderful to work with. Acquisitions editor Karen Clark saw potential in the manuscript I submitted, and her colleague, Rachel Stapleton, led me through the process of publishing my first book with grace and patience. I'm grateful to them both, as well as to managing editor Shannon Parr and editorial assistants David McLennan, Jellyn Ayudan, and Dulce Islas Lee. The two anonymous readers for the Press gave insightful notes that made this book so much better than it was before they read it. Art director Duncan Campbell worked his usual magic with his design of the book's cover—University of Regina Press books always look beautiful. John van der Woude worked a similar kind of magic with his design of the book's interior. Copy editor Kelly Laycock's feedback was invaluable, as was proofreader Rachel Taylor's. Patricia Furdek prepared the index with care and attention. Madeleine Maillet, marketing and publicity manager, and Erin Dunlop, sales and distribution manager, made it possible for this book to find its way into your hands, and I'm grateful for their efforts. Thank you to everybody at URP.

I'm also grateful to Peter Midgley for his keen editorial eye and thoughtful suggestions, and to Alex McPhee for the beautiful map that graces this book.

Thanks to Trevor Hopkin of University Advancement and Communications at the University of Regina for spending part of a Friday afternoon taking photographs of me walking on a grid road.

Many friends offered encouragement and support, including Glenn Gordon, Yens Pedersen, and Amy Snider. Other people, whose names I don't even know, did the same thing. If you remember stopping to offer a lift to a tall man walking on the outskirts of Regina in the summer of 2020, or if you gave him a friendly wave, or served him coffee and a sandwich, you played a part in this project. Thanks!

Finally, my biggest debt of gratitude, one I can never repay, goes to Christine Ramsay. She read draft after draft of this manuscript, carefully, suggesting necessary improvements; she drove out to pick me up when my legs and feet were too tired to carry me home many times during the summer of 2020; she shouldered burdens around our home while I was off wandering around somewhere; she never stopped believing in me and my writing. Christine, I am so lucky to have you in my life. This book is dedicated to you, with much love.

NOTES

PROLOGUE: THE REGINA INDIAN INDUSTRIAL SCHOOL CEMETERY

1 See David J. Wishart, "The Great Plains Region," in *Encyclopedia of the Great Plains*, ed. David J. Wishart (University of Nebraska Press, 2011), http://plainshumanities.unl.edu/encyclopedia/intro.html; and Ian Frazier, *Great Plains* (Farrar, Straus and Giroux, 1989), 12.

2 Trevor Herriot, *Grass, Sky, Song: Promise and Peril in the World of Grassland Birds* (HarperCollins, 2010), 17.

3 Herriot, *Grass, Sky, Song*, 17–18.

4 Herriot, *Grass, Sky, Song*, 18.

5 The fullest and most recent account of the Haudenosaunee and the Haldimand Tract is Susan M. Hill, *The Clay We Are Made Of: Haudenosaunee Land Tenure on the Grand River* (University of Manitoba Press, 2017).

6 "US Presidents—Hanadagá•yas," *Onondaga Nation: People of the Hills*, accessed May 20, 2020, https://www.onondaganation.org/history/us-presidents-hanadagayas/.

7 On my discovery of and response to this fact, see Ken Wilson, "Surrender No. 40," *The Goose* 20, no. 1 (2023), article 17, https://scholars.wlu.ca/thegoose/vol20/iss1/17/.

8 See "The Toronto Purchase Treaty, No. 13 (1805)," *Mississaugas of the Credit First Nation*, November 3, 2020, https://mncfn.ca/the-toronto-purchase-treaty-no-13-1805/. In 2010 the Mississaugas of the Credit First Nation

reached a settlement worth $145 million with the federal government for the Toronto Purchase claim and the Brant Tract claim.

9 I prefer using endonyms, the words First Nations use in their own languages to denote themselves, to exonyms, the words in other languages that outsiders use, when I can—when I know enough to do that without making a mistake. *nêhiyawak* is the plural noun that refers to the Plains Cree people, while *nêhiyaw* is the singular noun; *Anihšināpēk* is the plural noun for the Saulteaux, whereas *Anihšināpē* is the singular noun. In addition, *nêhiyawêwin* is the word that refers to the Plains Cree language, and *Anihšināpēmowin* is the language spoken by the Saulteaux. Standard Roman Orthography, one of the ways of writing nêhiyawêwin, doesn't use capital letters, even at the beginnings of sentences, and I follow that convention when I use words in that language in this book.

10 On the surrender of land and extinguishment of Indigenous title by the historical numbered treaties, see Sheldon Krasowski, *No Surrender: The Land Remains Indigenous* (University of Regina Press, 2019). The location where Regina has been built might be identified in other ways, however. For instance, Myke Agecoutay, CEO of Muscowpetung Saulteaux Business Development, has stated, in an interview with the *Regina Leader-Post*'s Larissa Kurz, that historical research commissioned by Muscowpetung Saulteaux Nation indicates that more than half of the city's area is its territory, according to the First Nation's 1875 adhesion to Treaty 4. See Larissa Kurz, "Muscowpetung FN Says City Has Been Sitting on Proposal for the Yards," *Regina Leader-Post*, August 13, 2024, https://leaderpost.com/news/local-news/city-hall/muscowpetung-fn-says-idea-of-baseball-stadium-at-yards-a-surprise-to-hear.

11 See Patrick Wolfe, "Settler Colonialism and the Elimination of the Native," *Journal of Genocide Research* 8, no. 4 (2006): 387–409, https://doi.org/10.1080/14623520601056240.

12 John Terpstra, *Daylighting Chedoke: Exploring Hamilton's Hidden Creek* (James Street North Books, 2018), 92.

13 Les Back, "Marchers and Steppers: Memory, City Life and Walking," in *Walking Through Social Research*, eds. Charlotte Bates and Alex Rhys-Taylor (Routledge, 2017), 22.

14 One of my nêhiyawêwin teachers, Solomon Ratt, told me that the word *môniyâw* is a transliteration of "Montréal" which came out of the fur trade. In nêhiyawêwin, for instance, Montreal Lake, which is located near Prince Albert, on the edge of Saskatchewan's boreal forest, is "*môniyâwi-sâkahikan*."

15 Natascia Lypny, "Residential School Cemetery Protected with Heritage Designation," *Regina Leader-Post*, September 26, 2016, https://leaderpost.com/news/local-news/residential-school-cemetery-protected-with-heritage-designation.

16 D.C. Fraser, "Regina Indian Industrial School Cemetery to Get Heritage Status," *Regina Leader-Post*, July 25, 2017, https://leaderpost.com/news/saskatchewan/regina-indian-industrial-school-cemetery-to-get-heritage-status.

17 Trudy Stewart and Janine Windolph, dirs., *RIIS from Amnesia* (short film), RIIS Media Project, October 28, 2015, https://www.youtube.com/watch?v=l8yfSM87Ces.

18 Bill Barry, *People Places: The Dictionary of Saskatchewan Place Names* (Centax Books & Distribution, 1998), 284.

19 "'First Step in Reconciliation' as Government Hands Over Residential School Cemetery," *CBC News*, June 25, 2019, https://www.cbc.ca/news/canada/saskatchewan/riis-residential-school-cemetery-land-transfer-1.5188585.

20 Truth and Reconciliation Commission of Canada (TRC), *Canada's Residential Schools*, vol. 4, *Missing Children and Unmarked Burials* (McGill-Queen's University Press, 2015), 133.

21 In September 2021, thirty-eight orange aluminum grave markers were installed on the site, donated by Pasqua First Nation and Pro Metal Industries. See Lynn Giesbrecht, "Grave Markers Donated for Regina Indian Industrial School Site," *Regina Leader-Post*, September 12, 2021, https://leaderpost.com/news/local-news/grave-markers-donated-for-regina-indian-industrial-school-site.

22 TRC, *Canada's Residential Schools*, vol. 4, 133.

23 John S. Milloy, *A National Crime: The Canadian Government and the Residential School System, 1879 to 1986* (University of Manitoba Press, 1999), 82.

24 TRC, *Canada's Residential Schools*, vol. 4, 79; Miranda J. Brady and Emily Hiltz, "The Archaeology of an Image: The Persistent Persuasion of Thomas Moore Keesick's Residential School Photographs," *TOPIA: Canadian Journal of Cultural Studies* 37 (Spring 2017): 68.

25 TRC, *Canada's Residential Schools*, vol. 4, 55.

26 Truth and Reconciliation Commission of Canada (TRC), *Canada's Residential Schools*, vol. 1, *The History*, pt. 1, *Origins to 1939* (McGill-Queen's University Press, 2015), 462.

27 TRC, *Canada's Residential Schools*, vol. 1, pt. 1, 460.

28 Milloy, *A National Crime*, 116–17; J.R. Miller, *Shingwauk's Vision: A History of Native Residential Schools* (University of Toronto Press, 1996), 291–92.

29 Milloy, *A National Crime*, 155; TRC, *Canada's Residential Schools*, vol. 1, pt. 1, 527.

30 TRC, *Canada's Residential Schools*, vol. 1, pt. 1, 574.

31 TRC, *Canada's Residential Schools*, vol. 4, 62–63; TRC, *Canada's Residential Schools*, vol. 1, pt. 1, 442.

32 TRC, *Canada's Residential Schools*, vol. 1, pt. 1, 442.

33 Douglas Stewart, *The Regina Indian Industrial School (1891–1910): Historical Overview and Chronological Narrative* (Benchmark Press, 2017), 9, 30.

34 James Daschuk, *Clearing the Plains: Disease, Politics of Starvation, and the Loss of Indigenous Life*, 2nd ed. (University of Regina Press, 2019), 100–1.

35 Milloy, *A National Crime*, 3.

36 Milloy, *A National Crime*, 5–6.

37 According to filmmaker Louise BigEagle, who directed the documentary film *I Am a Boy: Thomas Moore Keesick*, Keesick died of tuberculosis four years after he was sent home. See Brady and Hiltz, "The Archaeology of an Image," 68.

38 TRC, *Canada's Residential Schools*, vol. 1, pt. 1, 278–80.

39 Alexander Morris, *The Treaties of Canada with the Indians of Manitoba and the North-West Territories, Including the Negotiations on Which They Were Based, and Other Information Relating Thereto* (Belfords, Clark & Co., 1880; repr., Coles, 1971), 96. Citations refer to the Coles edition.

40 Morris, *The Treaties of Canada*, 118.

41 Stewart, *The Regina Indian Industrial School*, 123.

42 Stewart, *The Regina Indian Industrial School*, 31. The main school building burned down in 1948, and all the other buildings (the shops and stables, the carpenter's and principal's residences, the bakery, and the trades building) have been demolished.

43 TRC, *Canada's Residential Schools*, vol. 1, pt. 1, 319.

44 Sam Laskaris, "National Chief Says Canada's True Past Being Exposed," *Windspeaker*, February 14, 2022, https://windspeaker.com/news/windspeaker-news/national-chief-says-canadas-true-past-being-exposed.

45 TRC, *Canada's Residential Schools*, vol. 1, pt. 1, 271; Miller, *Shingwauk's Vision*, 353.

46 Trevor Sutter, "Province's Last Residential School Set for Closure," *Saskatoon Star-Phoenix*, July 2, 1998: A9.

47 Lee Maracle, *My Conversations With Canadians* (Book*hug Press, 2017), 34.

48 J. William Brennan, *Regina: An Illustrated History* (Lorimer, 1989), 12, 15.

49 Brian Titley, *The Frontier World of Edgar Dewdney* (University of British Columbia Press, 2000), 143.

50 See Titley, *The Frontier World of Edgar Dewdney*, 66–67; Daschuk, *Clearing the Plains*, 114–15; and Michael Asch, *On Being Here to Stay: Treaties and Aboriginal Rights in Canada* (University of Toronto Press, 2014), 161.

51 Kerry Benjoe, "What's in a Name? A Lot, According to Some Regina Residents," *Regina Leader-Post*, January 25, 2017, https://leaderpost.com/news/local-news/whats-in-a-name-a-lot-according-to-some-regina-residents.

52 Larissa Kurz, "'Shameful': Quick Debate Leads to 7–3 Vote Against New Name for Dewdney Ave.," *Regina Leader-Post*, August 21, 2024, https://

leaderpost.com/news/local-news/city-hall/no-new-name-for-dewdney-avenue-says-regina-city-council.

53 Doug Cuthand, "Canada Must Be Better Than Our History," *Saskatoon Star-Phoenix*, August 1, 2020, https://thestarphoenix.com/opinion/columnists/cuthand-canada-must-be-better-than-our-history.

54 Hailey Salvian, "No Charges Laid in GTH Investigation: RCMP," *CBC News*, July 25, 2018, https://www.cbc.ca/news/canada/saskatchewan/no-charges-laid-in-gth-land-deal-investigation-rcmp-1.4761263.

ONE: WEST/PAHKISIMOTÂHK

1 See John Davies, *Walking the M62* (Lulu Self-Publishing, 2007).

2 See Iain Sinclair, *London Orbital: A Walk Around the M25* (Penguin, 2003).

3 Sinclair, *London Orbital*, 272.

4 Robert Macfarlane, *The Old Ways: A Journey on Foot* (Penguin, 2013), 235.

5 For a detailed and lively account of these walks, see Matthew R. Anderson, *The Good Walk: Creating New Paths on Traditional Prairie Trails* (University of Regina Press, 2024).

6 On research-creation scholarship, see Natalie Loveless, *How to Make Art at the End of the World: A Manifesto for Research-Creation* (Duke University Press, 2019).

7 Andrew Suknaski, *Wood Mountain Poems* (Macmillan, 1976).

8 See Ken Wilson, "*Wood Mountain Walk*: Afterthoughts on a Pilgrimage for Andrew Suknaski," *International Journal of Religious Tourism and Pilgrimage* 7, no. 1 (2019): 123–34, https://arrow.tudublin.ie/ijrtp/vol7/iss1/13/; "*Wood Mountain Walk* and the Possibilities of Decolonization through Relationships with People and Land in Solo Walking Performance," *Canadian Theatre Review* 182, no. 2 (2020): 51–56; and "White Man Walking: Settler Ambulation in Colonised Spaces," in *Walking Bodies: Papers, Provocations, Actions from Walking's New Movements, the Conference*, eds. Helen Billinghurst, Claire Hind, and Phil Smith (Triarchy Press, 2020), 193–203.

9 Allison Aubrey, "Forest Bathing: A Retreat to Nature Can Boost Immunity and Mood," *NPR.org*, July 17, 2017, https://www.npr.org/sections/health-shots/2017/07/17/536676954/forest-bathing-a-retreat-to-nature-can-boost-immunity-and-mood.

10 Jonathan Raban, *Bad Land: An American Romance* (Vintage, 1996), 64, 85.

11 See Henry David Thoreau, "Walking," in *Essays: A Fully Annotated Edition*, ed. Jeffrey S. Cramer (Yale University Press, 2013), 243–80, https://doi.org/10.12987/9780300165623.

12 See Matthew R. Anderson, "Why Canadians Need the Right to Roam," *The*

Conversation, July 29, 2018, https://theconversation.com/why-canadians-need-the-right-to-roam-100497; and Ken Ilgunas, *This Land Is Our Land: How We Lost the Right to Roam and How to Take It Back* (Plume, 2018); see also Laura Sciarpelletti, "Changes to Sask. Trespassing Laws Come into Effect Jan. 1, Will Require Permission to Access Land," *CBC News*, December 16, 2021, https://www.cbc.ca/news/canada/saskatchewan/people-must-ask-rural-sask-property-owners-for-permission-to-access-property-1.6288061; and Robin Ganev, "Making Private Property in Rural Britain and Canada," *Active History*, March 23, 2022, https://activehistory.ca/2022/03/making-private-property-in-rural-britain-and-canada/.

13 Thia James, "Tackling Rural Crime Remains Focus for Province, Sask. Organizations," *Regina Leader-Post*, December 18, 2021, https://leaderpost.com/news/local-news/tackling-rural-crime-remains-focus-for-province-sask-organizations/wcm/4ba91ae7-2ee6-41d5-a96a-894194d9a8b3.

14 See Gina Starblanket and Dallas Hunt, *Storying Violence: Unravelling Colonial Narratives in the Stanley Trial* (ARP Books, 2020); Kent Roach, *Canadian Justice, Indigenous Justice: The Colten Boushie and Gerald Stanley Case* (McGill-Queen's University Press, 2019); and Harold R. Johnson, *Peace and Good Order: The Case for Indigenous Justice in Canada* (McClelland & Stewart, 2019).

15 Canadian Press, "Most Support Changing Sask. Trespassing Laws After Colten Boushie's Death: Survey," *CTV News*, November 15, 2018, https://www.ctvnews.ca/canada/most-support-changing-sask-trespassing-laws-after-colten-boushie-death-survey-1.4178884.

16 Doug Cuthand, "Trespass Law Amendment Shows No Respect for Treaty Rights," *Saskatoon Star-Phoenix*, January 22, 2022, https://thestarphoenix.com/opinion/columnists/cuthand-trespass-law-amendment-shows-no-respect-for-treaty-rights.

17 "The feat of surveying the fertile lands of the prairie provinces in a checkerboard fashion is one of the outstanding accomplishments of the early Canadian government," is the first sentence of James G. MacGregor's *Vision of an Ordered Land: The Story of the Dominion Land Survey* (Western Producer Prairie Books, 1981); see ix.

18 John C. Lehr, John Everitt, and Simon Evans, "The Making of the Prairie Landscape," *Prairie Forum* 33, no. 1 (2008): 5.

19 Lehr, Everitt, and Evans, "The Making of the Prairie Landscape," 5.

20 Tim Ingold, *Lines* (Routledge, 2016), 85.

21 Ingold, *Lines*, 85.

22 George Macaulay Trevelyan, "Walking," in *Clio, a Muse and Other Essays Literary and Pedestrian* (Longman, Greens, 1914), 67.

23 Trevelyan, "Walking," 68–69.

24 Trevelyan, "Walking," 69.

25 Trevelyan, "Walking," 69–70.
26 Trevelyan, "Walking," 70–71.
27 Trevelyan, "Walking," 71.
28 Ganev, "Making Private Property in Rural Britain and Canada."
29 Walt Whitman, "Song of the Open Road," in *Complete Poetry and Selected Prose*, ed. James E. Miller Jr. (Houghton Mifflin, 1959), 108, section 1, lines 1–3.
30 Whitman, "Song of the Open Road," 109–10, section 5, lines 6, 9.
31 Whitman, "Song of the Open Road," 111, section 9, lines 4–6.
32 Whitman, "Song of the Open Road," 115, section 15, lines 7–11.
33 See, for instance, Emily Talen, "Pedestrian Access as a Measure of Urban Quality," *Planning Practice and Research* 17, no. 3 (2002): 264–66, https://doi.org/10.1080/02697450220000563 4. Talen's research in Portland, Oregon, led to her conclusion that distances of a quarter mile or less are considered walkable by residents of that city. No similar research has been conducted into walkability in Regina, but it seems unlikely that Reginans are much different from Portlandians in regards to walking.
34 Marc Augé, *Non-Places: Introduction to an Anthropology of Supermodernity*, trans. John Howe (Verso, 1995), 86.
35 Augé, *Non-Places*, 86.
36 Augé, *Non-Places*, 96.
37 Zygmunt Bauman, *Liquid Modernity* (Polity, 2000), 102–3.
38 See Louis Althusser, "Ideology and Ideological State Apparatuses (Notes Towards an Investigation)," in *Lenin and Philosophy and Other Essays*, trans. Ben Brewster (NYU Press, 2001), 123.
39 Althusser, "Ideology and Ideological State Apparatuses," 123.
40 Trevor Herriot, *The Road Is How: A Prairie Pilgrimage Through Nature, Desire, and Soul* (Harper Perennial, 2014), 16–17.
41 Sylvia McAdam (Saysewahum), *Nationhood Interrupted: Revitalizing nêhiyaw Legal Systems* (Purich, 2015), 61.
42 John Borrows, *Canada's Indigenous Constitution* (University of Toronto Press, 2010), 84.
43 Harold R. Johnson, *The Power of Story: On Truth, the Trickster, and New Fictions for a New Era* (Biblioasis, 2022), 144–45.
44 Ariel Gordon, *Treed: Walking in Canada's Urban Forests* (Wolsak and Wynn, 2020), 49.
45 Don Hill, "Listening to Stones: Learning in Leroy Little Bear's Laboratory: Dialogue in the World Outside," *Alberta Views*, September 1, 2008, https://albertaviews.ca/listening-to-stones/.
46 Barb Pacholik, "Regina Bypass Opens to Traffic," *Regina Leader-Post*, October 29, 2019, A3.
47 Legislative Assembly of Saskatchewan, *Debates and Proceedings (Hansard)*, 28th Legislature, 38th Session, Vol. 60, No. 13A, November 15, 2018,

4859, http://docs.legassembly.sk.ca/legdocs/Legislative%20Assembly/Hansard/28L3S/181115Debates.pdf.

48 Pacholik, "Regina Bypass Opens to Traffic," A3.

49 Pacholik, "Regina Bypass Opens to Traffic," A3.

50 Pacholik, "Regina Bypass Opens to Traffic," A3.

51 Bill Barry reports that the source of Grand Coulee's name is unknown. See *People Places*, 150.

52 William Least Heat-Moon, *PrairyErth (a deep map)* (Mariner Books, 1999), 363.

53 Trevor Herriot, *Grass, Sky, Song: Promise and Peril in the World of Grassland Birds* (HarperCollins, 2010), 2; Jonathan Lambert, "We've Lost 3 Billion Birds Since 1970 in North America," *Science News*, September 19, 2019, https://www.sciencenews.org/article/3-billion-birds-lost-since-1970-north-america.

54 See James Daschuk, *Clearing the Plains: Disease, Politics of Starvation, and the Loss of Indigenous Life*, 2nd ed. (University of Regina Press, 2019), 99–126.

55 Katie Doke Sawatzky, "The State of Native Prairie in Saskatchewan," *PrairieCommons.ca*, October 1, 2018, http://www.prairiecommons.ca/?page_id=300; see also Katie Doke Sawatzky, "It's Time to Save the Prairie: Against a Bleak Climate Future, Our Grasslands Offer Hope," in *Divided: Populism, Polarization and Power in the New Saskatchewan*, eds. JoAnn Jaffe, Patricia W. Elliott, and Cora Sellers (Fernwood, 2021), 453–67; and Teal Fisher, Joanne Marchand, and Ericka Donald, "Saskatchewan Native Prairie Habitat Inventory: A Collaborative Study Between Saskatchewan Polytechnic and Environment Canada," unpublished research paper, June 23, 2020, 23.

56 Dan Kraus, "Why Canada's Prairies Are the World's Most Endangered Ecosystem," *Nature Conservancy of Canada*, October 24, 2016, https://www.natureconservancy.ca/en/blog/archive/grasslands-the-most.html.

57 Stephanie Kwetásel'wet Wood, "Meet the People Saving Canada's Native Grasslands," *The Narwhal*, July 31, 2020, https://thenarwhal.ca/carbon-cache-grasslands/.

58 Matthew R. Anderson, "Pilgrimage and the Challenging of a Canadian Foundational Myth," in *Pilgrimage in Practice: Narration, Reclamation and Healing*, eds. Ian S. McIntosh, E. Moore Quinn, and Vivian Keely (CABI, 2018), 153.

59 Simon Ash-Moccasin, "I Was Racially Profiled, Roughed Up, & Detailed by Police for Being Indigenous," *Briarpatch Magazine*, December 17, 2014, https://briarpatchmagazine.com/articles/view/i-was-racially-profiled.

60 Jennifer Ackerman, "Settlement Reached Four Years After Incident Between Indigenous Man and Regina Police," *Regina Leader-Post*, July 27, 2018,

https://leaderpost.com/news/local-news/settlement-reached-four-years-after-incident-between-indigenous-man-and-regina-police.

61 Adriana Christianson, "Sask. Woman Describes Threatening Encounter with Landowner," *980 CJME News*, September 14, 2018, https://www.cjme.com/2018/09/14/sask-woman-describes-threatening-encounter-with-landowner/.

62 Garnette Cadogan, "Walking While Black: Garnette Cadogan on the Realities of Being Black in America," *Literary Hub*, July 8, 2016, https://lithub.com/walking-while-black/; J. Drew Lanham, "9 Rules for the Black Birdwatcher," *Orion*, October 23, 2013, https://orionmagazine.org/article/9-rules-for-the-black-birdwatcher/.

63 Matt Vis, "Brayden Bushby, Convicted of Manslaughter in Trailer-Hitch Death of Indigenous Mom Barbara Kentner, to Serve 8 Years in Prison," *CBC News*, June 7, 2021, https://www.cbc.ca/amp/1.6056010.

64 For a discussion of the lack of safety experienced by pedestrians who are women, see Rebecca Solnit, *Wanderlust: A History of Walking* (Penguin, 2000), 232–46; for a contemporary Canadian account of what women experience while walking, see Tanis MacDonald, *Straggle: Adventures in Walking While Female* (Wolsak & Wynn, 2022), especially the essays "We, Megafauna" (9–21), "Veil, Valley, Viaduct" (131–39), and "Vigil" (145–55).

65 On this point, see Robin Wall Kimmerer, "Speaking of Nature: Finding Language That Affirms Our Kinship with the Natural World," *Orion*, March/April 2017, https://orionmagazine.org/article/speaking-of-nature/.

TWO: EAST/SÂKÂSTÊNOHK

1 Daniel Coleman, *Yardwork: A Biography of an Urban Place* (James Street North Books, 2017), 10.

2 Coleman, *Yardwork*, 10.

3 Vanessa Watts, "Indigenous Place-Thought and Agency Amongst Humans and Non-Humans (First Woman and Sky Woman Go On a European World Tour!)," *Decolonization: Indigeneity, Education & Society* 2, no. 1 (2013): 21, https://jps.library.utoronto.ca/index.php/des/article/view/19145/16234.

4 Watts, "Indigenous Place-Thought and Agency," 23.

5 Watts, "Indigenous Place-Thought and Agency," 23.

6 See Genesis 1:26 (King James Version): "And God said, Let us make man in our image, after our likeness: and let them have dominion over the fish of the sea, and over the fowl of the air, and over the cattle, and over all the earth, and over every creeping thing that creepeth upon the earth."

7 *Oxford English Dictionary*, s.v. "dominion (n)," July 2023, https://doi.org/10.1093/oed/6992135972.

8 On the Judeo-Christian origin story, the cosmology it creates, and the way that its restless movement makes relationships with the land difficult, see Coleman, *Yardwork*, 29–35. Settlers who brought other faith traditions with them to this place would see it through the lenses of other origin stories and cosmologies, which would no doubt affect the way they relate to the land. My focus on the faith tradition Coleman discusses reflects the fact that it's the one in which we both were raised; I'm not qualified to talk about other faith traditions, since I know so little about them.

9 See Trevor Herriot, *The Road Is How: A Prairie Pilgrimage Through Nature, Desire, and Soul* (HarperCollins, 2014).

10 Trevor Herriot, *Grass, Sky, Song: Promise and Peril in the World of Grassland Birds* (HarperCollins, 2010), 3.

11 Herriot, *Grass, Sky, Song*, 4.

12 Herriot, *Grass, Sky, Song*, 11.

13 Herriot, *Grass, Sky, Song*, 12.

14 Jeffrey A. Lockwood, *Prairie Soul: Finding Grace in the Earth Beneath My Feet* (Skinner House Books, 2004), 8.

15 Lockwood, *Prairie Soul*, 34–35.

16 Lockwood, *Prairie Soul*, 38.

17 Lockwood, *Prairie Soul*, 140–41.

18 Robinson, in Jill Carter, Karyn Recollet, and Dylan Robinson, "Interventions into the Maw of Old World Hunger: Frog Monsters, Kinstellatory Maps, and Radical Relationalities in a Project of Reworlding," in *Canadian Performance Histories and Historiographies*, New Essays in Canadian Theatre Vol. 7, ed. Heather Davis-Fisch (Playwrights Canada Press, 2017), 210.

19 Robinson, in Carter, Recollet, and Robinson, "Interventions into the Maw of Old World Hunger," 210.

20 Jack D. Forbes, *Columbus and Other Cannibals: The Wétiko Disease of Exploitation, Imperialism, and Terrorism*, rev. ed. (Seven Stories Press, 2008), 22.

21 Robin Wall Kimmerer, *Braiding Sweetgrass: Indigenous Wisdom, Scientific Knowledge, and the Teachings of Plants* (Milkweed Editions, 2013), 307.

22 Kristina Fagan Bidwell, "'Our New Storytellers': Cree Literature in Saskatchewan," in *The Literary History of Saskatchewan*, vol. 1, *Beginnings*, ed. David Carpenter (Coteau Books, 2013), 9–11.

23 Edward Ahenakew, "Cree Trickster Tales," *Journal of American Folklore* 42, no. 166 (1929): 352, https://www.jstor.org/stable/535231.

24 Ahenakew, "Cree Trickster Tales," 352.

25 Ahenakew, "Cree Trickster Tales," 352.

26 In Solomon Ratt's version of the story, the ermine enters the wîhtikow through its anus. Ahenakew may have bowdlerized the story for his settler

audience, who might have objected to a full representation of the wîhtikow's body. See Solomon Ratt, *kâ-pî-isi-kiskisiyân / The Way I Remember* (University of Regina Press, 2023), 323.

27 Ahenakew, "Cree Trickster Tales," 352–53.

28 Trevor Herriot, "The River Within Us," in *The Eye in the Thicket: Essays at a Natural History*, ed. Séan Virgo (Saskatoon: Thistledown, 2002), 110.

29 Herriot, "The River Within Us," 110.

30 Robinson, in Carter, Recollet, and Robinson, "Interventions into the Maw of Old World Hunger," 208.

31 Rebecca Solnit, *Hope in the Dark: Untold Histories, Wild Possibilities*, 3rd ed. (Haymarket Books, 2016), xiv.

32 "Why a Bypass?" *Regina Bypass Partners*, accessed May 12, 2020, https://www.reginabypass.ca/project/why-a-bypass/.

33 Adam Mann, "What's Up with That: Building Bigger Roads Makes Traffic Even Worse," *Wired*, June 17, 2014, https://www.wired.com/2014/06/wuwt-traffic-induced-demand/.

34 See Gilles Duranton and Matthew A. Turner, "The Fundamental Law of Road Congestion: Evidence from US Cities," *American Economic Review* 101, no. 6 (2011): 2616–52, http://www.aeaweb.org/articles.php?doi= 10.1257/aer.101.6.2616.

35 Joe Couture, "Councillor Pushes for Highway Bypass," *Regina Leader-Post*, February 20, 2010: A4.

36 Joe Couture, "Work Underway on West Regina Bypass," *Regina Leader-Post*, September 22, 2011: A3.

37 Couture, "Work Underway on West Regina Bypass," A3.

38 Bruce Johnstone, "Transport Hub Touted; Regina Distribution Centre Will See 1,400 Trucks Weekly When Fully Operational," *Saskatoon Star-Phoenix*, February 2, 2011: C6.

39 D.C. Fraser, "West Bypass Not Nearly as Busy as Projected When GTH Was Built: NDP," *Regina Leader-Post*, October 30, 2018, https://leaderpost.com/news/saskatchewan/west-bypass-not-nearly-as-busy-as-projected-when-gth-was-built-ndp.

40 Fraser, "West Bypass Not Nearly as Busy."

41 Harold Lerat (with Linda Ungar), *Treaty Promises, Indian Reality: Life on a Reserve* (Purich, 2005), 60.

42 Lerat, *Treaty Promises, Indian Reality*, 98–102.

43 Lerat, *Treaty Promises, Indian Reality*, 72.

44 Lerat, *Treaty Promises, Indian Reality*, 104–5.

45 Lerat, *Treaty Promises, Indian Reality*, 109–11.

46 Indigenous Services Canada, "Treaty Land Entitlement in Saskatchewan," April 11, 2017, https://www.sac-isc.gc.ca/eng/1100100034825/1611943779434.

47 Creeden Martell, "Awasis Solar Project to Provide Power for 2,500 Homes," *Regina Leader-Post*, November 9, 2022, https://leaderpost.com/news/local-

news/awasis-solar-project-to-provide-power-for-2500-homes.

48 Creeden Martell, "Construction Next Step After Wind Farm Deal Involving Cowessess," *Regina Leader-Post*, March 10, 2023, https://leaderpost.com/news/construction-next-step-after-wind-farm-deal-involving-cowessess.

THREE: SOUTH/SÂWANOHK

1 Robert Frost, "Nothing Gold Can Stay," in *The Poetry of Robert Frost*, ed. Edward Connery Lathem (Holt, Rinehart and Winston, 1969), 222–23, line 1.

2 David Sedaris, "Stepping Out: Living the Fitbit Life," *New Yorker*, June 23, 2014, https://www.newyorker.com/magazine/2014/06/30/stepping-out-3.

3 Charles Wilkins, *Walk to New York: A Journey Out of the Wilds of Canada* (Toronto: Viking Canada, 2004), 85.

4 Wilkins, *Walk to New York*, 85.

5 Wilkins, *Walk to New York*, 85.

6 Tara Isabella Burton, "The Prosperity Gospel, Explained: Why Joel Osteen Believes That Prayer Can Make You Rich," *Vox*, September 1, 2017, https://www.vox.com/identities/2017/9/1/15951874/prosperity-gospel-explained-why-joel-osteen-believes-prayer-can-make-you-rich-trump.

7 Burton, "The Prosperity Gospel, Explained."

8 Mike Rollo, dir., *The Broken Altar* (short film), 2013.

9 Percy Bysshe Shelley, "Mutability," in *Shelley's Poetry and Prose*, eds. Donald H. Reiman and Sharon B. Powers (Norton, 1977), 88.

10 Jeffrey A. Lockwood, *Prairie Soul: Finding Grace in the Earth Beneath My Feet* (Skinner House Books, 2004), 20.

11 Lockwood, *Prairie Soul*, 20.

12 Lockwood, *Prairie Soul*, 22.

13 Lockwood, *Prairie Soul*, 23.

14 Lockwood, *Prairie Soul*, 25.

15 Lockwood, *Prairie Soul*, 27.

16 Bettina Stoetzer, "Ruderal Ecologies: Rethinking Nature, Migration, and the Urban Landscape in Berlin," *Cultural Anthropology* 33, no. 2 (2018): 297.

17 Stoetzer, "Ruderal Ecologies," 297.

18 David Abram, *The Spell of the Sensuous: Perception and Language in a More-Than-Human World*, 2nd ed. (Vintage, 2017), 44.

19 Abram, *The Spell of the Sensuous*, 45.

20 Abram, *The Spell of the Sensuous*, 47.

21 Abram, *The Spell of the Sensuous*, 68.

22 Bill Barry, *People Places: The Dictionary of Saskatchewan Place Names* (Centax Books & Distribution, 1998), 310.

23 Frank Flegel, "Abandoned Church Deconsecrated," *Prairie Messenger*, May 2,

2018, 7, https://stpetersabbey.ca/wp/wp-content/uploads/2021/03/pm-05-02-2018.vol95_no44pdf-min-1.pdf.

24 J. William Brennan, *Regina: An Illustrated History* (James Lorimer & Company, 1989), 175.

25 Brennan, *Regina*, 175, 177.

26 Brennan, *Regina*, 177.

27 Bruce Johnstone, "Subdivision Worth $1B; New Neighbourhood Near Regina's Airport," *Regina Leader-Post*, July 10, 2007: A1.

28 Natascia Lypny, "Sherwood Reeve Removed; Inquiry Finds 'Horrendous' Conflict of Interest Issues; Under Review by RCMP," *Regina Leader-Post*, February 6, 2015: A1.

29 Natascia Lypny, "Wascana Village Plans Expire," *Regina Leader-Post*, January 12, 2016, https://leaderpost.com/news/local-news/wascana-village-plans-expire.

30 Charlotte McDonald, "How Many Earths Do We Need?," *BBC News*, June 16, 2015, https://www.bbc.com/news/magazine-33133712.

31 Robin Wall Kimmerer, "Speaking of Nature: Finding Language That Affirms Our Kinship with the Natural World," *Orion*, March/April 2017, https://orionmagazine.org/article/speaking-of-nature/.

32 Kimmerer, "Speaking of Nature."

33 Kimmerer, "Speaking of Nature."

34 Kimmerer, "Speaking of Nature."

35 Jeremy Lurgio, "Saving the Whanganui: Can Personhood Rescue a River?" *Guardian*, November 29, 2019, https://www.theguardian.com/world/2019/nov/30/saving-the-whanganui-can-personhood-rescue-a-river. Lurgio points out that while being recognized as a living being has not eliminated threats to its ecology, the new law might give the Whanganui a better chance of survival if the law holds people to account for their behaviour towards it. Other rivers, including the Magpie River in northern Quebec, have also been granted personhood; see Chloe Berge, "This Canadian River Is Now Legally a Person. It's Not the Only One," *National Geographic*, April 15, 2022, https://www.nationalgeographic.com/travel/article/these-rivers-are-now-considered-people-what-does-that-mean-for-travelers.

36 For one such attempt, see Ken Wilson, "Populus," *Queen's Quarterly* 130, no. 1 (2023): 146–59.

37 Trevor Herriot, *Grass, Sky, Song: Promise and Peril in the World of Grassland Birds* (HarperCollins, 2010), 36.

38 Herriot, *Grass, Sky, Song*, 37.

39 Herriot, *Grass, Sky, Song*, 37.

40 Kim Tallbear, "Dossier: Theorizing Queer Inhumanisms: An Indigenous Reflection on Working Beyond the Human/Nonhuman," *GLQ: A Journal of Lesbian and Gay Studies* 21, nos 2–3 (2015): 234.

41 Ella Deloria, "Meadow-lark and the Rattlesnake," in *Dakota Texts* (University of Nebraska Press, 2006), 81–82.
42 Tallbear, "Dossier: Theorizing Queer Inhumanisms," 235.
43 Tallbear, "Dossier: Theorizing Queer Inhumanisms," 234.
44 Herriot, *Grass, Sky, Song*, 42.
45 Vanessa Brown, "Province Introduces New Bypass," *Regina Leader-Post*, February 13, 2013: A3.
46 Brown, "Province Introduces New Bypass," A3.
47 Organization for Economic Co-operation and Development (OECD), *Public-Private Partnerships: In Pursuit of Risk Sharing and Value for Money* (OECD Publishing, 2008), 17, https://doi.org/10.1787/9789264046733-en.
48 OECD, *Public-Private Partnerships*, 20–21.
49 Craig Baird, "City Announces Substantial Completion of Wastewater Treatment Plant," *Regina Leader-Post*, December 20, 2016, https://leaderpost.com/news/local-news/city-announces-substantial-completion-of-water-treatment-plant.
50 Craig Baird, "What Will the Stadium's Final Price Tag Really Be?," *Regina Leader-Post*, June 9, 2017, https://leaderpost.com/news/local-news/what-will-the-stadiums-final-price-tag-really-be.
51 Bruce Johnstone, "P3s Positive, Not Always Perfect; Pros, Cons Discussed at Conference," *Regina Leader-Post*, June 4, 2013: D1.
52 Brown, "Province Introduces New Bypass," A3.
53 Pierre-André Hudon, "A Critique of Public-Private Partnerships in Quebec: Democratic Deficiencies and Unethical Procurement," *Public Integrity* 13, no. 3 (2011): 257, https://www.tandfonline.com/doi/abs/10.2753/PIN1099-9922130306.
54 Hudon, "A Critique of Public-Private Partnerships in Quebec," 270.
55 Bruce Johnstone, "To P3 or Not to P3?," *Regina Leader-Post*, October 26, 2013, B1.
56 Johnstone, "To P3 or not to P3?," B1.
57 Johnstone, "To P3 or not to P3?," B1.
58 Baird, "City Announces Substantial Completion of Wastewater Treatment Plant."
59 Alex MacPherson, "Early 'Concerns' Over Roof at Sask. Hospital 'Were Well-Founded': Email," *Saskatoon Star-Phoenix*, January 21, 2020, https://thestarphoenix.com/news/local-news/early-concerns-over-roof-at-sask-hospital-were-well-founded-saskbuilds-project-director; Arthur White-Crummey, "Hot Toilet Water at Sask. Hospital North Battleford Fires Up Debate in Legislature," *Regina Leader-Post*, June 24, 2020, https://leaderpost.com/news/saskatchewan/hot-toilet-water-at-sask-hospital-north-battleford-fires-up-debate-in-legislature.
60 See Adam Hunter, "Gov't Says Farm Equipment May Have to Drive On

Curb of New Balgonie Overpass," CBC *News*, July 31, 2017, https://www.cbc.ca/news/canada/saskatchewan/part-of-new-overpass-too-narrow-says-balgonie-farmer-1.4229553; and D.C. Fraser, "Province Responds to Concern New Bypass Roundabout Too Small for Big Vehicles," *Regina Leader-Post*, August 1, 2017, https://leaderpost.com/news/saskatchewan/province-responds-to-concern-new-bypass-roundabout-too-small-for-big-vehicles. More than a year later, the provincial government stated that the issue was "a minor deficiency" that had been repaired by VINCI, the project's private-sector partner, at no expense to the public; see Adam Hunter, "Regina Bypass Deficiency Costs Not a Concern for Taxpayers: Gov't," CBC *News*, November 17, 2018, https://www.cbc.ca/news/canada/saskatchewan/regina-bypass-deficiencies-1.4909460.

61 Natascia Lypny, "Feds Earmark $200M for Bypass Project; Private Firm Will Build, Operate Highway," *Regina Leader-Post*, May 6, 2014: A1.

62 "VINCI Construction," *VINCI*, February 29, 2024, https://www.vinci.com/vinci.nsf/en/item/business-line-vinci-construction.htm.

63 Canadian Press, "Saskatchewan Government Says Company Chosen to Build Bypass Disclosed Allegations," *Globe and Mail*, June 10, 2015, https://www.theglobeandmail.com/feeds/canadian-press/saskatchewan/saskatchewan-government-says-company-chosen-to-build-bypass-disclosed-allegations/article24910113/.

64 Legislative Assembly of Saskatchewan, Standing Committee on the Economy, *Verbatim Report (Hansard)*, 28th Legislature, No. 14, May 2, 2017, 291, https://docs.legassembly.sk.ca/legdocs/Legislative%20Committees/ECO/Debates/170502Debates-ECO.pdf.

65 Craig Slater, "Route Selected, Plans Ongoing," *Regina Leader-Post*, June 19, 2013: A1.

66 Emma Graney, "Bypass Costs Climbing; $1.88B Doesn't Include Land Purchases," *Regina Leader-Post*, August 6, 2015: A1.

67 Graney, "Bypass Costs Climbing," A1.

68 Murray Mandryk, "Sask. Party Bypasses Due Diligence," *Regina Leader-Post*, September 5, 2015: A6.

69 Murray Mandryk, "P3 Secrecy Disrespectful to Taxpayers," *Regina Leader-Post*, October 25, 2015: A8.

70 Murray Mandryk, "Government Fumbles the Infrastructure File," *Regina Leader-Post*, February 1, 2020: A10.

71 Mandryk, "Government Fumbles the Infrastructure File," A10.

72 Natascia Lypny, "Sask. Party Wins Majority," Saskatchewan Votes 2020, CBC *News*, https://newsinteractives.cbc.ca/elections/saskatchewan/2020/results/.

FOUR: NORTH/KÎWÊTINOHK

1 Jane Bennett, *Vibrant Matter: A Political Ecology of Things* (Duke University Press, 2010), vii.
2 Bennett, *Vibrant Matter*, viii.
3 Bennett, *Vibrant Matter*, 3–5.
4 Bennett, *Vibrant Matter*, 112–13.
5 On eating and "vibrant materiality," see Bennett, *Vibrant Matter*, 39–51.
6 See William Blake, preface to "Milton: a Poem in [1] 2 Books," *Blake Complete Writings: With Variant Readings*, 2nd ed., ed. Geoffrey Keynes (Oxford University Press, 1969), 481, line 8.
7 Bruno Latour, *Down to Earth: Politics in the New Climatic Regime*, trans. Catherine Porter (Polity, 2018), 93.
8 Latour, *Down to Earth*, 95.
9 Latour, *Down to Earth*, 95.
10 Zoe Todd, "An Indigenous Feminist's Take on the Ontological Turn: 'Ontology' Is Just Another Word for Colonialism," *Journal of Historical Sociology* 29, no. 1 (2016): 9, https://doi.org/10.1111/johs.12124.
11 Watts, "Indigenous Place-Thought and Agency," 30.
12 Leanne Betasamosake Simpson, "Land as Pedagogy: Nishnaabeg Intelligence and Rebellious Transformation," *Decolonization: Indigeneity, Education & Society* 3, no. 3 (2014): 19, https://jps.library.utoronto.ca/index.php/des/article/view/22170/17985.
13 Simpson, "Land as Pedagogy," 19.
14 Dwayne Donald, "We Need a New Story: Walking and the *wâhkôhtowin* Imagination," *Journal of the Canadian Association for Curriculum Studies* 18, no. 2 (2021): 55, https://doi.org/10.25071/1916-4467.40492.
15 Donald, "We Need a New Story," 55.
16 Donald, "We Need a New Story," 55–56.
17 Donald, "We Need a New Story," 56.
18 Donald, "We Need a New Story," 56.
19 Donald, "We Need a New Story," 61.
20 Donald, "We Need a New Story," 61.
21 Donald, "We Need a New Story," 61.
22 Donald, "We Need a New Story," 61.
23 Willie Ermine, "The Ethical Space of Engagement," *Indigenous Law Journal* 6, no. 1 (2007): 202, https://jps.library.utoronto.ca/index.php/ilj/article/view/27669/20400.
24 See Sharon Butala, *The Perfection of the Morning: An Apprenticeship in Nature* (Harper Perennial, 1995), 185–86.
25 Warren Cariou, "Haunted Prairie: Aboriginal 'Ghosts' and the Spectres of Settlement," *University of Toronto Quarterly* 75, no. 2 (2006): 728–29, https://doi.org/10.1353/utq.2006.0245.
26 Beth Cuthand, "For All the Settlers Who Secretly Sing," in *Native Poetry in*

Canada: A Contemporary Anthology, eds. Jeannette C. Armstrong and Lally Grauer (Broadview Press, 2001), 133–34.

27 Robert Macfarlane, *Landmarks* (Hamish Hamilton, 2015), 1.

28 Macfarlane, *Landmarks*, 2–3.

29 Macfarlane, *Landmarks*, 4–5.

30 Macfarlane, *Landmarks*, 5.

31 Macfarlane, *Landmarks*, 10.

32 Trevor Herriot, *Grass, Sky, Song: Promise and Peril in the World of Grassland Birds* (HarperCollins, 2010), 11.

33 Robin Wall Kimmerer, *Braiding Sweetgrass: Indigenous Wisdom, Scientific Knowledge, and the Teachings of Plants* (Milkweed Editions, 2013), 208.

34 Macfarlane, *Landmarks*, 10.

35 Arok Wolvengrey, *nêhiyawêwin: itwêwina/Cree: Words*, vol. 2 (University of Regina Press, 2001), 593.

36 Wolvengrey, *nêhiyawêwin*, vol. 2, 593.

37 Arok Wolvengrey, *nêhiyawêwin: itwêwina/Cree: Words*, vol. 1 (University of Regina Press, 2001), 238.

38 Wolvengrey, *nêhiyawêwin*, vol. 1, 218.

39 For various stories of the origin of the river's name, see Trevor Herriot, *River in a Dry Land: A Prairie Passage* (Stoddart, 2000), 8–14; see also Eleanor Brass, "Legend of Qu'Appelle," in *kisiskâciwan: Indigenous Voices from Where the River Flows Swiftly*, ed. Jesse Rae Archibald-Barber (University of Regina Press, 2018), 135–36.

40 Wolvengrey, *nêhiyawêwin*, vol. 2, 366.

41 Herriot, *River in a Dry Land*, 58.

42 Wolvengrey, *nêhiyawêwin*, vol. 1, 18.

43 See Herriot, *River in a Dry Land*, 57–98, for a description of the Aiktow Valley and its destruction.

44 See Solomon Ratt, *kâ-pî-isi-kiskisiyân / The Way I Remember* (University of Regina Press, 2023). Solomon helped with the vocabulary I've included in this section, and I'm grateful for his assistance.

45 Bill Barry, *People Places: The Dictionary of Saskatchewan Place Names* (Centax Books & Distribution, 1998), 80.

46 Barry, *People Places*, 80.

47 "Regina—Condie Nature Refuge," *Tourism Saskatchewan Canada*, accessed May 12, 2020, https://www.tourismsaskatchewan.com/listings/1002/regina---condie-nature-refuge.

FIVE: THE GLOBAL TRANSPORTATION HUB

1 Doreen Massey, "A Global Sense of Place," *Space, Place, and Gender* (University of Minnesota Press, 1994), 154–55.

2 Jane Jacobs, *The Economy of Cities* (Vintage, 1970), 129–30.

3 Jacobs, *The Economy of Cities*, 139–40.

4 Patricia Gober and Howard S. Wheater, "Socio-Hydrology and the Science-Policy Interface: A Case Study of the Saskatchewan River Basin," *Hydrology and Earth Systems Sciences* 18, no. 4 (2014): 1413–14, https://doi.org/10.5194/hess-18-1413-2014.

5 See Craig Welch, "Why Cape Town Is Running Out of Water, and Who's Next," *National Geographic*, March 5, 2018, https://www.nationalgeographic.com/science/article/cape-town-running-out-of-water-drought-taps-shutoff-other-cities; Krista Mahr, "How Cape Town Was Saved from Running Out of Water," The Upside, *Guardian*, May 4, 2018, https://www.theguardian.com/world/2018/may/04/back-from-the-brink-how-cape-town-cracked-its-water-crisis; "The 11 Cities Most Likely to Run Out of Drinking Water," *BBC News*, February 10, 2018, https://www.bbc.com/news/world-42982959.

6 Arthur White-Crummey, "Sask. Announces $4 Billion Project to Irrigate up to 500,000 Acres," *Regina Leader-Post*, July 2, 2020, https://leaderpost.com/news/saskatchewan/sask-announces-4-billion-project-to-irrigate-500000-acres; see also Jared Suchan and Shahid Azam, "Opinion: Much More Research Needs to Be Done into Diefenbaker Irrigation Project," *Regina-Leader-Post*, September 22, 2020, https://leaderpost.com/opinion/columnists/opinion-much-more-research-needs-to-be-done-into-diefenbaker-irrigation-project, and Robert Halliday, "Diefenbaker Project Not Worth the Cost," *Western Producer*, July 2, 2020, https://www.producer.com/opinion/diefenbaker-project-not-worth-the-cost/.

7 See Jane Jacobs, *The Death and Life of Great American Cities*, rev. ed. (Vintage, 1992).

8 Geoff Leo, "Government Defends 'Fake Map' of GTH to Sell Chinese Megamall as Artist's Rendering," CBC Investigates, *CBC News*, November 9, 2017, https://www.cbc.ca/news/canada/saskatchewan/government-defends-fake-map-of-gth-to-sell-chinese-megamall-as-artist-s-rendering-1.4393646.

9 Murray Lyons, "Inland Port Idea Floated: Ocean Containers Could Boost Economy," *Saskatoon Star-Phoenix*, April 13, 2006: C8.

10 Lyons, "Inland Port Idea Floated," C8.

11 Bruce Johnstone, "A Distribution Centre, 500,000 Square Feet of Space, 750 Jobs Within Two Years, and an Investment of $200 Million All Add Up to One Big Project (and More in the Works)," *Regina Leader-Post*, July 30, 2008: A1.

12 Johnstone, "A Distribution Centre," A1.

13 Johnstone, "A Distribution Centre," A1.

14 Bruce Johnstone, "Transport Hub Touted; Regina Distribution Centre Will See 1,400 Trucks Weekly When Fully Operational," *Saskatoon Star-Phoenix*, February 2, 2011: C6.

15 Johnstone, "A Distribution Centre," A1.

16 Johnstone, "A Distribution Centre," A1.

17 Angela Hall, "More Cash for Growing Transport Facility," *Regina Leader-Post*, January 7, 2009: A1.

18 Kerry Benjoe, "Regina Ready to Grow Its Borders," *Regina Leader-Post*, January 30, 2009: A1.

19 Ian Hamilton, "Fiacco Says Regina Can't Foot the Bill on Its Own," *Regina Leader-Post*, February 24, 2009: C1.

20 "Regina Approves Plan for Population of 500,000," *CBC News*, June 10, 2013, https://www.cbc.ca/news/canada/saskatchewan/regina-approves-plan-for-population-of-500-000-1.1396257.

21 See Globalspec, "Reach Stackers and ISO Container Handlers Information," accessed November 28, 2024, https://www.globalspec.com/learnmore/material_handling_packaging_equipment/material_handling_equipment/reach_stackers#:~:text=Reach%20stackers%20offer%20the%20ability,range%20of%20containers%20and%20cargo.

22 Rattra Y. Taylor, "Has Hub Met the Hype?; Some Question Whether the Original Vision for the Project Was Too Ambitious," *Regina Leader-Post*, August 29, 2015: G1.

23 Taylor, "Has Hub Met the Hype?" G1.

24 Taylor, "Has Hub Met the Hype?" G1.

25 Taylor, "Has Hub Met the Hype?" G1.

26 Geoff Leo, "Businessmen Made Millions on Regina Land That Wound Up in Taxpayers' Hands," CBC Investigates, *CBC News*, February 3, 2016, https://www.cbc.ca/news/canada/saskatchewan/businessmen-millions-regina-land-bill-boyd-1.3420479.

27 Geoff Leo, "The GTH Land Deal You've Never Heard Of—and Bill Boyd Won't Talk About," CBC Investigates, *CBC News*, October 16, 2016, https://www.cbc.ca/news/canada/saskatchewan/the-gth-land-deal-you-ve-never-heard-of-and-bill-boyd-won-t-talk-about-1.3800855.

28 Leo, "Businessmen Made Millions."

29 Leo, "Businessmen Made Millions."

30 Leo, "Businessmen Made Millions."

31 Leo, "Businessmen Made Millions."

32 Leo, "Businessmen Made Millions."

33 Leo, "Businessmen Made Millions."

34 Leo, "Businessmen Made Millions."

35 Geoff Leo, "SaskPower Bought $25M of GTH Land Just in Time to Fund Controversial Deal," CBC Investigates, *CBC News*, October 18, 2016, https://www.cbc.ca/news/canada/saskatchewan/saskpower-bought-25m-of-gth-land-just-in-time-to-fund-controversial-deal-1.3807286.

36 Leo, "SaskPower Bought $25M of GTH Land."

37 Leo, "Businessmen Made Millions."

38 Leo, "Businessmen Made Millions."

39 Leo, "Businessmen Made Millions."

40 Leo, "Businessmen Made Millions."

41 Leo, "Businessmen Made Millions."

42 Leo, "The GTH Land Deal You've Never Heard Of."

43 Leo, "The GTH Land Deal You've Never Heard Of."

44 Geoff Leo, "Irrigation Equipment from Chinese Immigration Scheme Would Water Land Farmed by Bill Boyd," CBC Investigates, *CBC News*, August 24, 2017, https://www.cbc.ca/news/canada/saskatchewan/irrigation-equipment-from-chinese-immigration-scheme-would-water-land-farmed-by-bill-boyd-1.4259310.

45 Geoff Leo, "Regina Land Deal 'Looks Like It's Not a Normal Transaction': Auditor," *CBC Saskatchewan*, February 5, 2016, https://www.cbc.ca/news/canada/saskatchewan/regina-land-deal-looks-like-it-s-not-a-normal-transaction-auditor-1.3435752.

46 "NDP Leader Cam Broten Calls for Judicial Inquiry into GTH Land Deal," *CBC News*, March 3, 2016, https://www.cbc.ca/news/canada/saskatchewan/ndp-leader-cam-broten-calls-for-judicial-inquiry-into-gth-land-deal-1.3474315.

47 Geoff Leo, "Sask. Government Charging $180K for Access to GTH Land Deal Documents," CBC Investigates, *CBC News*, May 3, 2016, https://www.cbc.ca/news/canada/saskatchewan/sask-government-charging-180k-for-access-to-gth-land-deal-documents-1.3564268.

48 "GTH Won't Release Land Deal Appraisal Because It Could 'Harm the Reputation' of Preparer," *CBC News*, May 9, 2016, https://www.cbc.ca/news/canada/saskatchewan/gth-won-t-release-land-deal-appraisal-because-it-could-harm-the-reputation-of-preparer-1.3570688.

49 Geoff Leo, "Commissioner Rebukes Government for 'Excessive Delays' in GTH Info Requests," CBC Investigates, *CBC News*, November 14, 2016, https://www.cbc.ca/news/canada/saskatchewan/commissioner-rebukes-government-for-excessive-delays-in-gth-info-requests-1.3850264.

50 Geoff Leo, "3 Strikes: Sask. Government Chastised Again for Handling of GTH Document Requests," *CBC News*, January 17, 2017, https://www.cbc.ca/news/canada/saskatchewan/3-strikes-sask-government-chastised-again-for-handling-of-gth-document-requests-1.3939695.

51 Geoff Leo, "Sask. Government Agreed to Transfer 300 Acres of GTH Land to CP for No Cost," CBC Investigates, *CBC News*, April 23, 2017, https://www.cbc.ca/news/canada/saskatchewan/global-transportation-hub-cp-regina-1.4068125.

52 Geoff Leo, "'Wrongdoing' in GTH News Release May Not Have Been the Right Word, Says Sask. Provincial Auditor," CBC Investigates, *CBC News*, November 10, 2016, https://www.cbc.ca/news/canada/saskatchewan/wrongdoing-in-gth-news-release-may-not-have-been-the-right-word-says-

sask-provincial-auditor-1.3846272.

53 "Government Paid Too Much for GTH Land: Sask. Provincial Auditor," CBC *Saskatchewan*, June 30, 2016, https://www.cbc.ca/news/canada/saskatchewan/government-paid-too-much-for-gth-land-sask-provincial-auditor-1.3659296.

54 Leo, "The GTH Land Deal You've Never Heard Of."

55 Geoff Leo, "Police Investigating GTH Land Deal, Committee Hears," CBC Investigates, *CBC News*, November 28, 2016, https://www.cbc.ca/news/canada/saskatchewan/police-investigating-gth-land-deal-committee-hears-1.3870876.

56 Hailey Salvian, "No Charges Laid in GTH Land Deal Investigation: RCMP," *CBC News*, July 25, 2018, https://www.cbc.ca/news/canada/saskatchewan/no-charges-laid-in-gth-land-deal-investigation-rcmp-1.4761263.

57 Salvian, "No Charges Laid in GTH Land Deal Investigation."

58 Salvian, "No Charges Laid in GTH Land Deal Investigation."

59 Nan Shepherd, *The Living Mountain* (Canongate, 2011), 1.

60 "Emterra Group," *Global Transportation Hub*, https://thegth.com/regulatory/current-businesses/emterra-group.

61 "Province Sets Course to Drop Global Transportation Hub; Fires CEO," *Regina Leader-Post*, January 4, 2019, https://leaderpost.com/news/politics/the-provincial-government-is-setting-a-course-to-divest-itself-of-the-controversial-global-transportation-hub.

62 "Province Sets Course to Drop Global Transportation Hub."

63 Paul Sinclair, "Selling Off Global Transportation Hub the Ultimate Dashed Dream; Facility Is Logical, Innovative Response to Saskatchewan Issues," *Regina Leader-Post*, August 1, 2018: A6.

64 Sinclair, "Selling Off Global Transportation Hub," A6.

65 Sinclair, "Selling Off Global Transportation Hub," A6.

66 Amanda Short, "Colliers Taking Over GTH Operations Amid Land Sale Concerns," *Regina Leader-Post*, September 20, 2019: A7.

67 Murray Mandryk, "Time Ripe to Rethink Purpose of GTH," *Regina Leader-Post*, January 4, 2020: A5.

68 Murray Mandryk, "$2B Spending Begs for Recall of the Legislature," *Regina Leader-Post*, May 8, 2020: A4.

69 Arthur White-Crummey, "GTH Now $46 Million in Debt and Still Not Selling Land," *Regina Leader-Post*, July 30, 2020, https://leaderpost.com/news/saskatchewan/gth-now-46-million-in-debt-and-still-not-selling-land/wcm/6176b42e-a2ea-4815-8fbe-a5d8e0e89347/.

70 Padraig Moran, "Video of RCMP Hitting Inuk Man with Truck Shows Police Choosing Violence Over Protection, Says Lawyer," The Current, CBC *Radio*, June 5, 2020, https://www.cbc.ca/radio/thecurrent/the-current-for-june-5-2020-1.5599723/video-of-rcmp-hitting-inuk-man-with-truck-shows-

police-choosing-violence-over-protection-says-lawyer-1.5599847.

71 James Daschuk, *Clearing the Plains: Disease, Politics of Starvation, and the Loss of Indigenous Life*, 2nd ed. (University of Regina Press, 2019), 159–80.

72 Patrick Wolfe, "Settler Colonialism and the Elimination of the Native," *Journal of Genocide Research* 8, no. 4 (2006): 387, https://doi.org/10.1080/14623520601056240.

73 Wolfe, "Settler Colonialism and the Elimination of the Native," 387.

74 Wolfe, "Settler Colonialism and the Elimination of the Native," 388.

75 Wolfe, "Settler Colonialism and the Elimination of the Native," 388.

76 Quoted in Brian Titley, *A Narrow Vision: Duncan Campbell Scott and the Administration of Indian Affairs in Canada* (University of British Columbia Press, 1986), 50.

77 Quoted in Titley, *A Narrow Vision*, 50.

78 Duncan Campbell Scott, "The Onondaga Madonna," *The Poems of Duncan Campbell Scott* (McClelland & Stewart, 1926), 230; Duncan Campbell Scott, "Powassan's Drum," *The Poems of Duncan Campbell Scott* (McClelland & Stewart, 1926), 59–63.

79 Duncan Campbell Scott, "The Height of Land," *The Poems of Duncan Campbell Scott* (McClelland & Stewart, 1926), 46–51; Sarah Krotz, "Shadows of Indian Title: The Territorial Underpinnings of 'The Height of Land,'" *Canadian Literature*, no. 204 (Spring 2010): 93, https://doi.org/10.14288/cl.v0i204.192871.

80 F.R. Scott, "Laurentian Shield," in *Leaving the Shade of the Middle Ground: The Poetry of F.R. Scott*, ed. Laura Moss (Wilfred Laurier University Press, 2011), 2, lines 4–5.

81 Laura Moss, "Biographical Note," in *Leaving the Shade of the Middle Ground: The Poetry of F.R. Scott*, ed. Laura Moss (Wilfred Laurier University Press, 2011), x.

82 Marilyn Dumont, "Letter to Sir John A. Macdonald," *A Really Good Brown Girl* (Brick Books, 1996), 52, lines 13–18.

83 Dumont, "Letter to Sir John A. Macdonald," 52, line 20.

84 Jennifer Andrews, "Irony, Métis Style: Reading the Poetry of Marilyn Dumont and Gregory Scofield," *Canadian Poetry: Studies, Documents, Reviews* 50 (2002): 18, https://canadianpoetry.org/wp-content/uploads/2020/03/Studies-1-50.pdf.

85 Dumont, "Letter to Sir John A. Macdonald," 52, lines 27–30.

86 Dumont, "Letter to Sir John A. Macdonald," 52, line 23.

87 Jim Coyle, "Canada 150: When a Man with an Eagle Feather Thwarted the High and Mighty," *Toronto Star*, May 27, 2017, https://www.thestar.com/news/insight/canada-150-when-a-man-with-an-eagle-feather-thwarted-the-high-and-mighty/article_12365086-be6d-5f31-85c5-1211aac6affc.html; see also Tabitha de Bruin, "Elijah Harper," in *The Canadian Encyclopedia*, July

31, 2013, https://www.thecanadianencyclopedia.ca/en/article/elijah-harper.

88 See, for instance, Aaron Mills/Waabishki Ma'iingan, "What Is a Treaty? On Contract and Mutual Aid," in *The Right Relationship: Reimagining the Implementation of Historical Treaties*, eds. John Borrows and Michael Coyle (University of Toronto Press, 2017), 220.

89 Coyle, "When a Man with an Eagle Feather Thwarted the High and Mighty."

90 Dylan Robinson, "Intergenerational Sense, Intergenerational Responsibility," in *Arts of Engagement: Taking Aesthetic Action In and Beyond the Truth and Reconciliation Commission of Canada*, eds. Dylan Robinson and Keavy Martin (Wilfred Laurier University Press, 2016), 63. Italics are Robinson's.

91 Robinson, "Intergenerational Sense, Intergenerational Responsibility," 63.

92 Wolfe, "Settler Colonialism and the Elimination of the Native," 388.

93 Trevor Herriot, *Towards a Prairie Atonement* (University of Regina Press, 2016), 13.

SIX: THE LAY OF THE LAND

1 Margaret Hryniuk and Meta Perry, *Regina: A City of Beautiful Homes* (First Writing, 1994), 7.

2 Robert Macfarlane, *The Old Ways: A Journey on Foot* (Penguin, 2013), 17.

3 Macfarlane, *The Old Ways*, 17–18.

4 Charlotte Bates, "Desire Lines: Walking in Woolwich," in *Walking Through Social Research*, eds. Charlotte Bates and Alex Rhys-Taylor (Routledge, 2017), 55.

5 Bates, "Desire Lines," 56.

6 James Holston, *The Modernist City: An Anthropological Critique of Brasília* (University of Chicago Press, 1989), 141.

7 E.A. Christiansen, "The Wisconsinan Deglaciation, of Southern Saskatchewan and Adjacent Areas," *Canadian Journal of Earth Sciences* 16, no. 4 (1979): 916.

8 Christiansen, "The Wisconsinan Deglaciation," 926.

9 Janis Dale, "Proglacial Lakes," in *The Encyclopedia of Saskatchewan: A Living Legacy* (Canadian Plains Research Center, 2005), 726.

10 Dale, "Proglacial Lakes," 726.

11 Dale, "Proglacial Lakes," 726.

12 Daria Coneghan, "Regina," in *The Encyclopedia of Saskatchewan: A Living Legacy* (Canadian Plains Research Center, 2005), 744.

13 Craig Mod, "The Glorious, Almost-Disconnected Boredom of My Walk in Japan," The Big Story, *Wired*, May 29, 2019, https://www.wired.com/story/six-weeks-100s-miles-hours-glorious-boredom-japan/.

14 Mod, "The Glorious, Almost-Disconnected Boredom of My Walk in Japan."

15 Natascia Lypny, "'They Just Don't Care': Landowners Anxious over Regina Bypass Impact," *Regina Leader-Post*, August 21, 2015, https://leaderpost.com/news/local-news/they-just-dont-care-landowners-anxious-over-regina-bypass-impact.

16 James H. Shaw, "How Many Bison Originally Populated Western Rangelands?" *Rangelands* 17, no. 5 (1995): 150, https://journals.uair.arizona.edu/index.php/rangelands/article/viewFile/11258/10531.

17 Bill Waiser, *A World We Have Lost: Saskatchewan Before 1905* (Fifth House, 2016), 420.

18 Waiser, *A World We Have Lost*, 497.

19 Ernest Hemingway, *The Sun Also Rises* (Scribner's, 1954), 136.

20 Waiser, *A World We Have Lost*, 500.

21 Waiser, *A World We Have Lost*, 500.

22 Waiser, *A World We Have Lost*, 501.

23 Waiser, *A World We Have Lost*, 501.

24 James Daschuk, *Clearing the Plains: Disease, Politics of Starvation, and the Loss of Indigenous Life*, 2nd ed. (University of Regina Press, 2019), 114–15, 151.

25 Daschuk, *Clearing the Plains*, 114.

26 Daschuk, *Clearing the Plains*, 114.

27 Daschuk, *Clearing the Plains*, 114.

28 Daschuk, *Clearing the Plains*, 102, 121, 124.

29 Daschuk, *Clearing the Plains*, 132.

30 Daschuk, *Clearing the Plains*, 115, 138–43.

31 Daschuk, *Clearing the Plains*, 123.

32 F. Laurie Barron, "The Indian Pass System in the Canadian West, 1882–1935," in *Immigration and Settlement*, 1870–1939, ed. Gregory P. Marchildon (Canadian Plains Research Center, 2009), 214.

33 See *The Pass System*, dir. Alex Williams (Tamarack Productions, 2015), available at http://thepasssystem.ca.

34 Daschuk, *Clearing the Plains*, 153–54; Brian Titley, *The Frontier World of Edgar Dewdney* (University of British Columbia Press, 2000), 50.

35 Daschuk, *Clearing the Plains*, 127–28.

36 Waiser, *A World We Have Lost*, 573.

37 Andrew C. Isenberg, *The Destruction of the Bison: An Environmental History, 1750–1920* (Cambridge University Press, 2000), 2.

38 Wes Olson and Johane Janelle, *The Ecological Buffalo: On the Trail of a Keystone Species* (University of Regina Press, 2022), 11.

39 Olson and Janelle, *The Ecological Buffalo*, 12.

40 Waiser, *A World We Have Lost*, 341.

41 Waiser, *A World We Have Lost*, 420.

42 Isenberg, *The Destruction of the Bison*, 93.

43 Kendall Latimer, "Sask. Advocates Raise Concerns About 20-Year Plan to

Clear Cut Boreal Forest," CBC *News*, August 29, 2019, https://www.cbc.ca/news/canada/saskatchewan/people-call-more-consultation-prince-albert-forest-management-1.5262070.

44 Isenberg, *The Destruction of the Bison*, 3.

45 Isenberg, *The Destruction of the Bison*, 130.

46 Isenberg, *The Destruction of the Bison*, 131.

47 Isenberg, *The Destruction of the Bison*, 136.

48 Isenberg, *The Destruction of the Bison*, 162.

49 Isenberg, *The Destruction of the Bison*, 3.

50 Ryan Crosschild et al., "Awakening Buffalo Consciousness: Lessons, Theory, and Practice from the Buffalo Treaty," *Wicazo Sa Review* 36, no. 1 (2021): 10, https://doi.org/10.1353/wic.2021.a903665; Robert Wooster, "Miles, Nelson (1839–1925)," in *Encyclopedia of the Great Plains*, ed. David J. Wishart (University of Nebraska Press, 2011), http://plainshumanities.unl.edu/encyclopedia/doc/egp.war.028.

51 Crosschild et al., "Awakening Buffalo Consciousness," 10–11; Gary Trogdon, "Sheridan, Philip (1831–1888)," in *Encyclopedia of the Great Plains*, ed. Gary J. Wishart (University of Nebraska Press, 2011), http://plainshumanities.unl.edu/encyclopedia/doc/egp.war.042.xml.

52 Isenberg, *The Destruction of the Bison*, 144–50.

53 Isenberg, *The Destruction of the Bison*, 164–65.

54 Jennifer Brower, *Lost Tracks: Buffalo National Park, 1908–1939* (Athabasca University Press, 2008), 4–5.

55 Candace Savage, *Geography of Blood: Unearthing Memory from a Prairie Landscape* (Greystone Books, 2012), 43.

56 Canadian Press, "Large Herd of Bison Still on the Loose Near Tisdale," *Regina Leader-Post*, December 15, 2015, https://leaderpost.com/news/saskatchewan/large-herd-of-roaming-bison-still-on-the-loose-near-tisdale.

57 Tennessa Wild, "Sask. Bison Home After Winter of Roaming Free," *Western Producer*, July 14, 2016, https://www.producer.com/2016/07/sask-bison-back-home-after-winter-of-roaming-free/.

58 Tasha Hubbard, "Buffalo Genocide in Nineteenth-Century North America: 'Kill, Skin, and Sell,'" in *Colonial Genocide in Indigenous North America*, eds. Andrew Woolford, Jeff Benvenuto, and Alexander Laban Hinton (Duke University Press, 2014), 293.

59 Hubbard, "Buffalo Genocide," 295.

60 Hubbard, "Buffalo Genocide," 301.

61 Hubbard, "Buffalo Genocide," 302.

62 Hubbard, "Buffalo Genocide," 302–3.

63 Leroy Little Bear, "Jagged Worldviews Colliding," in *Reclaiming Indigenous Voice and Vision*, ed. Marie Battiste (UBC Press, 2000), 78–79.

64 Little Bear, "Jagged Worldviews Colliding," 84.

65 Crosschild et al., "Awakening Buffalo Consciousness," 6.
66 Crosschild et al., "Awakening Buffalo Consciousness," 14.
67 Crosschild et al., "Awakening Buffalo Consciousness," 15.
68 Chelsea Vowel, *Buffalo Is the New Buffalo: Stories* (Arsenal Pulp Press, 2022), 21.
69 See *The Buffalo: A Treaty of Cooperation, Renewal, and Restoration*, https://www.buffalotreaty.com.
70 Crosschild et al., "Awakening Buffalo Consciousness," 16.
71 Crosschild et al., "Awakening Buffalo Consciousness," 8.
72 Crosschild et al., "Awakening Buffalo Consciousness," 16; see also Leanne Betasamosake Simpson, *As We Have Always Done: Indigenous Freedom Through Radical Resistance* (University of Minnesota Press, 2017), 55–70.
73 Simpson, *As We Have Always Done*, 20.
74 Crosschild et al., "Awakening Buffalo Consciousness," 12–13.
75 Crosschild et al., "Awakening Buffalo Consciousness," 17–18.
76 Crosschild et al., "Awakening Buffalo Consciousness," 20.
77 Ken Zontek, *Buffalo Nation: American Indian Efforts to Restore the Bison* (University of Nebraska Press, 2007), 43–44.
78 Zontek, *Buffalo Nation*, 152.
79 Karen Gardiner, "How Canadian Bison Have Been Brought Back from the Brink in Saskatchewan," *National Geographic*, June 3, 2023, https://www.nationalgeographic.com/travel/article/canadian-bison-brought-back-saskatchewan.
80 Gardiner, "How Canadian Bison Have Been Brought Back."
81 Mouhamad Rachini, "Indigenous-led Bison Repopulation Projects Are Helping the Animal Thrive Again in Alberta," The Current, *CBC Radio*, May 26, 2023, https://www.cbc.ca/radio/thecurrent/bison-repopulation-alberta-1.6856433.
82 "Canada Reintroduces Bison to Banff National Park After More Than a Century," *Guardian*, February 13, 2017, https://www.theguardian.com/world/2017/feb/13/canada-reintroduces-bison-banff-national-park.
83 Rebecca Solnit, *Hope in the Dark: Untold Histories, Wild Possibilities*, 3rd ed. (Haymarket Books, 2016), xiv.
84 Robert Macfarlane, *The Wild Places* (Penguin, 2008), 90–91, 95.

SEVEN: FUTURES TRADING

1 Naomi Klein, "Dancing the World into Being: A Conversation with Idle No More's Leanne Simpson," *Yes Magazine*, March 6, 2013, https://www.yesmagazine.org/social-justice/2013/03/06/dancing-the-world-into-being-a-conversation-with-idle-no-more-leanne-simpson/.

2 Irene Spry, *The Palliser Expedition: The Dramatic Story of Western Canadian Exploration 1857–1860*, 2nd ed. (Fifth House, 1995), 6–7.

3 Spry, *The Palliser Expedition*, 6-7.

4 Captain John Palliser, *The Journals, Detailed Reports, and Observations Relative to the Exploration, By Captain Palliser, of that Portion of British North America, Which, in Latitude, Lies Between the British Boundary Line and the Height of Land or Watershed of the Northern or Frozen Ocean Respectively, and in Longitude, Between the Western Shore of Lake Superior and the Pacific Ocean During the Years 1857, 1858, 1859, and 1860* (George Edward Eyre and William Spottiswoode, 1863), 52; available from Canadiana by CKRN, https://www.canadiana.ca/view/oocihm.9_01593/53.

5 Spry, *The Palliser Expedition*, 63.

6 W.F. Rannie, "Summer Rainfall on the Prairies During the Palliser and Hind Expeditions, 1857–59," *Prairie Forum* 31, no. 1 (2006): 20.

7 Henry Youle Hind, *Narrative of the Canadian Red River Exploration Expedition of 1857 and of the Assinniboine and Saskatchewan Exploring Expedition of 1858*, vol. 2 (Longman, Green, Longman, and Roberts, 1860), 234; available from Canadiana by CKRN, https://www.canadiana.ca/view/oocihm.35700.

8 Hind, *Narrative of the Canadian Red River Exploring Expedition*, 234–35.

9 For a map of the ecoregions of the Western Canadian prairies, see Gregory P. Marchildon, Suren Kulshreshtha, Elaine Wheaton, and Dave Sauchyn, "Drought and Institutional Adaptation in the Great Plains of Alberta and Saskatchewan, 1914–1939," *Natural Hazards* 45 (2008): 394, https://doi.org/10.1007/s11069-007-9175-5.

10 S.A. Wolfe, C.H. Hugenholtz, and Olav B. Lian, "Palliser's Triangle: Reconstructing the 'Central Desert' of the Southwestern Canadian Prairies During the Late 1850s," *The Holocene* 23, no. 5 (2013): 699, https://doi.org/10.1177/0959683612470179.

11 Wolfe, Hugenholtz, and Lian, "Palliser's Triangle," 700.

12 Wolfe, Hugenholtz, and Lian, "Palliser's Triangle," 700.

13 David J. Sauchyn and Alwynne B. Beaudoin, "Recent Environmental Change in the Southwestern Canadian Plains," *Canadian Geographer* 42, no. 4 (1998): 348, https://doi.org/10.1111/J.1541-0064.1998.TB01350.X.

14 Rannie, "Summer Rainfall on the Prairies," 34.

15 Rannie, "Summer Rainfall on the Prairies," 35–36.

16 W.A. Waiser, *The Field Naturalist: John Macoun, the Geological Survey, and Natural Science* (University of Toronto Press, 1989), 36.

17 Roger L. Welch, "The Myth of the American Desert," *Nebraska History* 52, no. 3 (1971): 256–57.

18 George Mercer Dawson, *Report on the Geology and Resources of the Region in the Vicinity of the Forty-Ninth Parallel from the Lake of the Woods to the*

Rocky Mountains, with Lists of Plants and Animals Collected and Notes on the Fossils (Dawson Brothers, 1875), 291, https://hdl.handle.net/2027/aeu.ark:/13960/t6pz5wn9t.

19 Waiser, *The Field Naturalist*, 47.

20 Waiser, *The Field Naturalist*, 47.

21 Janis Dale, "Proglacial Lakes," in *The Encyclopedia of Saskatchewan: A Living Legacy* (Canadian Plains Research Center, 2005), 726.

22 W.A. Waiser, "A Willing Scapegoat: John Macoun and the Route of the CPR," in *Immigration and Settlement, 1870–1939*, ed. Gregory P. Marchildon (Canadian Plains Research Center, 2009), 67–68.

23 Trevor Herriot, *Grass, Sky, Song: Promise and Peril in the World of Grassland Birds* (HarperCollins, 2010), 109.

24 John Borrows, *Canada's Indigenous Constitution* (University of Toronto Press, 2010), 17.

25 Borrows, *Canada's Indigenous Constitution*, 17–18.

26 Borrows, *Canada's Indigenous Constitution*, 18.

27 Sylvia McAdam (Saysewahum), *Nationhood Interrupted: Revitalizing nêhiyaw Legal Systems* (Purich, 2015), 76.

28 Borrows, *Canada's Indigenous Constitution*, 17.

29 Borrows, *Canada's Indigenous Constitution*, 17.

30 Harold Johnson, *Two Families: Treaties and Government* (Purich, 2007), 23.

31 Johnson, *Two Families*, 23.

32 Eve Tuck and K. Wayne Yang, "Decolonization Is Not a Metaphor," *Decolonization: Indigeneity, Education & Society* 1, no. 1 (2012): 7. https://jps.library.utoronto.ca/index.php/des/article/view/18630.

33 Eva Mackey, *Unsettled Expectations Uncertainty, Land and Settler Decolonization* (Fernwood, 2016), 38.

34 Mackey, *Unsettled Expectations*, 125–26.

35 Emma Battell Lowman and Adam J. Barker. *Settler: Identity and Colonialism in 21st Century Canada* (Fernwood, 2015), 111.

36 Truth and Reconciliation Commission of Canada (TRC), *Honouring the Truth, Reconciling for the Future: Summary of the Final Report of the Truth and Reconciliation Commission of Canada* (Truth and Reconciliation Commission of Canada, 2015), 6.

37 TRC, *Honouring the Truth, Reconciling for the Future*, 187.

38 TRC, *Honouring the Truth, Reconciling for the Future*, 43.

39 Lowman and Barker, *Settler*, 112.

40 Lowman and Barker, *Settler*, 112.

41 Tuck and Yang, "Decolonization Is Not a Metaphor," 36.

42 Eve Tuck and Rubén A. Gaztambide-Fernández, "Curriculum, Replacement, and Settler Futurity," *Journal of Curriculum Theorizing* 29, no. 1 (2013): 80, https://journal.jctonline.org/index.php/jct/article/view/411.

43 Andrew Baldwin, "Whiteness and Futurity: Towards a Research Agenda," *Progress in Human Geography* 36, no. 2 (2012): 173, https://doi.org/10.1177/0309132511414603.

44 *Oxford English Dictionary*, s.v. "commensurate (adj.)," June 2024, https://doi.org/10.1093/OED/3187118747.

45 Tuck and Yang, "Decolonization Is Not a Metaphor," 12.

46 Tuck and Yang, "Decolonization Is Not a Metaphor," 17.

47 Tuck and Yang, "Decolonization Is Not a Metaphor," 17.

48 Alexander Morris, *The Treaties of Canada with the Indians of Manitoba and the North-West Territories, Including the Negotiations on Which They Were Based, and Other Information Relating Thereto* (Belfords, Clark & Co., 1880; repr., Coles, 1971).

49 Whether the terms offered to First Nations in the written treaty texts were in fact "fair and just," of course, is a question that continues to be debated today. Given the amount of land allegedly surrendered, and the relatively small amount of money offered in exchange, it seems unlikely that those terms were "fair and just."

50 Morris, *The Treaties of Canada*, 16.

51 Morris, *The Treaties of Canada*, 143–44.

52 Morris, *The Treaties of Canada*, 331.

53 Sheldon Krasowski, *No Surrender: The Land Remains Indigenous* (University of Regina Press, 2019), 158–59.

54 See James Daschuk, *Clearing the Plains: Disease, Politics of Starvation, and the Loss of Indigenous Life*, 2nd ed. (University of Regina Press, 2019), 99–126, for a discussion of the federal government's failure to live up to the promises it made to First Nations in the immediate aftermath of the treaty negotiations. That failure continues. In July 2024, however, the Supreme Court of Canada determined that the Crown had breached the promises it made to First Nations in the Robinson Treaties in northern Ontario, opening the way for the payment of billions of dollars in compensation to those First Nations by the governments of Ontario and Canada. That decision could have implications for other historical treaties in Canada. See Bridget Gilbride et al., "Restoule Decision Finds the Crown Breached Its Promises to Robinson Treaty Beneficiaries," *Fasken*, August 8, 2024, https://www.fasken.com/en/knowledge/2024/08/restoule-decision-finds-the-crown-breached-its-promise.

55 Leanne Betasamosake Simpson, *As We Have Always Done: Indigenous Freedom Through Radical Resistance* (University of Minnesota Press, 2017), 99.

56 Harold Cardinal, *The Unjust Society: The Tragedy of Canada's Indians* (Hurtig, 1969), 28.

57 Cardinal, *The Unjust Society*, 39.

58 Julie Jai, "Bargains Made in Bad Times: How Principles from Modern Treaties Can Reinvigorate Historic Treaties," in *The Right Relationship: Reimagining the Implementation of Historical Treaties*, ed. John Borrows and Michael Coyle (University of Toronto Press, 2017), 128–29.

59 Harold Cardinal and Walter Hildebrandt, *Treaty Elders of Saskatchewan: Our Dream Is That Our Peoples Will One Day Be Clearly Recognized as Nations* (University of Calgary Press, 2000), 15.

60 Jai, "Bargains Made in Bad Times," 130.

61 Johnson, *Two Families*, 13–14. Johnson's use of this term does not prevent him from offering a scathing critique of settler behaviour and Indigenous-settler relations in this book.

62 Borrows, *Canada's Indigenous Constitution*, 26.

63 Aaron Mills/Waabishki Ma'iingan, "What Is a Treaty? On Contract and Mutual Aid," in *The Right Relationship: Reimagining the Implementation of Historical Treaties*, eds. John Borrows and Michael Coyle (University of Toronto Press, 2017), 220.

64 Mills, "What Is a Treaty?," 220–21.

65 Mills, "What Is a Treaty?," 222. For the Supreme Court of Canada decision, see *Tsilhqot'in Nation v British Columbia*, 2014 SCC 44, [2014] 2 SCR 256.

66 Mills, "What Is a Treaty?," 224.

67 Mills, "What Is a Treaty?," 225.

68 Mills, "What Is a Treaty?," 229.

69 Mills, "What Is a Treaty?," 237–38. Borrows suggests that it's possible that representatives of the Cree and Lakota nations were present at the negotiations of the Treaty of Niagara, which may indicate that the metaphor of the Covenant Chain has some purchase in Western Canada. See John Borrows, "Wampum at Niagara: The Royal Proclamation, Canadian Legal History, and Self-Government," in *Aboriginal and Treaty Rights in Canada: Essays on Law, Equality, and Respect for Difference*, ed. Michael Asch (UBC Press, 1998), 163.

70 Mills, "What is a Treaty?," 241.

71 See Borrows, *Canada's Indigenous Constitution*.

72 Gina Starblanket and Dallas Hunt, *Storying Violence: Unravelling Colonial Narratives in the Stanley Trial* (ARP Books, 2020), 107.

73 Starblanket and Hunt, *Storying Violence*, 108.

74 Starblanket and Hunt, *Storying Violence*, 108.

75 Starblanket and Hunt, *Storying Violence*, 108.

76 Starblanket and Hunt, *Storying Violence*, 109.

77 Starblanket and Hunt, *Storying Violence*, 109.

78 Starblanket and Hunt, *Storying Violence*, 109.

79 Starblanket and Hunt, *Storying Violence*, 110.

80 Robin DiAngelo, *White Fragility: Why It's So Hard for White People to Talk*

About Racism (Beacon Press, 2018), 2.

81 DiAngelo, *White Fragility*, 2.

82 Lee Maracle, *My Conversations With Canadians* (Book*hug Press, 2017), 34.

83 Lowman and Barker, *Settler*, 105–6.

84 Rebecca Solnit, *Hope in the Dark: Untold Histories, Wild Possibilities*, 3rd ed. (Haymarket Books, 2016), xiv.

85 Starblanket and Hunt, *Storying Violence*, 110.

86 Starblanket and Hunt, *Storying Violence*, 111.

87 Starblanket and Hunt, *Storying Violence*, 116.

88 Starblanket and Hunt, *Storying Violence*, 116–17.

89 Albert Memmi, *The Colonizer and The Colonized*, exp. ed., trans. Howard Greenfield (Beacon Press, 1991), 43.

90 Lowman and Barker, *Settler*, 16.

91 Clare Land, *Decolonizing Solidarity: Dilemmas and Directions for Supporters of Indigenous Struggles* (Zed Books, 2015), 2.

92 Land, *Decolonizing Solidarity*, 2–3.

93 Land, *Decolonizing Solidarity*, 20.

94 Land, *Decolonizing Solidarity*, 22.

95 Land, *Decolonizing Solidarity*, 29.

96 Land, *Decolonizing Solidarity*, 29.

97 Land, *Decolonizing Solidarity*, 33.

98 Land,, *Decolonizing Solidarity*, 128–29.

99 Land, *Decolonizing Solidarity*, 129.

100 Land, *Decolonizing Solidarity*, 130–31.

101 Land, *Decolonizing Solidarity*, 132.

102 Land, *Decolonizing Solidarity*, 150.

103 Land, *Decolonizing Solidarity*, 151.

104 Land, *Decolonizing Solidarity*, 154.

105 Land, *Decolonizing Solidarity*, 155.

106 Land, *Decolonizing Solidarity*, 163

107 Land, *Decolonizing Solidarity*, 164.

108 Tuck and Yang, "Decolonization Is Not a Metaphor," 19.

109 Tuck and Yang, "Decolonization Is Not a Metaphor," 19.

110 Justin Brake, "How Canada Can Give Land Back," *Breach Magazine*, January 29, 2022, https://breachmedia.ca/how-canada-can-give-land-back/.

111 Brake, "How Canada Can Give Land Back."

112 Hayden King and Shiri Pasternak, *Land Back: A Yellowhead Institute Red Paper* (Yellowhead Institute, 2019), https://redpaper.yellowheadinstitute.org/wp-content/uploads/2019/10/red-paper-report-final.pdf.

113 See Kendall Latimer, "Crown Land Sales Chip Away at Remaining Natural Prairie, Says Sask. Naturalist," *CBC News*, October 6, 2017, https://www.cbc.ca/news/canada/saskatchewan/sask-crown-land-needs-protection-says-

activist-1.4343523.

114 Dayne Patterson, "Carry the Kettle Nakoda Nation Asks Court to Declare Sask. Gov't Failed Duties in Crown Land Sales," *CBC News*, March 25, 2022, https://www.cbc.ca/news/canada/saskatchewan/crown-land-sales-carry-the-kettle-judicial-review-1.6397759.

115 On walking as an embodied territorial acknowledgment, see Ken Wilson, "Walking as Embodied Territorial Acknowledgment: Thinking About Place-Based Relationships from the Side of the Road," *Performance Matters* 7, nos 1–2 (2021): 97–115; and Ken Wilson and Matthew Robert Anderson, "The Promise and Peril of Walking Indigenous Territorial Recognitions Carried Out by Settlers," *International Journal of Religious Tourism and Pilgrimage* 9, no. 2 (2021): article 7, https://arrow.tudublin.ie/ijrtp/vol9/iss2/7/; on "walking-with," see Stephanie Springgay and Sarah E. Truman, *Walking Methodologies in a More-than-Human World: WalkingLab* (Routledge, 2018), 11.

116 Michael Asch, *On Being Here to Stay: Treaties and Aboriginal Rights in Canada* (University of Toronto Press, 2014), 152.

117 Asch, *On Being Here to Stay*, 165.

EIGHT: TREATY, KINSHIP, CEREMONY

1 Tim Ingold, "The Temporality of Landscape," *World Archaeology* 25, no. 2 (1993): 166, https://doi.org/10.1080/00438243.1993.9980235.

2 Yi-Fu Tuan, *Space and Place: The Perspective of Experience* (University of Minnesota Press, 1977), 184.

3 "What is 'Rupert's Land'?" *Centre for Rupert's Land Studies*, University of Winnipeg, n.d., https://www.uwinnipeg.ca/rupertsland/about-us/what-is-rupertsland.html.

4 Sheldon Krasowski, *No Surrender: The Land Remains Indigenous* (University of Regina Press, 2019), 148.

5 Alexander Morris, *The Treaties of Canada with the Indians of Manitoba and the North-West Territories, Including the Negotiations on Which They Were Based, and Other Information Relating Thereto* (Belfords, Clark & Co., 1880; repr., Coles, 1971), 92–93, 96.

6 Morris, *The Treaties of Canada*, 95–96.

7 Morris, *The Treaties of Canada*, 108–9.

8 Morris, *The Treaties of Canada*, 117.

9 Morris, *The Treaties of Canada*, 101.

10 Morris, *The Treaties of Canada*, 102.

11 Morris, *The Treaties of Canada*, 104.

12 Morris, *The Treaties of Canada*, 106.

13 Krasowski, *No Surrender*, 151.
14 Krasowski, *No Surrender*, 151–52.
15 Krasowski, *No Surrender*, 152.
16 Krasowski, *No Surrender*, 152.
17 Morris, *The Treaties of Canada*, 106.
18 Morris, *The Treaties of Canada*, 115.
19 Arthur J. Ray, Jim Miller, and Frank Tough, *Bounty and Benevolence: A History of Saskatchewan Treaties* (McGill-Queen's University Press, 2002), 112.
20 Morris, *The Treaties of Canada*, 108.
21 Ray, Miller, and Tough, *Bounty and Benevolence*, 112.
22 Harold Cardinal and Walter Hildebrandt, *Treaty Elders of Saskatchewan: Our Dream Is That Our Peoples Will One Day Be Clearly Recognized as Nations* (University of Calgary Press, 2000), 58.
23 Sylvia McAdam (Saysewahum), *Nationhood Interrupted: Revitalizing nêhiyaw Legal Systems* (Purich, 2015), 55.
24 Harold Johnson, *Two Families: Treaties and Government* (Purich, 2007), 13.
25 Krasowski, *No Surrender*, 157.
26 Krasowski, *No Surrender*, 158.
27 Andrew R. Thompson, "Resource Rights," in *The Canadian Encyclopedia*, February 7, 2006, https://www.thecanadianencyclopedia.ca/en/article/resource-rights; on the Federation of Sovereign Indigenous Nations' legal fight to reclaim those mineral rights, see Will McLernon, "First Nations Lay Claim to All Critical Minerals and Rare Earth Elements in Saskatchewan," CBC *News*, March 30, 2023, https://www.cbc.ca/news/canada/saskatchewan/first-nations-lay-claim-to-all-critical-mineral-rare-earth-minerals-1.6795871.
28 Krasowski, *No Surrender*, 158.
29 Krasowski, *No Surrender*, 158–59.
30 Krasowski, *No Surrender*, 160.
31 Krasowski, *No Surrender*, 160.
32 Krasowski, *No Surrender*, 159–60.
33 Krasowski, *No Surrender*, 160.
34 Michael Asch, *On Being Here to Stay: Treaties and Aboriginal Rights in Canada* (University of Toronto Press, 2014), 90.
35 Cardinal and Hildebrandt, *Treaty Elders of Saskatchewan*, 34.
36 Cardinal and Hildebrandt, *Treaty Elders of Saskatchewan*, 34.
37 Aimée Craft, *Breathing Life into the Stone Fort Treaty: An Anishinabe Understanding of Treaty One* (Purich, 2013), 92–93.
38 Joe Hyslop, Harry Bone, and the Treaty & Dakota Elders of Manitoba with contributions by the AMC Council of Elders, *Dtantu Balai Betl Nahidei: Our Relations to the Newcomers*, Treaty Elders' Teachings, Vol. 3 (Treaty Relations Commission of Manitoba, 2015), 159.

39 Krasowski, *No Surrender*, 154.
40 Krasowski, *No Surrender*, 155.
41 Ray, Miller, and Tough, *Bounty and Benevolence*, 107–9.
42 Johnson, *Two Families*, 27.
43 Cardinal and Hildebrant, *Treaty Elders of Saskatchewan*, 31-32.
44 Cardinal and Hildebrant, *Treaty Elders of Saskatchewan*, 31–32.
45 Morris, *The Treaties of Canada*, 97.
46 Krasowski, *No Surrender*, 164.
47 Krasowski, *No Surrender*, 164.
48 Morris, *The Treaties of Canada*, 115.
49 Morris, *The Treaties of Canada*, 122–23.
50 Morris, *The Treaties of Canada*, 122–23.
51 Asch, *On Being Here to Stay*, 97–98.
52 Asch, *On Being Here to Stay*, 97.
53 Harold Cardinal, *The Unjust Society: The Tragedy of Canada's Indians* (Hurtig, 1969), 8.
54 Asch, *On Being Here to Stay*, 161.
55 Morris, *The Treaties of Canada*, 285.
56 See Blair Stonechild and Bill Waiser, *Loyal Till Death: Indians and the North-West Rebellion*, 2nd ed. (Fifth House, 2010).
57 Morris, *The Treaties of Canada*, 285–92.
58 James Daschuk, *Clearing the Plains: Disease, Politics of Starvation, and the Loss of Indigenous Life*, 2nd ed. (University of Regina Press, 2019), 95.
59 Morris, *The Treaties of Canada*, 113.
60 Morris, *The Treaties of Canada*, 113.
61 Krasowski, *No Surrender*, 272.
62 Krasowski, *No Surrender*, 276–77.
63 Krasowski, *No Surrender*, 277–78.
64 Craft, *Breathing Life into the Stone Fort Treaty*, 107.
65 Craft, *Breathing Life into the Stone Fort Treaty*, 108.
66 Craft, *Breathing Life into the Stone Fort Treaty*, 108.
67 Craft, *Breathing Life into the Stone Fort Treaty*, 113.
68 Michael Coyle, "As Long as the Sun Shines: Recognizing That Treaties Were Intended to Last," in *The Right Relationship: Reimagining the Implementation of Historical Treaties*, ed. John Borrows and Michael Coyle (University of Toronto Press, 2017), 60.
69 Coyle, "As Long as the Sun Shines," 61.
70 John Borrows, "Wampum at Niagara: The Royal Proclamation, Canadian Legal History, and Self-Government," in *Aboriginal and Treaty Rights in Canada: Essays on Law, Equality, and Respect for Difference*, ed. Michael Asch (UBC Press, 1998), 163.
71 Julie Jai, "Bargains Made in Bad Times: How Principles from Modern

Treaties Can Reinvigorate Historic Treaties," in *The Right Relationship: Reimagining the Implementation of Historical Treaties*, ed. John Borrows and Michael Coyle (University of Toronto Press, 2017), 121.

72 Aaron Mills/Waabishki Ma'iingan, "What Is a Treaty? On Contract and Mutual Aid," in *The Right Relationship: Reimagining the Implementation of Historical Treaties*, eds. John Borrows and Michael Coyle (University of Toronto Press, 2017), 238.

73 Mills, "What Is a Treaty?," 241.

74 See Jai, "Bargains Made in Bad Times," 109–18.

75 Mark D. Walters, "Rights and Remedies Within Common Law and Indigenous Legal Traditions: Can the Covenant Chain Be Judicially Enforced Today?" in *The Right Relationship: Reimagining the Implementation of Historical Treaties*, ed. John Borrows and Michael Coyle (University of Toronto Press, 2017), 204.

76 Asch, *On Being Here to Stay*, 99.

77 Gina Starblanket and Dallas Hunt, *Storying Violence: Unravelling Colonial Narratives in the Stanley Trial* (ARP Books, 2020), 108.

NINE: FLYING-UP MOON

1 Nan Shepherd, *The Living Mountain* (Canongate, 2011), 90.

2 Shepherd, *The Living Mountain*, 91.

3 Aldo Leopold, "The Outlook for Farm Wildlife [1945]," in *The River of the Mother of God and Other Essays by Aldo Leopold*, eds. Susan L. Flader and J. Baird Callicott (University of Wisconsin Press, 1992), 323.

4 Leopold, "The Outlook for Farm Wildlife," 324.

5 Leopold, "The Outlook for Farm Wildlife," 325.

6 Leopold, "The Outlook for Farm Wildlife," 326.

7 Leopold, "The Outlook for Farm Wildlife," 326.

8 On glyphosate and cancer, see Carey Gillam, "People Exposed to Weed Killer Chemical Have Cancer Biomarkers in Urine," *Guardian*, January 20, 2023, https://www.theguardian.com/us-news/2023/jan/20/glyphosate-weedkiller-cancer-biomarkers-urine-study.

9 Trevor Herriot, *Grass, Sky, Song: Promise and Peril in the World of Grassland Birds* (HarperCollins, 2010), 157.

10 Herriot, *Grass, Sky, Song*, 157–58.

11 Herriot, *Grass, Sky, Song*, 159.

12 Herriot, *Grass, Sky, Song*, 159–60.

13 Herriot, *Grass, Sky, Song*, 160–61.

14 Herriot, *Grass, Sky, Song*, 161.

15 Elizabeth Pennisi, "Three Billion North American Birds Have Vanished

Since 1970, Surveys Show," *Science*, September 19, 2019, https://www.sciencemag.org/news/2019/09/three-billion-north-american-birds-have-vanished-1970-surveys-show.

16 Stephen Leahy, "Huge Decline in Songbirds Linked to Common Insecticide," *National Geographic*, September 12, 2019, https://www.nationalgeographic.com/environment/2019/09/widely-used-pesticide-makes-birds-lose-weight/#close.

17 Nathan Rott, "The World Lost Two-Thirds of Its Wildlife in 50 Years. We Are to Blame," Environment and Energy Collaborative Special Series, *NPR*, September 10, 2020, https://www.npr.org/2020/09/10/911500907/the-world-lost-two-thirds-of-its-wildlife-in-50-years-we-are-to-blame.

18 Patrick Wolfe, "Settler Colonialism and the Elimination of the Native," *Journal of Genocide Research* 8, no. 4 (2006): 388, https://doi.org/10.1080/14623520601056240.

19 See Bob Joseph, *21 Things You May Not Know About the Indian Act: Helping Canadians Make Reconciliation with Indigenous Peoples a Reality* (Page Two, 2018).

20 See Sarah Carter, *Lost Harvests: Prairie Indian Reserve Farmers and Government Policy*, 2nd. ed. (McGill-Queen's University Press, 2019).

21 See F. Laurie Barron, "The Indian Pass System in the Canadian West, 1882–1935," in *Immigration and Settlement*, 1870–1939, ed. Gregory P. Marchildon (Canadian Plains Research Center, 2009), 213–33.

22 See *Reclaiming Power and Place: The Final Report of the National Inquiry into Missing and Murdered Indigenous Women and Girls*, 2 vols., 2019, https://www.mmiwg-ffada.ca/final-report/.

23 See Harold R. Johnson, *Peace and Good Order: The Case for Indigenous Justice in Canada* (McClelland & Stewart, 2019), 1–15; and Kent Roach, *Canadian Justice, Indigenous Injustice: The Colten Boushie and Gerald Stanley Case* (McGill-Queen's University Press, 2019), 207–40.

24 On the struggle to get Saskatchewan's government to come up with a workable strategy to reduce the number of suicides in northern Saskatchewan, see Emily Rae Pasiuk, "Twice-Rejected Suicide Prevention Bill Passes in Sask. Legislature," *CBC News*, April 30, 2021, https://www.cbc.ca/news/canada/saskatchewan/suicide-prevention-bill-saskatchewan-doyle-vermette-1.6010335.

25 Eve Tuck and K. Wayne Yang, "Decolonization Is Not a Metaphor," *Decolonization: Indigeneity, Education & Society* 1, no. 1 (2012): 21, https://jps.library.utoronto.ca/index.php/des/article/view/18630.

EPILOGUE: LOOKING BACK

1 See Ken Wilson, "'Elms at Night' and 'Outside the Museum (For George F. Ledingham),'" *The Goose* 19, no. 2 (2022): article 11, https://scholars.wlu.ca/thegoose/vol19/iss2/11/; "Populus," *Queen's Quarterly* 130, no. 1 (2023): 146–59; and "Surrender No. 40," *The Goose* 20, no. 1 (2023): article 17, https://scholars.wlu.ca/thegoose/vol20/iss1/17/.

2 Alexander Quon, "Regina City Council Votes Against Renaming Dewdney Avenue," *CBC News*, August 21, 2024, https://www.cbc.ca/news/canada/saskatchewan/dewdney-avenue-renaming-efforts-fails-1.7301498#.

3 Quon, "Regina City Council Votes Against Renaming Dewdney Avenue."

4 Quon, "Regina City Council Votes Against Renaming Dewdney Avenue."

5 On the city's Indigenous framework, see Larissa Kurz, "Indigenous Framework Could Be 'a Win for Everybody,' Says FNUniv Expert," *Regina Leader-Post*, October 15, 2023, https://leaderpost.com/news/local-news/city-hall/indigenous-framework-could-be-a-win-for-everybody-says-fnuniv-expert.

6 Donovan Maess, "'An Explicit Endorsement': Regina City Council Votes Down Motion to Rename Dewdney Avenue," *CTV News Regina*, August 21, 2024, https://regina.ctvnews.ca/an-explicit-endorsement-regina-city-council-votes-down-motion-to-rename-dewdney-avenue-1.7009666.

7 Larissa Kurz, "'Shameful': Quick Debates Leads to 7-3 Vote Against New Name for Dewdney Ave.," *Regina Leader-Post*, August 21, 2024, https://leaderpost.com/news/local-news/city-hall/no-new-name-for-dewdney-avenue-says-regina-city-council.

8 Kurz, "'Shameful.'"

9 City officials approached BigEagle-Kequahtooway in 2016 for assistance with issues related to truth and reconciliation, including changing the name of Dewdney Avenue; council's rejection of her efforts left her feeling that the city doesn't care about the concerns of Indigenous people. See Louise BigEagle, "Regina City Council's Rejection of Dewdney Avenue Renaming Disappointing for Advocate, Researchers," *CBC News*, August 24, 2024, https://www.cbc.ca/news/canada/saskatchewan/regina-council-dewdney-avenue-renaming-reaction-1.7303983.

10 Candace Savage and Meghan Mickelson, "Opinion: Saskatoon Freeway Plan a Remnant of Rejected Urban Thinking," *Saskatoon Star-Phoenix*, April 10, 2024, https://thestarphoenix.com/opinion/columnists/opinion-saskatoon-freeway-plan-a-remnant-of-rejected-urban-thinking; see also Bryn Levy, "Saskatoon City Council Passes Freeway Route Endorsement, Approves Borrowing for Solar Farm," *Saskatoon Star-Phoenix*, May 29, 2024, https://thestarphoenix.com/news/local-news/saskatoon-city-council-passes-freeway-route-endorsement-approves-borrowing-for-solar-farm.

11 Geoff Leo, "Sask. 'Moving Forward' with $1.15B Lake Diefenbaker Irrigation Project Despite Incomplete Feasibility Study," In Depth, *CBC News*, August

21, 2024, https://www.cbc.ca/news/canada/saskatchewan/sask-moving-forward-with-1-15b-lake-diefenbaker-irrigation-project-despite-incomplete-feasibility-study-1.7296727.

12 KPMG, "Economic Analysis: Westside Irrigation Rehabilitation Project," September 2024, 4, https://diefenbakerirrigation.ca/wp-content/uploads/2024/11/WIRP-Economic-Analysis.pdf.

13 KPMG, "Economic Analysis," 4.

14 Geoff Leo, "Economists Say Review of Sask. Irrigation Megaproject Shows Cost Would Exceed Return to Provincial Government," *CBC News*, October 8, 2024, https://www.cbc.ca/news/canada/saskatchewan/cost-benefit-review-irrigation-megaproject-1.7337364.

15 Leo, "Economists Say."

16 Leo, "Economists Say."

17 Leo, "Sask. 'Moving Forward.'"

18 Leo, "Sask. 'Moving Forward.'"

19 Leo, "Economists Say."

20 Leo, "Economists Say."

21 Leo, "Economists Say."

22 Leo, "Economists Say."

23 Drew Anderson, "Construction Starts Soon on Saskatchewan's Largest Infrastructure Project—Ever. Here's What You Need to Know," *The Narwhal*, October 18, 2024, https://thenarwhal.ca/saskatchewan-election-lake-diefenbaker-irrigation/.

24 Anderson, "Construction Starts Soon."

25 Anderson, "Construction Starts Soon."

26 Alexander Quon, "FSIN Raises Concerns About Lack of Consultation as Sask. Announces Work on Irrigation Project," *CBC News*, March 15, 2024, https://www.cbc.ca/news/canada/saskatchewan/fsin-raises-concerns-about-lack-of-consultation-as-sask-announces-work-on-irrigation-project-1.7145267.

27 Alexandre Silberman, "In Saskatchewan, North America's Third Largest Inland River Delta Is Under Threat," *CBC News*, August 8, 2024, https://www.cbc.ca/news/canada/saskatchewan/saskatchewan-river-delta-lake-diefenbaker-1.7288013.

28 Anderson, "Construction Starts Soon."

29 Phil Tank, "Sask. Plans Irrigation from Depleted Diefenbaker Watershed," *Regina Leader-Post*, March 27, 2024, https://leaderpost.com/opinion/columnists/phil-tank-sask-plans-irrigation-from-depleted-diefenbaker-watershed/wcm/d640b5fc-2186-4a9d-989c-de8b8ba8734a.

30 On the Anthropocene, see Erle C. Ellis, *Anthropocene: A Very Short Introduction* (Oxford University Press, 2018). Much has been written on the science of climate change and the responses of writers and artists to it;

see, for example, Amy Brady and Tajja Isen, eds., *The World As We Knew It: Dispatches from a Changing Climate* (Catapult, 2022); Heather Davis and Etienne Turpin, eds., *Art in the Anthropocene: Encounters Among Aesthetics, Politics, Environments and Epistemologies* (Open Humanities Press, 2015); David J. Gibson and Jonathan A. Newman, eds., *Grasslands and Climate Change* (Cambridge University Press, 2019); Barry Lopez, *Embrace Fearlessly the Burning World: Essays* (Random House, 2023); Kathryn Mockler, ed., *Watch Your Head: Writers and Artists Respond to the Climate Crisis* (Coach House Books, 2020); Anna Tsing et al., eds., *Arts of Living on a Damaged Planet: Ghosts and Monsters of the Anthropocene* (University of Minnesota Press, 2017); and Catriona Sandilands, ed., *Rising Tides: Reflections for Climate Changing Times* (Caitlin Press, 2019). One recent artistic reflection on climate change that I found deeply moving was Amy Snider's *Crushed*; see Amy Snider, "Crushed, August 20–27th 2024, Fifth Parallel Gallery, University of Regina," *Precipice*, August 4, 2024, https://amysnider.ca/2024/08/04/crushed-august-20-27th-2024-fifth-parallel-gallery-university-of-regina/.

31 Annie Hylton, "How Scott Moe Moved Saskatchewan—and Canada—Further Right," *Walrus*, July 23, 2024, https://thewalrus.ca/scott-moe/.

32 Kendall Latimer, "Experts Say Sask. RMs' Vote Against Climate Change Policies Not Rooted in Fact," *CBC News*, March 31, 2024, https://www.cbc.ca/news/canada/saskatoon/sarm-resolution-climate-change-agriculture-1.7158627.

33 Murray Mandryk, "Our Long, Hard Journey: Treaty 4 and 150 Years of Unfulfilled Promises," *Regina Leader-Post*, September 14, 2024, https://leaderpost.com/feature/our-long-hard-journey-treaty-4-and-150-years-of-unfulfilled-promises.

34 Doug Cuthand, "Treaty 4 Marks 150 Years with a Legacy of Broken Promises," *Saskatoon Star-Phoenix*, September 14, 2024, https://thestarphoenix.com/opinion/columnists/cuthand-150th-anniversary-treaty-signing-broken-promises.

35 Cuthand, "Treaty 4 Marks 150 Years with a Legacy of Broken Promises."

36 "Fort Qu'Appelle, Sask., Gathering Celebrates 150th Anniversary of Treaty 4," *CBC News*, September 15, 2024, https://www.cbc.ca/news/canada/saskatchewan/treaty-4-gathering-sask-150-anniversary-1.7323820.

37 "Fort Qu'Appelle, Sask., Gathering."

38 Alexander Morris, *The Treaties of Canada with the Indians of Manitoba and the North-West Territories, Including the Negotiations on Which They Were Based, and Other Information Relating Thereto* (Belfords, Clark & Co., 1880; repr., Coles, 1971), 115.

39 "Cargill Canola Crusher to Be Built in Global Transportation Hub," *Regina Leader-Post*, August 17, 2021, https://leaderpost.com/news/local-news/

cargill-canola-crusher-to-be-built-in-global-transportation-hub.

40 "Cargill Canola Crusher"; "Cargill Passes Halfway Mark on Regina Canola Crush Plant Construction," *RealAgriculture.com*, July 16, 2024, https://www.realagriculture.com/2024/07/cargill-passes-halfway-mark-on-regina-canola-crush-plant-construction/.

41 "SaskPower Grants $95M Contract to Finish Operations Hub at GTH," *Regina Leader-Post*, August 12, 2024, https://leaderpost.com/news/saskatchewan/saskpower-grants-95m-contract-to-finish-operations-hub-at-gth; "Morguard Investments," *GTH: Global Transportation Hub*, accessed August 10, 2024, https://thegth.com/regulatory/current-businesses/morguard-investments; "SLGA," *GTH: Global Transportation Hub*, accessed August 10, 2024, https://thegth.com/regulatory/current-businesses/saskatchewan-liquor-and-gaming-authority; "Regina Operations and Maintenance Complex," *SaskPower*, accessed August 10, 2024, https://www.saskpower.com/our-power-future/infrastructure-projects/construction-projects/planning-and-construction-projects/regina-operations-and-maintenance-complex.

42 For a list, see "Current Businesses," *GTH: Global Transportation Hub*, accessed August 10, 2024, https://thegth.com/regulatory/current-businesses.

43 "SaskPower Grants $95M Contract to Finish Operations Hub at GTH"; "Annual Report for 2023-24 Global Transportation Hub," March 31, 2024, 7, 12, https://thegth.com/wp-content/uploads/2024/12/GTH-Annual-Report-2023-24-Final.pdf.

BIBLIOGRAPHY

Abram, David. *The Spell of the Sensuous: Perception and Language in a More-Than-Human World.* 2nd ed. Vintage, 2017.

Ackerman, Jennifer. "Settlement Reached Four Years After Incident Between Indigenous Man and Regina Police." *Regina Leader-Post*, July 27, 2018. https://leaderpost.com/news/local-news/settlement-reached-four-years-after-incident-between-indigenous-man-and-regina-police.

Ahenakew, Edward. "Cree Trickster Tales." *Journal of American Folklore* 42, no. 166 (1929): 309–53. https://www.jstor.org/stable/535231.

Althusser, Louis. "Ideology and Ideological State Apparatuses (Notes Towards an Investigation)." In *Lenin and Philosophy and Other Essays*, translated by Ben Brewster. NYU Press, 2001.

Anderson, Drew. "Construction Starts Soon on Saskatchewan's Largest Infrastructure Project—Ever. Here's What You Need to Know." *The Narwhal*, October 18, 2024. https://thenarwhal.ca/saskatchewan-election-lake-diefenbaker-irrigation/.

Anderson, Matthew R. *The Good Walk: Creating New Paths on Traditional Prairie Trails.* University of Regina Press, 2024.

———. "Pilgrimage and the Challenging of a Canadian Foundational Myth." In *Pilgrimage in Practice: Narration, Reclamation and*

Healing, edited by Ian S. McIntosh, E. Moore Quinn, and Vivian Keely. CABI, 2018.

———. "Why Canadians Need the Right to Roam." *The Conversation.* July 29, 2018. https://theconversation.com/why-canadians-need-the-right-to-roam-100497.

Andrews, Jennifer. "Irony, Métis Style: Reading the Poetry of Marilyn Dumont and Gregory Schofield." *Canadian Poetry: Studies, Documents, Reviews* 50 (2002): 6–31. https://canadianpoetry.org/wp-content/uploads/2020/03/Studies-1-50.pdf.

Asch, Michael. *On Being Here to Stay: Treaties and Aboriginal Rights in Canada.* University of Toronto Press, 2014.

Ash-Moccasin, Simon. "I Was Racially Profiled, Roughed Up, & Detained by Police for Being Indigenous." *Briarpatch Magazine*, December 17, 2014. https://briarpatchmagazine.com/articles/view/i-was-racially-profiled.

Aubrey, Allison. "Forest Bathing: A Retreat to Nature Can Boost Immunity and Mood." *NPR.org*, July 17, 2017. https://www.npr.org/sections/health-shots/2017/07/17/536676954/forest-bathing-a-retreat-to-nature-can-boost-immunity-and-mood.

Augé, Marc. *Non-Places: Introduction to an Anthropology of Supermodernity.* Translated by John Howe. Verso, 1995.

Back, Les. "Marchers and Steppers: Memory, City Life and Walking." In *Walking Through Social Research*, edited by Charlotte Bates and Alex Rhys-Taylor. Routledge, 2017.

Baird, Craig. "City Announces Substantial Completion of Wastewater Treatment Plant." *Regina Leader-Post*, December 20, 2016. https://leaderpost.com/news/local-news/city-announces-substantial-completion-of-water-treatment-plant.

———. "What Will the Stadium's Final Price Tag Really Be?" *Regina Leader-Post*, June 9, 2017. https://leaderpost.com/news/local-news/what-will-the-stadiums-final-price-tag-really-be.

Baldwin, Andrew. "Whiteness and Futurity: Towards a Research Agenda." *Progress in Human Geography* 36, no. 2 (2012): 172–87. https://doi.org/10.1177/0309132511414603.

Barron, F. Laurie. "The Indian Pass System in the Canadian West, 1882–1935." In *Immigration and Settlement, 1870–1939*, edited by Gregory P. Marchildon. Canadian Plains Research Center, 2009.

Barry, Bill. *People Places: The Dictionary of Saskatchewan Place Names.* Canadian Plains Research Center, 1997.

Bates, Charlotte. "Desire Lines: Walking in Woolwich." In *Walking Through Social Research*, edited by Charlotte Bates and Alex Rhys-Taylor. Routledge, 2017.

Bauman, Zygmunt. *Liquid Modernity.* Polity, 2000.

BBC *News.* "The 11 Cities Most Likely to Run Out of Drinking Water." February 10, 2018. https://www.bbc.com/news/world-42982959.

Benjoe, Kerry. "Regina Ready to Grow Its Borders." *Regina Leader-Post*, January 30, 2009: A1.

———. "What's in a Name? A Lot, According to Some Regina Residents." *Regina Leader-Post*, January 25, 2017. https://leaderpost.com/news/local-news/whats-in-a-name-a-lot-according-to-some-regina-residents.

Bennett, Jane. *Vibrant Matter: A Political Ecology of Things.* Duke University Press, 2010.

Berge, Chloe. "This Canadian River Is Now Legally a Person. It's Not the Only One." *National Geographic*, April 15, 2022. https://www.nationalgeographic.com/travel/article/these-rivers-are-now-considered-people-what-does-that-mean-for-travelers.

Bidwell, Kristina Fagan. "'Our New Storytellers': Cree Literature in Saskatchewan." In *The Literary History of Saskatchewan*, vol. 1, *Beginnings*, edited by David Carpenter. Coteau Books, 2013.

BigEagle, Louise. "Regina City Council's Rejection of Dewdney Avenue Renaming Disappointing for Advocate, Researchers." CBC *News*, August 24, 2024. https://www.cbc.ca/news/canada/saskatchewan/regina-council-dewdney-avenue-renaming-reaction-1.7303983.

Blake, William. Preface to "Milton: a Poem in [1] 2 Books." *Blake Complete Writings: With Variant Readings.* 2nd ed. Edited by Geoffrey Keynes. Oxford University Press, 1969.

Borrows, John. *Canada's Indigenous Constitution.* University of Toronto Press, 2010.

———. "Wampum at Niagara: The Royal Proclamation, Canadian Legal History, and Self-Government." In *Aboriginal and Treaty Rights in Canada: Essays on Law, Equality, and Respect for Difference*, edited by Michael Asch. UBC Press, 1998.

Brady, Amy, and Tajja Isen, eds. *The World As We Knew It: Dispatches from a Changing Climate.* Catapult, 2022.

Brady, Miranda J., and Emily Hiltz. "The Archaeology of an Image: The Persistent Persuasion of Thomas Moore Keesick's Residential School Photographs." TOPIA: *Canadian Journal of Cultural Studies* 37 (Spring 2017): 61–85. https://utpjournals.press/doi/pdf/10.3138/topia.37.61.

Brake, Justin. "How Canada Can Give Land Back." *Breach Magazine*, January 29, 2022. https://breachmedia.ca/how-canada-can-give-land-back/.

Brass, Eleanor. "Legend of Qu'Appelle." In *kisiskâciwan: Indigenous Voices from Where the River Flows Swiftly*, edited by Jesse Rae Archibald-Barber. University of Regina Press, 2018.

Brennan, J. William. *Regina: An Illustrated History*. James Lorimer & Company, 1989.

Brower, Jennifer. *Lost Tracks: Buffalo National Park, 1908–1939*. Athabasca University Press, 2008.

Brown, Vanessa. "Province Introduces New Bypass." *Regina Leader-Post*, February 13, 2013: A3.

The Buffalo: A Treaty of Cooperation, Renewal, and Restoration. https://www.buffalotreaty.com.

Burton, Tara Isabella. "The Prosperity Gospel, Explained: Why Joel Osteen Believes That Prayer Can Make You Rich." *Vox*, September 1, 2017. https://www.vox.com/identities/2017/9/1/15951874/prosperity-gospel-explained-why-joel-osteen-believes-prayer-can-make-you-rich-trump.

Butala, Sharon. *The Perfection of the Morning: An Apprenticeship in Nature*. Harper Perennial, 1995.

Cadogan, Garnette. "Walking While Black: Garnette Cadogan on the Realities of Being Black in America." *Literary Hub*, July 8, 2016. https://lithub.com/walking-while-black/.

Canadian Press. "Large Herd of Bison Still on the Loose Near Tisdale." *Regina Leader-Post*, December 15, 2015. https://leaderpost.com/news/saskatchewan/large-herd-of-roaming-bison-still-on-the-loose-near-tisdale.

———. "Most Support Changing Sask. Trespassing Laws After Colten Boushie's Death: Survey." CTV *News*, November 15, 2018. https://www.ctvnews.ca/canada/most-support-changing-sask-trespassing-laws-after-colten-boushie-death-survey-1.4178884.

———. "Saskatchewan Government Says Company Chosen to Build Bypass Disclosed Allegations." *Globe and Mail*, June 10, 2015. https://www.theglobeandmail.com/feeds/canadian-press/saskatchewan/saskatchewan-government-says-company-chosen-to-build-bypass-disclosed-allegations/article24910113/.

Cardinal, Harold. *The Unjust Society: The Tragedy of Canada's Indians*. Hurtig, 1969.

Cardinal, Harold, and Walter Hildebrandt. *Treaty Elders of Saskatchewan: Our Dream Is That Our Peoples Will One Day Be Clearly Recognized as Nations*. University of Calgary Press, 2000.

"Cargill Canola Crusher to Be Built in Global Transportation Hub." *Regina Leader-Post*, August 17, 2021. https://leaderpost.com/news/local-news/cargill-canola-crusher-to-be-built-in-global-transportation-hub.

"Cargill Passes Halfway Mark on Regina Canola Crush Plant Construction." *RealAgriculture.com*, July 16, 2024. https://www.realagriculture.com/2024/07/cargill-passes-halfway-mark-on-regina-canola-crush-plant-construction/.

Cariou, Warren. "Haunted Prairie: Aboriginal 'Ghosts' and the Spectres of Settlement." *University of Toronto Quarterly* 75, no. 2 (2006): 727–34. https://doi.org/10.1353/utq.2006.0245.

Carter, Jill, Karyn Recollet, and Dylan Robinson. "Interventions into the Maw of Old World Hunger: Frog Monsters, Kinstellatory Maps, and Radical Relationalities in a Project of Reworlding." In *Canadian Performance Histories and Historiographies*. New Essays in Canadian Theatre Vol. 7. Edited by Heather Davis-Fisch. Playwrights Canada Press, 2017.

Carter, Sarah. *Lost Harvests: Prairie Indian Reserve Farmers and Government Policy*. 2nd ed. McGill-Queen's University Press, 2019.

CBC News. "'First Step in Reconciliation' as Government Hands Over Residential School Cemetery." June 25, 2019. https://www.cbc.ca/news/canada/saskatchewan/riis-residential-school-cemetery-land-transfer-1.5188585.

———. "Fort Qu'Appelle, Sask., Gathering Celebrates 150th Anniversary of Treaty 4." September 15, 2024. https://www.cbc.ca/news/canada/saskatchewan/treaty-4-gathering-sask-150-anniversary-1.7323820.

———. "Government Paid Too Much for GTH Land: Sask. Provincial Auditor." June 30, 2016. https://www.cbc.ca/news/canada/saskatchewan/provincial-auditor-saskatchewan-gth-highways-1.3659296.

———. "GTH Won't Release Land Deal Appraisal Because It Could 'Harm the Reputation' of Preparer." CBC Investigates. May 9, 2016. https://www.cbc.ca/news/canada/saskatchewan/global-transportation-hub-release-land-deal-appraisal-1.3570688.

———. "NDP Leader Cam Broten Calls for Judicial Inquiry into GTH Land Deal." March 3, 2016. https://www.cbc.ca/news/canada/saskatchewan/ndp-broten-gth-land-deal-inquiry-saskachewan-1.3474315.

———. "Regina Approves Plan for Population of 500,000." June 10, 2013. https://www.cbc.ca/news/canada/saskatchewan/regina-approves-plan-for-population-of-500-000-1.1396257.

Centre for Rupert's Land Studies. "What Is 'Rupert's Land'?" University of Winnipeg, n.d. https://www.uwinnipeg.ca/rupertsland/about-us/what-is-rupertsland.html.

Christiansen, E.A. "The Wisconsinan Deglaciation, of Southern Saskatchewan and Adjacent Areas." *Canadian Journal of Earth Sciences* 16, no. 4 (1979): 913–38. https://doi.org/10.1139/e79-079.

Christianson, Adriana. "Sask. Woman Describes Threatening Encounter with Landowner." *980 CJME News*, September 14, 2018. https://www.cjme.com/2018/09/14/sask-woman-describes-threatening-encounter-with-landowner/.

Coleman, Daniel. *Yardwork: A Biography of an Urban Place*. James Street North Books, 2017.

Coneghan, Daria. "Regina." In *The Encyclopedia of Saskatchewan: A Living Legacy*. Canadian Plains Research Center, 2005.

Couture, Joe. "Councillor Pushes for Highway Bypass." *Regina Leader-Post*, February 20, 2010: A4.

———. "Work Underway on West Regina Bypass." *Regina Leader-Post*, September 22, 2011: A13.

Coyle, Jim. "Canada 150: When a Man with an Eagle Feather Thwarted the High and Mighty." *Toronto Star*, May 27, 2017. https://www.thestar.com/news/insight/canada-150-when-a-man-with-an-eagle-feather-thwarted-the-high-and-mighty/article_12365086-be6d-5f31-85c5-1211aac6affc.html.

Coyle, Michael. "As Long as the Sun Shines: Recognizing That Treaties Were Intended to Last." In *The Right Relationship: Reimagining the Implementation of Historical Treaties*, edited by John Borrows and Michael Coyle. University of Toronto Press, 2017.

Craft, Aimée. *Breathing Life into the Stone Fort Treaty: An Anishinabe Understanding of Treaty One*. Purich, 2013.

Crosschild, Ryan, Gina Starblanket, Daniel Voth, Tasha Hubbard, and Leroy Little Bear. "Awakening Buffalo Consciousness: Lessons, Theory, and Practice from the Buffalo Treaty." *Wicazo Sa Review* 36, no. 1 (2021): 5–29. https://doi.org/10.1353/wic.2021.a903665.

Cuthand, Beth. "For All the Settlers Who Secretly Sing." In *Native Poetry in Canada: A Contemporary Anthology*, edited by Jeannette C. Armstrong and Lally Grauer. Broadview Press, 2001.

Cuthand, Doug. "Canada Must Be Better Than Our History." *Saskatoon Star-Phoenix*, August 1, 2020. https://thestarphoenix.com/opinion/columnists/cuthand-canada-must-be-better-than-our-history.

———. "Treaty 4 Marks 150 Years with Legacy of Broken Promises." *Saskatoon Star-Phoenix*, September 14, 2024. https://thestarphoenix.com/opinion/columnists/cuthand-150th-anniversary-treaty-signing-broken-promises.

———. "Trespass Law Amendment Shows No Respect for Treaty Rights." *Saskatoon Star-Phoenix*, January 22, 2022. https://thestarphoenix.com/opinion/columnists/cuthand-trespass-law-amendment-shows-no-respect-for-treaty-rights.

Dale, Janis. "Proglacial Lakes." In *The Encyclopedia of Saskatchewan: A Living Legacy*. Canadian Plains Research Center, 2005.

Daschuk, James. *Clearing the Plains: Disease, Politics of Starvation, and the Loss of Indigenous Life*. 2nd ed. University of Regina Press, 2019.

Davies, John. *Walking the M62*. Lulu Self-Publishing, 2007.

Davis, Heather, and Etienne Turpin, eds. *Art in the Anthropocene: Encounters Among Aesthetics, Politics, Environments and Epistemologies*. Open Humanities Press, 2015.

Dawson, George Mercer. *Report on the Geology and Resources of the Region in the Vicinity of the Forty-Ninth Parallel from the Lake of the Woods to the Rocky Mountains, with Lists of Plants and Animals Collected and Notes on the Fossils*. Dawson Brothers, 1875. https://hdl.handle.net/2027/aeu.ark:/13960/t6pz5wn9t.

de Bruin, Tabitha. "Elijah Harper." In *The Canadian Encyclopedia*. Article published July 31, 2013; last modified May 30, 2024. https://www.thecanadianencyclopedia.ca/en/article/elijah-harper.

Deloria, Ella. "Meadow-lark and the Rattlesnake." In *Dakota Texts*. University of Nebraska Press, 2006.

DiAngelo, Robin. *White Fragility: Why It's So Hard for White People to Talk About Racism*. Beacon Press, 2018.

Donald, Dwayne. "We Need a New Story: Walking and the *wâhkôhtowin* Imagination." *Journal of the Canadian Association for Curriculum Studies* 18, no. 2 (2021): 53–63. https://doi.org/10.25071/1916-4467.40492.

Dumont, Marilyn. "Letter to Sir John A. Macdonald." *A Really Good Brown Girl*. Brick Books, 1996.

Duranton, Gilles, and Matthew A. Turner. "The Fundamental Law of Road Congestion: Evidence from US Cities." *American Economic Review* 101, no. 6 (2011): 2616–52. http://www.aeaweb.org/articles.php?doi=10.1257/aer.101.6.2616.

Ellis, Erle C. *Anthropocene: A Very Short Introduction*. Oxford University Press, 2018.

Ermine, Willie. "The Ethical Space of Engagement." *Indigenous Law Journal* 6, no. 1 (2007): 193–203. https://jps.library.utoronto.ca/index.php/ilj/article/view/27669/20400.

Fisher, Teal, Joanne Marchand, and Ericka Donald. "Saskatchewan Native Prairie Habitat Inventory: A Collaborative Study Between Saskatchewan Polytechnic and Environment Canada." Unpublished research paper. June 23, 2020.

Frank Flegel, "Abandoned Church Deconsecrated," *Prairie Messenger*, May 2, 2018, 7, https://stpetersabbey.ca/wp/wp-content/uploads/2021/03/PM-05-02-2018.vol95_no44pdf-min-1.pdf.

Forbes, Jack D. *Columbus and Other Cannibals: The Wétiko Disease of Exploitation, Imperialism, and Terrorism*. Rev. ed. Seven Stories Press, 2008.

Fraser, D.C. "Province Responds to Concern New Bypass Roundabout Too Small for Big Vehicles." *Regina Leader-Post*, August 1, 2017. https://leaderpost.com/news/saskatchewan/province-responds-to-concern-new-bypass-roundabout-too-small-for-big-vehicles.

———. "Regina Indian Industrial School Cemetery to Get Heritage Status." *Regina Leader-Post*, July 25, 2017. https://leaderpost.com/

news/saskatchewan/regina-indian-industrial-school-cemetery-to-get-heritage-status.

———. "West Bypass Not Nearly as Busy as Projected When GTH Was Built: NDP." *Regina Leader-Post*, October 30, 2018. https://leaderpost.com/news/saskatchewan/west-bypass-not-nearly-as-busy-as-projected-when-gth-was-built-ndp.

Frazier, Ian. *Great Plains.* Farrar, Straus and Giroux, 1989.

Frost, Robert. "Nothing Gold Can Stay." In *The Poetry of Robert Frost*, edited by Edward Connery Lathem. Holt, Rinehart and Winston, 1969.

Ganev, Robin. "Making Private Property in Rural Britain and Canada." *Active History*, March 23, 2022. https://activehistory.ca/2022/03/making-private-property-in-rural-britain-and-canada/.

Gardiner, Karen. "How Canadian Bison Have Been Brought Back from the Brink in Saskatchewan." *National Geographic*, June 3, 2023. https://www.nationalgeographic.com/travel/article/canadian-bison-brought-back-saskatchewan.

Gibson, David J., and Jonathan A. Newman, eds. *Grasslands and Climate Change.* Cambridge University Press, 2019.

Giesbrecht, Lynn. "Grave Markers Donated for Regina Indian Industrial School Site." *Regina Leader-Post*, September 12, 2021. https://leaderpost.com/news/local-news/grave-markers-donated-for-regina-indian-industrial-school-site.

Gilbride, Bridget, Emilie Bundock, Marie-Pierre Boudreau, Niall Rand, Nao Garcia-Ahmad, and Samuel Gesterfer. "Restoule Decision Finds the Crown Breached Its Promises to Robinson Treaty Beneficiaries." *Fasken*, August 8, 2024. https://www.fasken.com/en/knowledge/2024/08/restoule-decision-finds-the-crown-breached-its-promise.

Gillam, Carey. "People Exposed to Weed Killer Chemical Have Cancer Biomarkers in Urine: Study." *Guardian*, January 20, 2023. https://www.theguardian.com/us-news/2023/jan/20/glyphosate-weedkiller-cancer-biomarkers-urine-study.

Globalspec. "Reach Stackers and ISO Container Handlers Information." Accessed November 28, 2024. https://www.globalspec.com/learnmore/material_handling_packaging_equipment/material_handling_equipment/reach_stackers.

Gober, Patricia, and Howard S. Wheater. "Socio-Hydrology and the Science-Policy Interface: A Case Study of the Saskatchewan River

Basin." *Hydrology and Earth System Sciences* 18, no. 4 (2014): 1413–22. https://doi.org/10.5194/hess-18-1413-2014.

Gordon, Ariel. *Treed: Walking in Canada's Urban Forests*. Wolsak and Wynn, 2020.

Graney, Emma. "Bypass Costs Climbing; $1.88B Doesn't Include Land Purchases." *Regina Leader-Post*, August 6, 2015: A1.

GTH *Global Transportation Hub*. "Annual Report for 2023-24 Global Transportation Hub." March 31, 2024. https://thegth.com/wp-content/uploads/2024/12/GTH-Annual-Report-2023-24-Final.pdf.

———. "Current Businesses." Accessed August 10, 2024. https://thegth.com/regulatory/current-businesses.

———. "Emterra Group." Accessed August 10, 2024. https://thegth.com/regulatory/current-businesses/emterra-group.

———. "Morguard Investments." Accessed August 10, 2024. https://thegth.com/regulatory/current-businesses/morguard-investments.

———. "SLGA." Accessed August 10, 2024. https://thegth.com/regulatory/current-businesses/saskatchewan-liquor-and-gaming-authority.

Guardian. "Canada Reintroduces Bison to Banff National Park After More Than a Century." February 13, 2017. https://www.theguardian.com/world/2017/feb/13/canada-reintroduces-bison-banff-national-park.

Hall, Angela. "More Cash for Growing Transport Facility." *Regina Leader-Post*, January 7, 2009: A1.

Halliday, Robert. "Diefenbaker Project Not Worth the Cost." *Western Producer*, July 2, 2020. https://www.producer.com/opinion/diefenbaker-project-not-worth-the-cost/.

Hamilton, Ian. "Fiacco Says Regina Can't Foot the Bill on Its Own." *Regina Leader-Post*, February 24, 2009: C1.

Hemingway, Ernest. *The Sun Also Rises*. Scribner's, 1954.

Herriot, Trevor. *Grass, Sky, Song: Promise and Peril in the World of Grassland Birds*. HarperCollins, 2010.

———. *River in a Dry Land: A Prairie Passage*. Stoddart, 2000.

———. "The River Within Us." In *The Eye in the Thicket: Essays at a Natural History*, edited by Seán Virgo. Thistledown, 2002.

———. *The Road Is How: A Prairie Pilgrimage Through Nature, Desire, and Soul*. HarperCollins, 2014.

———. *Towards a Prairie Atonement*. University of Regina Press, 2016.

Hill, Don. "Listening to Stones: Learning in Leroy Little Bear's Laboratory: Dialogue in the World Outside." *Alberta Views*, September 1, 2008. https://albertaviews.ca/listening-to-stones/.

Hill, Susan M. *The Clay We Are Made Of: Haudenosaunee Land Tenure on the Grand River*. University of Manitoba Press, 2017.

Hind, Henry Youle. *Narrative of the Canadian Red River Exploring Expedition of 1857 and of the Assinniboine and Saskatchewan Exploring Expedition of 1858*. 2 vols. Longman, Green, Longman, and Roberts, 1860. Canadiana by CKRN. https://www.canadiana.ca/view/oocihm.35700/9.

Holston, James. *The Modernist City: An Anthropological Critique of Brasília*. University of Chicago Press, 1989.

Hunter, Adam. "Gov't Says Farm Equipment May Have to Drive On Curb of New Balgonie Overpass." *CBC News*, July 31, 2017. https://www.cbc.ca/news/canada/saskatchewan/part-of-new-overpass-too-narrow-says-balgonie-farmer-1.4229553.

———. "Regina Bypass Deficiency Costs Not a Concern for Taxpayers: Gov't." *CBC News*, November 17, 2018. https://www.cbc.ca/news/canada/saskatchewan/regina-bypass-deficiencies-1.4909460.

Hryniuk, Margaret, and Meta Perry. *Regina: A City of Beautiful Homes*. First Writing, 1994.

Hubbard, Tasha. "Buffalo Genocide in Nineteenth-Century North America: 'Kill, Skin, and Sell.'" In *Colonial Genocide in Indigenous North America*, edited by Andrew Woolford, Jeff Benvenuto, and Alexander Laban Hinton. Duke University Press, 2014.

Hudon, Pierre-André. "A Critique of Public-Private Partnerships in Quebec: Democratic Deficiencies and Unethical Procurement." *Public Integrity* 13, no. 3 (2011): 257–74. https://www.tandfonline.com/doi/abs/10.2753/PIN1099-9922130306.

Hylton, Annie. "How Scott Moe Moved Saskatchewan—and Canada—Further Right." *Walrus*, July 23, 2024. https://thewalrus.ca/scott-moe.

Hyslop, Joe, Harry Bone, and the Treaty & Dakota Elders of Manitoba with contributions by the AMC Council of Elders, *Dtantu Balai Betl Nahidei: Our Relations to the Newcomers*. Treaty Elders' Teachings, Vol. 3. Treaty Relations Commission of Manitoba, 2015.

Ilgunas, Ken. *This Land Is Our Land: How We Lost the Right to Roam and How to Take It Back*. Plume, 2018.

Indigenous Services Canada. "Treaty Land Entitlement in Saskatchewan." April 11, 2017. https://www.sac-isc.gc.ca/eng/1100100034825/1611943779434.

Ingold, Tim. *Lines*. Routledge, 2016.

———. "The Temporality of Landscape." *World Archaeology* 25, no. 2 (1993): 152–72. https://doi.org/10.1080/00438243.1993.9980235.

Isenberg, Andrew C. *The Destruction of the Bison: An Environmental History, 1750–1920*. Cambridge University Press, 2000.

Jacobs, Jane. *The Death and Life of Great American Cities*. Rev. ed. Vintage, 1992.

———. *The Economy of Cities*. Vintage, 1970.

Jai, Julie. "Bargains Made in Bad Times: How Principles from Modern Treaties Can Reinvigorate Historic Treaties." In *The Right Relationship: Reimagining the Implementation of Historical Treaties*, edited by John Borrows and Michael Coyle. University of Toronto Press, 2017.

James, Thia. "Tackling Rural Crime Remains Focus for Province, Sask. Organizations." *Regina Leader-Post*, December 18, 2021. https://leaderpost.com/news/local-news/tackling-rural-crime-remains-focus-for-province-sask-organizations/wcm/4ba91ae7-2ee6-41d5-a96a-894194d9a8b3.

Johnson, Harold R. *Peace and Good Order: The Case for Indigenous Justice in Canada*. McClelland & Stewart, 2019.

———. *The Power of Story: On Truth, the Trickster, and New Fictions for a New Era*. Biblioasis, 2022.

———. *Two Families: Treaties and Government*. Purich, 2007.

Johnstone, Bruce. "A Distribution Centre, 500,000 Square Feet of Space, 750 Jobs Within Two Years, and an Investment of $200 Million All Add Up to One Big Project (and More in the Works)." *Regina Leader-Post*, July 30, 2008: A1.

———. "P3s Positive, Not Always Perfect: Pros, Cons Discussed at Conference." *Regina Leader-Post*, June 4, 2013: D1.

———. "Subdivision Worth $1B; New Neighbourhood Near Regina's Airport." *Regina Leader-Post*, July 10, 2007: A1.

———. "To P3 or Not to P3?" *Regina Leader-Post*, October 26, 2013: B1.

———. "Transport Hub Touted; Regina Distribution Centre Will See 1,400 Trucks Weekly When Fully Operational." *Saskatoon Star-Phoenix*, February 2, 2011: C6.

Joseph, Bob. *21 Things You May Not Know About the Indian Act: Helping Canadians Make Reconciliation with Indigenous Peoples a Reality.* Page Two Press, 2018.

Kimmerer, Robin Wall. *Braiding Sweetgrass: Indigenous Wisdom, Scientific Knowledge, and the Teachings of Plants.* Milkweed Editions, 2013.

———. "Speaking of Nature: Finding Language That Affirms Our Kinship with the Natural World." *Orion*, March/April 2017. https://orionmagazine.org/article/speaking-of-nature/.

King, Hayden, and Shiri Pasternak. *Land Back: A Yellowhead Institute Red Paper.* Yellowhead Institute, 2019. https://redpaper.yellowheadinstitute.org/wp-content/uploads/2019/10/red-paper-report-final.pdf.

Klein, Naomi. "Dancing the World into Being: A Conversation with Idle No More's Leanne Simpson." *Yes Magazine*, March 6, 2013. https://www.yesmagazine.org/social-justice/2013/03/06/dancing-the-world-into-being-a-conversation-with-idle-no-more-leanne-simpson/.

KPMG. "Economic Analysis: Westside Irrigation Rehabilitation Project." September 2024. https://diefenbakerirrigation.ca/wp-content/uploads/2024/11/WIRP-Economic-Analysis.pdf.

Krasowski, Sheldon. *No Surrender: The Land Remains Indigenous.* University of Regina Press, 2019.

Kraus, Dan. "Why Canada's Prairies Are the World's Most Endangered Ecosystem." *Nature Conservancy of Canada*, October 24, 2016. https://www.natureconservancy.ca/en/blog/archive/grasslands-the-most.html.

Krotz, Sarah. "Shadows of Indian Title: The Territorial Underpinnings of 'The Height of Land.'" *Canadian Literature*, no. 204 (Spring 2010): 85–101. https://doi.org/10.14288/cl.v0i204.192871.

Kurz, Larissa. "Indigenous Framework Could Be 'a Win for Everybody,' Says FNUniv Expert." *Regina Leader-Post*, October 15, 2023. https://leaderpost.com/news/local-news/city-hall/indigenous-framework-could-be-a-win-for-everybody-says-fnuniv-expert.

———. "Muscowpetung FN Says City Has Been Sitting on Proposal for the Yards." *Regina Leader-Post*, August 13, 2024. https://leaderpost.com/news/local-news/city-hall/muscowpetung-fn-says-idea-of-baseball-stadium-at-yards-a-surprise-to-hear.

———. "'Shameful': Quick Debate Leads to 7-3 Vote Against New Name for Dewdney Ave." *Regina Leader-Post*, August 21, 2024. https://leaderpost.com/news/local-news/city-hall/no-new-name-for-dewdney-avenue-says-regina-city-council.

Land, Clare. *Decolonizing Solidarity: Dilemmas and Directions for Supporters of Indigenous Struggles*. Zed Books, 2015.

Lanham, J. Drew. "9 Rules for the Black Birdwatcher." *Orion*, October 23, 2013. https://orionmagazine.org/article/9-rules-for-the-black-birdwatcher.

Laskaris, Sam. "National Chief Says Canada's True Past Being Exposed." *Windspeaker*, February 14, 2022. https://windspeaker.com/news/windspeaker-news/national-chief-says-canadas-true-past-being-exposed.

Latimer, Kendall. "Crown Land Sales Chip Away at Remaining Natural Prairie, Says Sask. Naturalist." *CBC News*, October 6, 2017. https://www.cbc.ca/news/canada/saskatchewan/sask-crown-land-needs-protection-says-activist-1.4343523.

———. "Experts Say Sask. RMs' Vote Against Climate Change Policies Not Rooted in Fact." *CBC News*, March 31, 2024. https://www.cbc.ca/news/canada/saskatoon/sarm-resolution-climate-change-agriculture-1.7158627.

———. "Sask. Advocates Raise Concerns About 20-Year Plan to Clear Cut Boreal Forest." *CBC News*, August 29, 2019. https://www.cbc.ca/news/canada/saskatchewan/people-call-more-consultation-prince-albert-forest-management-1.5262070.

Latour, Bruno. *Down to Earth: Politics in the New Climatic Regime*. Translated by Catherine Porter. Polity, 2018.

Leahy, Stephen. "Huge Decline in Songbirds Linked to Common Insecticide." *National Geographic*, September 12, 2019. https://www.nationalgeographic.com/environment/2019/09/widely-used-pesticide-makes-birds-lose-weight/#close.

Least Heat-Moon, William. *PrairyErth (a deep map)*. Mariner Books, 1999.

Legislative Assembly of Saskatchewan. *Debates and Proceedings (Hansard)*. 28th Legislature, 38th Session, Vol. 60, No. 13A. November 15, 2018. http://docs.legassembly.sk.ca/legdocs/Legislative%20Assembly/Hansard/28L3S/181115Debates.pdf.

———. Standing Committee on the Economy. *Hansard Verbatim Report*. 28th Legislature, No. 14. May 2, 2017. https://docs.legassembly

.sk.ca/legdocs/Legislative%20Committees/ECO/Debates/170502Debates-ECO.pdf.

Lehr, John C., John Everitt, and Simon Evans. "The Making of the Prairie Landscape." *Prairie Forum* 33, no. 1 (2008): 1–38.

Leo, Geoff. "3 Strikes: Sask. Government Chastised Again for Handling of GTH Document Requests." *CBC News*, January 17, 2017. https://www.cbc.ca/news/canada/saskatchewan/gth-information-privacy-commissioner-3rd-saskatchewan-government-1.3939695.

———. "Businessmen Made Millions on Regina Land That Wound Up in Taxpayers' Hands." CBC Investigates. *CBC News*, February 3, 2016. https://www.cbc.ca/news/canada/saskatchewan/businessmen-millions-regina-land-bill-boyd-1.3420479.

———. "Commissioner Rebukes Government for 'Excessive Delays' in GTH Info Requests." CBC Investigates. *CBC News*, November 14, 2016. https://www.cbc.ca/news/canada/saskatchewan/gth-foip-commissioner-requests-saskatchewan-1.3850264.

———. "Economists Say Review of Sask. Irrigation Megaproject Shows Cost Would Exceed Return to Provincial Government." *CBC News*, October 8, 2024. https://www.cbc.ca/news/canada/saskatchewan/cost-benefit-review-irrigation-megaproject-1.7337364.

———. "Government Defends 'Fake Map' of GTH to Sell Chinese Megamall as Artist's Rendering." CBC Investigates. *CBC News*, November 9, 2017. https://www.cbc.ca/news/canada/saskatchewan/government-defends-fake-map-of-gth-to-sell-chinese-megamall-as-artist-s-rendering-1.4393646.

———. "The GTH Land Deal You've Never Heard Of—and Bill Boyd Won't Talk About." CBC Investigates. *CBC News*, October 16, 2016. https://www.cbc.ca/news/canada/saskatchewan/gth-land-deal-bill-boyd-never-heard-of-1.3800855.

———. "Irrigation Equipment from Chinese Immigration Scheme Would Water Land Farmed by Bill Boyd." CBC Investigates. *CBC News*, August 24, 2017. https://www.cbc.ca/news/canada/saskatchewan/irrigation-equipment-from-chinese-immigration-scheme-would-water-land-farmed-by-bill-boyd-1.4259310.

———. "Police Investigating GTH Land Deal, Committee Hears." CBC Investigates. *CBC News*, November 28, 2016. https://www.cbc.ca/news/canada/saskatchewan/police-investigating-gth-land-deal-1.3870876.

———. "Regina Land Deal 'Looks Like It's Not a Normal Transaction': Auditor." CBC Investigates. *CBC News*, February 5, 2016. https://www.cbc.ca/news/canada/saskatchewan/regina-land-deal-normal-transaction-auditor-1.3435752.

———. "Sask. Government Agreed to Transfer 300 Acres of GTH Land to CP for No Cost." CBC Investigates. *CBC News*, April 23, 2017. https://www.cbc.ca/news/canada/saskatchewan/global-transportation-hub-cp-regina-1.4068125.

———. "Sask. Government Charging $180K for Access to GTH Land Deal Documents." CBC Investigates. *CBC News*, May 3, 2016. https://www.cbc.ca/news/canada/saskatchewan/government-charging-access-global-transportation-hub-land-deal-1.3564268.

———. "SaskPower Bought $25M of GTH Land Just in Time to Fund Controversial Deal." CBC Investigates. *CBC News*, October 18, 2016. https://www.cbc.ca/news/canada/saskatchewan/saskpower-bought-25-million-gth-land-controversial-deal-1.3807286.

———. "'Wrongdoing' in GTH News Release May Not Have Been the Right Word, Says Sask. Provincial Auditor." CBC Investigates. *CBC News*, November 10, 2016. https://www.cbc.ca/news/canada/saskatchewan/wrongdoing-in-gth-news-release-may-not-have-been-the-right-word-says-sask-provincial-auditor-1.3846272.

Leopold, Aldo. "The Outlook for Farm Wildlife [1945]." In *The River of the Mother of God and Other Essays by Aldo Leopold*, edited by Susan L. Flader and J. Baird Callicott. University of Wisconsin Press, 1992.

Lerat, Harold (with Linda Ungar). *Treaty Promises, Indian Reality: Life on a Reserve*. Purich, 2005.

Levy, Bryn. "Saskatoon City Council Passes Freeway Route Endorsement, Approves Borrowing for Solar Farm." *Saskatoon Star-Phoenix*, May 29, 2024. https://thestarphoenix.com/news/local-news/saskatoon-city-council-passes-freeway-route-endorsement-approves-borrowing-for-solar-farm.

Little Bear, Leroy. "Jagged Worldviews Colliding." In *Reclaiming Indigenous Voice and Vision*, edited by Marie Battiste. UBC Press, 2000.

Lockwood, Jeffrey A. *Prairie Soul: Finding Grace in the Earth Beneath My Feet*. Skinner House Books, 2004.

Lopez, Barry. *Embrace Fearlessly the Burning World: Essays*. Random House, 2023.

Loveless, Natalie. *How to Make Art at the End of the World: A Manifesto for Research-Creation*. Duke University Press, 2019.

Lowman, Emma Battell, and Adam J. Barker. *Settler: Identity and Colonialism in 21st Century Canada*. Fernwood, 2015.

Lurgio, Jeremy. "Saving the Whanganui: Can Personhood Rescue a River?" *Guardian*. November 29, 2019. https://www.theguardian.com/world/2019/nov/30/saving-the-whanganui-can-personhood-rescue-a-river.

Lyons, Murray. "Inland Port Idea Floated: Ocean Containers Could Boost Economy." *Saskatoon Star-Phoenix*, April 13, 2006: C8.

Lypny, Natascia. "Feds Earmark $200M for Bypass Project; Private Firm Will Build, Operate Highway." *Regina Leader-Post*, May 6, 2014: A1.

———. "Residential School Cemetery Protected with Heritage Designation." *Regina Leader-Post*, September 26, 2016. https://leaderpost.com/news/local-news/residential-school-cemetery-to-get-heritage-status.

———. "Sask. Party Wins Majority." Saskatchewan Votes 2020. *CBC News*. https://newsinteractives.cbc.ca/elections/saskatchewan/2020/results/.

———. "Sherwood Reeve Removed; Inquiry Finds 'Horrendous' Conflict of Interest Issues; Under Review by RCMP." *Regina Leader-Post*, February 6, 2015: A1.

———. "'They Just Don't Care': Landowners Anxious over Regina Bypass Impact." *Regina Leader-Post*, August 21, 2015. https://leaderpost.com/news/local-news/they-just-dont-care-landowners-anxious-over-regina-bypass-impact.

———. "Wascana Village Plans Expire." *Regina Leader-Post*, January 12, 2016. https://leaderpost.com/news/local-news/wascana-village-plans-expire.

MacDonald, Tanis. *Straggle: Adventures in Walking While Female*. Wolsak & Wynn, 2022.

Macfarlane, Robert. *Landmarks*. Hamish Hamilton, 2015.

———. *The Old Ways: A Journey on Foot*. Penguin, 2013.

———. *The Wild Places*. Penguin, 2008.

MacGregor, James G. *Vision of an Ordered Land: The Story of the Dominion Land Survey*. Western Producer Prairie Books, 1981.

Mackey, Eva. *Unsettled Expectations: Uncertainty, Land and Settler Decolonization*. Fernwood, 2016.

MacPherson, Alex. "Early 'Concerns' Over Roof at Sask. Hospital 'Were Well-Founded': Email." *Saskatoon Star-Phoenix*, January 21, 2020. https://thestarphoenix.com/news/local-news/early-concerns-over-roof-at-sask-hospital-were-well-founded-saskbuilds-project-director.

Maess, Donovan. "'An Explicit Endorsement': Regina City Council Votes Down Motion to Rename Dewdney Avenue." *CTV News Regina*, August 21, 2024. https://regina.ctvnews.ca/an-explicit-endorsement-regina-city-council-votes-down-motion-to-rename-dewdney-avenue-1.7009666.

Mahr, Krista. "How Cape Town Was Saved from Running Out of Water." The Upside, *Guardian*, May 4, 2018. https://www.theguardian.com/world/2018/may/04/back-from-the-brink-how-cape-town-cracked-its-water-crisis.

Mandryk, Murray. "$2B Spending Begs for Recall of the Legislature." *Regina Leader-Post*, May 8, 2020: A4.

———. "Government Fumbles the Infrastructure File." *Regina Leader-Post*, February 1, 2020: A10.

———. "Our Long, Hard Journey: Treaty 4 and 150 Years of Unfulfilled Promises." *Regina Leader-Post*, September 14, 2024. https://leaderpost.com/feature/our-long-hard-journey-treaty-4-and-150-years-of-unfulfilled-promises.

———. "P3 Secrecy Disrespectful to Taxpayers." *Regina Leader-Post*, October 25, 2015: A8.

———. "Sask. Party Bypasses Due Diligence." *Regina Leader-Post*, September 5, 2015: A6.

———. "Time Ripe to Rethink Purpose of GTH." *Regina Leader-Post*, January 4, 2020: A5.

Mann, Adam. "What's Up with That: Building Bigger Roads Makes Traffic Even Worse." *Wired*, June 17, 2014. https://www.wired.com/2014/06/wuwt-traffic-induced-demand/.

Maracle, Lee. *My Conversations With Canadians*. Book*hug Press, 2017.

Marchildon, Gregory P., Suren Kulshreshtha, Elaine Wheaton, and Dave Sauchyn. "Drought and Institutional Adaptation in the Great Plains of Alberta and Saskatchewan, 1914–1939." *Natural Hazards* 45 (2008): 391–411. https://doi.org/10.1007/s11069-007-9175-5.

Martell, Creeden. "Awasis Solar Project to Provide Power for 2,500 Homes." *Regina Leader-Post*, November 9, 2022. https://leaderpost.com/news/local-news/awasis-solar-project-to-provide-power-for-2500-homes.

———. "Construction Next Step After Wind Farm Deal Involving Cowessess." *Regina Leader-Post*, March 10, 2023. https://leaderpost.com/news/construction-next-step-after-wind-farm-deal-involving-cowessess.

Massey, Doreen. "A Global Sense of Place." In *Space, Place, and Gender*. University of Minnesota Press, 1994.

McAdam, Sylvia (Saysewahum). *Nationhood Interrupted: Revitalizing nêhiyaw Legal Systems*. Purich, 2015.

McDonald, Charlotte. "How Many Earths Do We Need?" *BBC News*, June 16, 2015. https://www.bbc.com/news/magazine-33133712.

McLernon, Will. "First Nations Lay Claim to All Critical Minerals and Rare Earth Elements in Saskatchewan." *CBC News*, March 30, 2023. https://www.cbc.ca/news/canada/saskatchewan/first-nations-lay-claim-to-all-critical-mineral-rare-earth-minerals-1.6795871.

Memmi, Albert. *The Colonizer and The Colonized*. Exp. ed. Translated by Howard Greenfield. Beacon Press, 1991.

Miller, J.R. *Shingwauk's Vision: A History of Native Residential Schools*. University of Toronto Press, 1996.

Milloy, John S. *A National Crime: The Canadian Government and the Residential School System, 1879 to 1986*. University of Manitoba Press, 1999.

Mills, Aaron/Ma'iingan, Waabishki. "What Is a Treaty? On Contract and Mutual Aid." In *The Right Relationship: Reimagining the Implementation of Historical Treaties*, edited by John Borrows and Michael Coyle. University of Toronto Press, 2017.

Mississaugas of the Credit First Nation. "The Toronto Purchase Treaty No. 13 (1805)." November 3, 2020. https://mncfn.ca/the-toronto-purchase-treaty-no-13-1805/.

Mockler, Kathryn, ed. *Watch Your Head: Writers and Artists Respond to the Climate Crisis*. Coach House Books, 2020.

Mod, Craig. "The Glorious, Almost-Disconnected Boredom of My Walk in Japan." The Big Story, *Wired*, May 29, 2019. https://www.wired.com/story/six-weeks-100s-miles-hours-glorious-boredom-japan.

Moran, Padraig. "Video of RCMP Hitting Inuk Man with Truck Shows Police Choosing Violence Over Protection, Says Lawyer." The Current. *CBC Radio*, June 5, 2020. https://www.cbc.ca/radio/thecurrent/the-current-for-june-5-2020-1.5599723/video-of-rcmp-hitting-inuk-man-with-truck-shows-police-choosing-violence-over-protection-says-lawyer-1.5599847.

Morris, Alexander. *The Treaties of Canada with the Indians of Manitoba and the North-West Territories, Including the Negotiations on Which They Were Based, and Other Information Relating Thereto.* Belfords, Clark & Co., 1880. Reprint, Coles, 1971.

Moss, Laura. "Biographical Note." In *Leaving the Shade of the Middle Ground: The Poetry of F.R. Scott*, edited by Laura Moss. Wilfrid Laurier University Press, 2011.

National Inquiry into Missing and Murdered Indigenous Women and Girls. *Reclaiming Power and Place: The Final Report of the National Inquiry into Missing and Murdered Indigenous Women and Girls.* 2 vols. 2019. https://www.mmiwg-ffada.ca/final-report/.

Olson, Wes, and Johane Janelle. *The Ecological Buffalo: On the Trail of a Keystone Species.* University of Regina Press, 2022.

Onondaga Nation: People of the Hills. "US Presidents–Hanadagá•yas." Accessed May 20, 2020. https://www.onondaganation.org/history/us-presidents-hanadagayas/.

Organisation for Economic Co-operation and Development. *Public-Private Partnerships: In Pursuit of Risk Sharing and Value for Money.* OECD Publishing, 2008. https://doi.org/10.1787/9789264046733-en.

Pacholik, Barb. "Regina Bypass Opens to Traffic." *Regina Leader-Post*, October 29, 2019: A3.

Palliser, Captain John. *The Journals, Detailed Reports, and Observations Relative to the Exploration, By Captain Palliser, of that Portion of British North America, Which, in Latitude, Lies Between the British Boundary Line and the Height of Land or Watershed of the Northern or Frozen Ocean Respectively, and in Longitude, Between the Western Shore of Lake Superior and the Pacific Ocean During the Years 1857, 1858, 1859, and 1860.* George Edward Eyre and William Spottiswoode, 1863. Canadiana by CKRN. https://www.canadiana.ca/view/oocihm.9_01593/53.

Pasiuk, Emily Rae. "Twice-Rejected Suicide Prevention Bill Passes in Sask. Legislature." *CBC News*, April 30, 2021. https://www.cbc.ca/

news/canada/saskatchewan/suicide-prevention-bill-saskatchewan-doyle-vermette-1.6010335.

Patterson, Dayne. "Carry the Kettle Nakoda Nation Asks Court to Declare Sask. Gov't Failed Duties in Crown Land Sales." CBC *News*, March 25, 2022. https://www.cbc.ca/news/canada/saskatchewan/crown-land-sales-carry-the-kettle-judicial-review-1.6397759.

Pennisi, Elizabeth. "Three Billion North American Birds Have Vanished Since 1970, Surveys Show." *Science*, September 19, 2019. https://www.sciencemag.org/news/2019/09/three-billion-north-american-birds-have-vanished-1970-surveys-show.

Quon, Alexander. "FSIN Raises Concerns About Lack of Consultation as Sask. Announces Work on Irrigation Project." CBC *News*, March 15, 2024. https://www.cbc.ca/news/canada/saskatchewan/fsin-raises-concerns-about-lack-of-consultation-as-sask-announces-work-on-irrigation-project-1.7145267.

———. "Regina City Council Votes Against Renaming Dewdney Avenue." CBC *News*, August 21, 2024. https://www.cbc.ca/news/canada/saskatchewan/dewdney-avenue-renaming-efforts-fails-1.7301498#.

Raban, Jonathan. *Bad Land: An American Romance*. Vintage, 1996.

Rachini, Mouhamad. "Indigenous-led Bison Repopulation Projects Are Helping the Animal Thrive Again in Alberta." The Current. CBC *Radio*, May 26, 2023. https://www.cbc.ca/radio/thecurrent/bison-repopulation-alberta-1.6856433.

Rannie, W.F. "Summer Rainfall on the Prairies During the Palliser and Hind Expeditions, 1857–59." *Prairie Forum* 31, no. 1 (2006): 17–38.

Ratt, Solomon. *kâ-pî-isi-kiskisiyân / The Way I Remember*. University of Regina Press, 2023.

Ray, Arthur J., Jim Miller, and Frank Tough. *Bounty and Benevolence: A History of Saskatchewan Treaties*. McGill-Queen's University Press, 2002.

Regina Bypass Partners. "Why a Bypass?" Accessed May 12, 2020. https://www.reginabypass.ca/project/why-a-bypass/.

Regina Leader-Post. "Province Sets Course to Drop Global Transportation Hub; Fires CEO." January 4, 2019. https://leaderpost.com/news/politics/the-provincial-government-is-setting-a-course-to-divest-itself-of-the-controversial-global-transportation-hub.

———. “SaskPower Grants $95M Contract to Finish Operations Hub at GTH.” August 12, 2024. https://leaderpost.com/news/saskatchewan/saskpower-grants-95m-contract-to-finish-operations-hub-at-gth.

Roach, Kent. *Canadian Justice, Indigenous Injustice: The Gerald Stanley and Colten Boushie Case*. McGill-Queen’s University Press, 2019.

Robinson, Dylan. “Intergenerational Sense, Intergenerational Responsibility.” In *Arts of Engagement: Taking Aesthetic Action In and Beyond the Truth and Reconciliation Commission of Canada*, edited by Dylan Robinson and Keavy Martin. Wilfrid Laurier University Press, 2016.

Rollo, Mike, dir. *The Broken Altar* (short film). 2013.

Rott, Nathan. “The World Lost Two-Thirds of Its Wildlife in 50 Years. We Are to Blame.” Environment and Energy Collaborative Special Series, *NPR*, September 10, 2020. https://www.npr.org/2020/09/10/911500907/the-world-lost-two-thirds-of-its-wildlife-in-50-years-we-are-to-blame.

Salvian, Hailey. “No Charges Laid in GTH Investigation: RCMP.” *CBC News*, July 25, 2018. https://cbc.ca/news/canada/saskatchewan/no-charges-laid-in-gth-land-deal-investigation-rcmp-1.4761263.

Sandilands, Catriona, ed. *Rising Tides: Reflections for Climate Changing Times*. Caitlin Press, 2019.

SaskPower. “Regina Operations and Maintenance Complex.” Accessed August 10, 2024. https://www.saskpower.com/our-power-future/infrastructure-projects/construction-projects/planning-and-construction-projects/regina-operations-and-maintenance-complex.

Sauchyn, David J., and Alwynne B. Beaudoin. “Recent Environmental Change in the Southwestern Canadian Plains.” *Canadian Geographer* 42, no. 4 (1998): 337–53. https://doi.org/10.1111/J.1541-0064.1998.TB01350.X.

Savage, Candace. *Geography of Blood: Unearthing Memory from a Prairie Landscape*. Greystone Books, 2012.

Savage, Candace, and Meghan Mickelson. “Opinion: Saskatoon Freeway Plan a Remnant of Rejected Urban Thinking.” *Saskatoon StarPhoenix*, April 10, 2024. https://thestarphoenix.com/opinion/columnists/opinion-saskatoon-freeway-plan-a-remnant-of-rejected-urban-thinking.

Sawatzky, Katie Doke. "It's Time to Save the Prairie: Against a Bleak Climate Future, Our Grasslands Offer Hope." In *Divided: Populism, Polarization and Power in the New Saskatchewan*, edited by JoAnn Jaffe, Patricia W. Elliott, and Cora Sellers. Fernwood, 2021.

———. "The State of Native Prairie in Saskatchewan." *PrairieCommons.ca*, October 1, 2018. http://www.prairiecommons.ca/?page_id=300.

Sciarpelletti, Laura. "Changes to Sask. Trespassing Laws Come into Effect Jan. 1, Will Require Permission to Access Land." *CBC News*, December 16, 2021. https://www.cbc.ca/news/canada/saskatchewan/people-must-ask-rural-sask-property-owners-for-permission-to-access-property-1.6288061.

Scott, Duncan Campbell. "The Height of Land." In *The Poems of Duncan Campbell Scott*. McClelland & Stewart, 1926.

———. "The Onondaga Madonna." In *The Poems of Duncan Campbell Scott*. McClelland & Stewart, 1926.

———. "Powassan's Drum." In *The Poems of Duncan Campbell Scott*. McClelland & Stewart, 1926.

Scott, F.R. "Laurentian Shield." In *Leaving the Shade of the Middle Ground: The Poetry of F.R. Scott*, edited by Laura Moss. Wilfred Laurier University Press, 2011.

Sedaris, David. "Stepping Out: Living the Fitbit Life." *New Yorker*, June 23, 2014. https://www.newyorker.com/magazine/2014/06/30/stepping-out-3.

Shaw, James H. "How Many Bison Originally Populated Western Rangelands?" *Rangelands* 17, no. 5 (1995): 148–50. https://journals.uair.arizona.edu/index.php/rangelands/article/viewFile/11258/10531.

Shelley, Percy Bysshe. "Mutability." In *Shelley's Poetry and Prose*, edited by Donald H. Reiman and Sharon B. Powers. W.W. Norton, 1977.

Shepherd, Nan. *The Living Mountain*. Canongate, 2011.

Short, Amanda. "Colliers Taking Over GTH Operations Amid Land Sale Concerns." *Regina Leader-Post*, September 20, 2019: A7.

Silberman, Alexandre. "In Saskatchewan, North America's Third Largest Inland River Delta Is Under Threat." *CBC News*, August 8, 2024. https://www.cbc.ca/news/canada/saskatchewan/saskatchewan-river-delta-lake-diefenbaker-1.7288013.

Simpson, Leanne Betasamosake. *As We Have Always Done: Indigenous Freedom Through Radical Resistance*. University of Minnesota Press, 2017.

———. "Land as Pedagogy: Nishnaabeg Intelligence and Rebellious Transformation." *Decolonization: Indigeneity, Education & Society* 3, no. 3 (2014): 1–25. https://jps.library.utoronto.ca/index.php/des/article/view/22170/17985.

Sinclair, Iain. *London Orbital: A Walk Around the M25*. Penguin, 2003.

Sinclair, Paul. "Selling Off Global Transportation Hub the Ultimate Dashed Dream; Facility Is Logical, Innovative Response to Saskatchewan Issues." *Regina Leader-Post*, August 1, 2018: A6.

Slater, Craig. "Route Selected, Plans Ongoing." *Regina Leader-Post*, June 19, 2013: A1.

Snider, Amy. "Crushed, August 20-27th 2024, Fifth Parallel Gallery, University of Regina." *Precipice*, August 4, 2024. https://amysnider.ca/2024/08/04/crushed-august-20-27th-2024-fifth-parallel-gallery-university-of-regina/.

Solnit, Rebecca. *Hope in the Dark: Untold Histories, Wild Possibilities*. 3rd ed. Haymarket, 2016.

———. *Wanderlust: A History of Walking*. Penguin, 2000.

Springgay, Stephanie, and Sarah E. Truman. *Walking Methodologies in a More-than-Human World: WalkingLab*. Routledge, 2018.

Spry, Irene M. *The Palliser Expedition: The Dramatic Story of Western Canadian Exploration 1857–1860*. 2nd ed. Fifth House, 1995.

Starblanket, Gina, and Dallas Hunt. *Storying Violence: Unravelling Colonial Narratives in the Stanley Trial*. ARP Books, 2020.

Stewart, Douglas. *The Regina Indian Industrial School (1891–1910): Historical Overview and Chronological Narrative*. Benchmark Press, 2017.

Stewart, Trudy, and Janine Windolph, dirs. *RIIS from Amnesia* (short film). RIIS Media Project, October 28, 2015. https://www.youtube.com/watch?v=l8yfSM87Ces.

Stoetzer, Bettina. "Ruderal Ecologies: Rethinking Nature, Migration, and the Urban Landscape in Berlin." *Cultural Anthropology* 33, no. 2 (2018): 295–323. https://doi.org/10.14506/ca33.2.09.

Stonechild, Blair, and Bill Waiser. *Loyal Till Death: Indians and the North-West Rebellion*. 2nd ed. Fifth House, 2010.

Suchan, Jared, and Shahid Azam. "Opinion: Much More Research Needs to Be Done into Diefenbaker Irrigation Project." *Regina-Leader-Post*, September 22, 2020. https://leaderpost.com/opinion/columnists/opinion-much-more-research-needs-to-be-done-into-diefenbaker-irrigation-project.

Suknaski, Andrew. *Wood Mountain Poems.* Macmillan, 1976.

Sutter, Trevor. "Province's Last Residential School Set for Closure." *Saskatoon Star-Phoenix*, July 2, 1998: A9.

Talen, Emily. "Pedestrian Access as a Measure of Urban Quality." *Planning Practice and Research* 17, no. 3 (2002): 257–78. https://doi.org/10.1080/026974502200005634.

Tallbear, Kim. "Dossier: Theorizing Queer Inhumanisms: An Indigenous Reflection on Working Beyond the Human/Nonhuman." *GLQ: A Journal of Lesbian and Gay Studies* 21, nos 2–3 (2015): 230–35.

Tank, Phil. "Sask. Plans Irrigation from Depleted Diefenbaker Watershed." *Regina Leader-Post*, March 27, 2024. https://leaderpost.com/opinion/columnists/phil-tank-sask-plans-irrigation-from-depleted-diefenbaker-watershed.

Taylor, Rattra Y. "Has Hub Met the Hype?; Some Question Whether the Original Vision for the Project Was Too Ambitious." *Regina Leader-Post*, August 29, 2015: G1.

Terpstra, John. *Daylighting Chedoke: Exploring Hamilton's Hidden Creek.* James Street North Books, 2018.

Thompson, Andrew R. "Resource Rights." In *The Canadian Encyclopedia.* Article published February 7, 2006; last modified December 16, 2013. https://www.thecanadianencyclopedia.ca/en/article/resource-rights.

Thoreau, Henry David. "Walking." In *Essays: A Fully Annotated Edition*, edited by Jeffrey S. Cramer. Yale University Press, 2013. https://doi.org/10.12987/9780300165623.

Titley, Brian. *The Frontier World of Edgar Dewdney.* University of British Columbia Press, 2000.

———. *A Narrow Vision: Duncan Campbell Scott and the Administration of Indian Affairs in Canada.* University of British Columbia Press, 1986.

Todd, Zoe. "An Indigenous Feminist's Take on the Ontological Turn: 'Ontology' Is Just Another Word for Colonialism." *Journal of*

Historical Sociology 29, no. 1 (2016): 4–22. https://doi.org/10.1111/johs.12124.

Tourism Saskatchewan Canada. "Regina—Condie Nature Refuge." Accessed May 12, 2020. https://tourismsaskatchewan.com/listings/1002/regina---condie-nature-refuge.

Trevelyan, George Macaulay. "Walking." In *Clio, a Muse and Other Essays Literary and Pedestrian*. Longmans, Green and Co., 1914.

Trogdon, Gary. "Sheridan, Philip (1831–1888)." In *Encyclopedia of the Great Plains*, edited by Gary J. Wishart. University of Nebraska Press, 2011. http://plainshumanities.unl.edu/encyclopedia/doc/egp.war.042.xml.

Truth and Reconciliation Commission of Canada (TRC). *Canada's Residential Schools*, vol. 1, *The History*, pt. 1, *Origins to 1939*. The Final Report of the Truth and Reconciliation Commission of Canada, McGill-Queen's University Press, 2015.

———. *Canada's Residential Schools*, vol. 4, *Missing Children and Unmarked Burials*. The Final Report of the Truth and Reconciliation Commission of Canada. McGill-Queen's University Press, 2015.

———. *Honouring the Truth, Reconciling for the Future: Summary of the Final Report of the Truth and Reconciliation Commission of Canada*. Truth and Reconciliation Commission of Canada, 2015.

Tsing, Anna Lowenhaupt, Nils Bubandt, Elaine Gan, and Heather Anne Swanson, eds. *Arts of Living on a Damaged Planet: Ghosts and Monsters of the Anthropocene*. University of Minnesota Press, 2017.

Tuan, Yi-Fu. *Space and Place: The Perspective of Experience*. University of Minnesota Press, 1977.

Tuck, Eve, and Rubén A. Gaztambide-Fernández. "Curriculum, Replacement, and Settler Futurity." *Journal of Curriculum Theorizing* 29, no. 1 (2013): 72–89. https://journal.jctonline.org/index.php/jct/article/view/411.

Tuck, Eve, and K. Wayne Yang. "Decolonization Is Not a Metaphor." *Decolonization: Indigeneity, Education & Society* 1, no. 1 (2012): 1–40. https://jps.library.utoronto.ca/index.php/des/article/view/18630.

VINCI. "VINCI Construction." February 29, 2024. https://www.vinci.com/vinci.nsf/en/item/business-line-vinci-construction.htm.

Vis, Matt. "Brayden Bushby, Convicted of Manslaughter in Trailer-Hitch Death of Indigenous Mom Barbara Kentner, to Serve 8 Years in Prison." CBC *News*, June 7, 2021. https://www.cbc.ca/amp/1.6056010.

Vowel, Chelsea. *Buffalo Is the New Buffalo: Stories.* Arsenal Pulp Press, 2022.

Waiser, Bill. *A World We Have Lost: Saskatchewan Before 1905.* Fifth House, 2016.

Waiser, W.A (Bill). *The Field Naturalist: John Macoun, the Geological Survey, and Natural Science.* University of Toronto Press, 1989.

———. "A Willing Scapegoat: John Macoun and the Route of the CPR." In *Immigration and Settlement, 1870–1939*, edited by Gregory P. Marchildon. Canadian Plains Research Center, 2009.

Walters, Mark D. "Rights and Remedies Within Common Law and Indigenous Legal Traditions: Can the Covenant Chain Be Judicially Enforced Today?" In *The Right Relationship: Reimagining the Implementation of Historical Treaties*, edited by John Borrows and Michael Coyle. University of Toronto Press, 2017.

Watts, Vanessa. "Indigenous Place-Thought and Agency Amongst Humans and Non-Humans (First Woman and Sky Woman Go on a European World Tour!)." *Decolonization: Indigeneity, Education & Society* 2, no. 1 (2013): 20–34. https://jps.library.utoronto.ca/index.php/des/article/view/19145/16234.

Welch, Craig. "Why Cape Town Is Running Out of Water, and Who's Next." *National Geographic*, March 5, 2018. https://www.nationalgeographic.com/science/article/cape-town-running-out-of-water-drought-taps-shutoff-other-cities.

Welch, Roger L. "The Myth of the American Desert." *Nebraska History* 52, no. 3 (1971): 255–65.

White-Crummey, Arthur. "GTH Now $46 Million in Debt and Still Not Selling Land." *Regina Leader-Post*, July 30, 2020. https://leaderpost.com/news/saskatchewan/gth-now-46-million-in-debt-and-still-not-selling-land.

———. "Hot Toilet Water at Sask. Hospital North Battleford Fires Up Debate in Legislature." *Regina Leader-Post*, June 24, 2020. https://leaderpost.co/news/saskatchewan/hot-toilet-water-at-sask-hospital-north-battleford-fires-up-debate-in-legislature.

———. "Sask. Announces $4 Billion Project to Irrigate up to 500,000 Acres," *Regina Leader-Post*, July 2, 2020, https://leaderpost.com/

news/saskatchewan/sask-announces-4-billion-project-to-irrigate-500000-acres.

Whitman, Walt. "Song of the Open Road." In *Complete Poetry and Selected Prose*, edited by James E. Miller Jr. Houghton Mifflin, 1959.

Wild, Tennessa. "Sask. Bison Home After Winter of Roaming Free." *Western Producer*, July 14, 2016. https://www.producer.com/2016/07/sask-bison-back-home-after-winter-of-roaming-free/.

Wilkins, Charles. *Walk to New York: A Journey Out of the Wilds of Canada*. Viking Canada, 2004.

Williams, Alex, dir. *The Pass System* (documentary film). Tamarack Productions, 2015. http://thepasssystem.ca.

Wilson, Ken. "'Elms at Night' and 'Outside the Museum (for George F. Ledingham).'" *The Goose* 19, no. 2 (2022): article 11. https://scholars.wlu.ca/thegoose/vol19/iss2/11/.

———. "Populus." *Queen's Quarterly* 130, no. 1 (2023): 146–59.

———. "Surrender No. 40." *The Goose* 20, no. 1 (2023): article 17. https://scholars.wlu.ca/thegoose/vol20/iss1/17/.

———. "Walking as Embodied Territorial Acknowledgment: Thinking About Place-Based Relationships from the Side of the Road." *Performance Matters* 7, nos 1–2 (2021): 97–115. https://performancematters-thejournal.com/index.php/pm/article/view/317.

———. "White Man Walking: Settler Ambulation in Colonized Spaces." In *Walking Bodies: Papers, Provocations, Actions from Walking's New Movements, the Conference*, edited by Helen Billinghurst, Claire Hind, and Phil Smith. Triarchy Press, 2020.

———. "*Wood Mountain Walk*: Afterthoughts on a Pilgrimage for Andrew Suknaski." *International Journal of Religious Tourism and Pilgrimage* 7, no. 1 (2019): 123–34. https://doi.org/10.21427/czey-xw12.

———. "*Wood Mountain Walk* and the Possibilities of Decolonization through Relationships with People and Land in Solo Walking Performance." *Canadian Theatre Review* 182, no. 2 (2020): 51–56. http://dx.doi.org/10.3138/ctr.182.010.

Wilson, Ken, and Matthew R. Anderson. "The Promise and Peril of Walking Indigenous Territorial Recognitions Carried Out by Settlers." *International Journal of Religious Tourism and Pilgrimage* 9, no. 2 (2021): article 7. https://doi.org/10.21427/wmx8-e578.

Wishart, David J. "The Great Plains Region." In *The Encyclopedia of the Great Plains*, edited by David J. Wishart. University of Nebraska Press, 2011. http://plainshumanities.unl.edu/encyclopedia/intro.html.

Wolfe, Patrick. "Settler Colonialism and the Elimination of the Native." *Journal of Genocide Research* 8, no. 4 (2006): 387–409. https://doi.org/10.1080/14623520601056240.

Wolfe, S.A., C.H. Hugenholtz, and Olav B. Lian. "Palliser's Triangle: Reconstructing the 'Central Desert' of the Southwestern Canadian Prairies During the Late 1850s." *The Holocene* 23, no. 5 (2013): 699–707. https://doi.org/10.1177/0959683612470179.

Wolvengrey, Arok. *nêhiyawêwin: itwêwina/Cree: Words*. 2 vols. University of Regina Press, 2001.

Wood, Stephanie Kwetásel'wet. "Meet the People Saving Canada's Native Grasslands." *The Narwhal*, July 31, 2020. https://thenarwhal.ca/carbon-cache-grasslands/.

Wooster, Robert. "Miles, Nelson (1839–1925)." In *Encyclopedia of the Great Plains*, edited by David J. Wishart. University of Nebraska Press, 2011. http://plainshumanities.unl.edu/encyclopedia/doc/egp.war.028.

Zontek, Ken. *Buffalo Nation: American Indian Efforts to Restore the Bison*. University of Nebraska Press, 2007.

INDEX

G

T

Y

Z

PHOTO: TREVOR HOPKIN

KEN WILSON is a settler who lives on Treaty 4 territory in oskana kâ-asastêki (Regina, Saskatchewan), where he teaches English courses at the University of Regina. *Walking the Bypass* is his first book; its manuscript won the 2022 City of Regina Writing Award.